# THE PLATO
# READER

# THE PLATO
# READER

## T.D.J. CHAPPELL

EDINBURGH UNIVERSITY PRESS

© T.D.J. Chappell, 1996

Edinburgh University Press Ltd
22 George Square, Edinburgh

Typeset in 11/13pt Times Roman
by Hewer Text Composition Services, Edinburgh, and
printed and bound in Great Britain

A CIP record for this book is available from the
British Library

ISBN 0 7486 0788 9

# CONTENTS

# PART VI: KNOWLEDGE AND THE FORMS (II)

# EPILOGUE: PLATO ON WRITING PHILOSOPHY

# PREFACE

This volume uses brief, newly translated selections from as many as possible of Plato's works, to give the reader a better idea of the astonishing range of Plato's thought and interests than could be got just from reading any one of Plato's works.

It is also meant to provoke the reader to read far more Plato than is included here; it is not meant to provide a limit, but a flying start, to further explorations. Plato believed that the most any book of philosophy can ever do is to incite its readers to inquire for themselves. For him any book at all is not an end in itself, but merely a beginning. That must be doubly true for books which, like this one, are compiled from other books.

Some points about the readings. First, the readings are all taken direct from Plato's works, with no abridgement or trimming except as indicated. Their order within the Parts, and the order of the Parts themselves, is meant, broadly, to mirror what I take to be the order of development of Plato's thought; none the less, they are not precisely chronologically arranged. Sixteen of the 35 extant works of Plato are represented here, but there are perhaps 19 others, though some of these are generally agreed to be spurious. Most of the works are dramatic dialogues with numerous characters; but there are also seven Letters. I say little about the characters in the dialogues, or about the probable dates of composition, dramatic settings or voices – not because these are uninteresting topics, but because they are too interesting: there is too much that could be said about them for half-measures to be attractive. Some directions for those who want to pursue these topics will be found in the Suggestions for Further Reading. Any first-person narrator in the readings who is not otherwise identified is always Socrates.

The readings are numbered, for ease of reference, from 1 to 46. The reader will see that there are also numbers in the headings and margins of the selections (34d10, 589c3, etc.). These derive from the page numberings in the great Renaissance edition of Plato edited by Robert Stephanus. The first number refers to a page, the letter to a paragraph, and the second number to a line in the paragraph. The main drawback with this system is that Stephanus' edition had three volumes. So, for example, page 410 occurs in all three of Cratylus, Republic and Cleitophon, because these three works were in Stephanus' volumes I, II and III respectively. Thus the standard means of reference to Platonic *loci* not only cites page, paragraph and line, but also gives the name of the dialogue in question.

Last, the translations. Many of Plato's terms have special resonances specific to his philosophy; it is vital not to disguise it when he is using a term in a technical sense. I have therefore tried, so far as possible, to use a limited range of translations for what I take to be Platonic terms of special significance. Thus *dynamis* is always '(causal) power' or 'causal influence'; *doxa* is always either 'belief' or 'opinion'; and *arete* is always 'virtue'.

Some cases prove intractable. No single English word corresponds neatly to *logos* (word/definition/account/reason/ argument/rationality), *kinesis* (change/movement/process), *aitia* (explanation/cause/reason), *kalos* (beautiful/handsome/ fine/honourable). Moreover Plato himself often varies his vocabulary. For example, to express the relation of particular to Form he uses such terms as *metekhein* (literally 'hold in common with'), *metalambanein* ('take in common with'), *koinonein* ('share'). In Greek, readers have to recognise for themselves that all these are words for the same concept (if indeed they are); likewise in this translation.

For some difficult cases, like the Forms, I have a special policy: the use of capitals to pick out key terms. For Plato does not only use, for example, *eidos* to refer to the famous Forms of his theory of forms – though he often uses *eidos* in ways which may well be ancestors of that usage (as in readings 5 and 8), or, as some hold, descendants of it (as in reading 42). (See also readings 19 and 23, where I have sometimes used 'aspect' to translate another usage of *eidos*.) I have therefore capitalised 'Form' when it translates *eidos* in a context where the theory of Forms is evidently under discussion, and left it in lower case elsewhere. Likewise with related terminology: *idea* becomes sometimes 'universal' but usually 'Universal'; *genos* generally becomes 'Class', not 'class', *to on* becomes mostly 'What Is', not 'what is'; and *ousia* 'Being', not 'being', and so on.

In the case of *theos* I have adopted a reverse convention, writing 'god' not 'God'. 'God' is a monotheistic term of art which, strictly speaking, has no plural. But *theos* in Plato's usage can go into the plural almost without Plato noticing: Plato is no monotheist, and even if he were, his 'God' would not be the highest reality.

My thanks are due to Neil Cooper, Terence Irwin, Margaret McCabe, David Sedley, Richard Sorabji, Nicholas White and David Wiggins, for encouragement in the early stages of the project; and to Nicola Carr, Jonathan Price and Rita Winter of Edinburgh University Press, for overseeing it to completion. Richard Stalley gave some useful comments on contents. Specimens of my translations were read and criticised by first-year philosophy students at UEA; also by David Bostock, Lesley Brown, Alec Fisher, Martin Hollis, Dory Scaltsas and, most meticulously of all, Tom Braun. I am very grateful to all for their help, though they will see that I have not always had the sense to take their advice.

This book is dedicated to the memory of my daughter, Caitlin Frances Richardson.

Tim Chappell
Philosophy Sector, UEA
Norwich, UK

PRELUDE

✦✦

# THE DEATH OF
SOCRATES

# 1. APOLOGY 19A–23B

✦✦

## SOCRATES' DEFENCE AT HIS TRIAL, AND HIS CONFESSION OF IGNORANCE

19a9   Let us take up, from the beginning, the question of what slander it is that has aroused people's enmity against me, and on which Meletus[1] was relying when he brought this indictment against me. Very well: how did my slanderers slander me? Let me read out what one would call these slanderers' affidavit – if they had the guts to present it in court: 'Socrates acts criminally by being a busybody and inquiring into what is under the earth and in the heavens; he makes the weaker argument the stronger one, and he teaches other people to do the same.'

19c1   It is something like this, anyway; you yourselves have seen this sort of slander at work in Aristophanes' comedy,[2] where someone called 'Socrates' is whirled around in a basket, pronouncing that he is walking on thin air and drivelling so many other sorts of drivel – about things that *I* know neither the first thing nor the last thing about.

19c7   I don't say this to belittle that kind of learning, if there is anyone who really is wise about such matters; I wouldn't want to bring on myself a suit from Meletus on so grave a charge as that! All I say, gentlemen justices, is that I have nothing to do with these inquiries. And I cite, as witnesses to this, the majority of yourselves. Those among you who have ever heard me in discussion – and that means many of you: I ask you to speak out now, gentlemen, and inform the others in the court, if at any time any of you has heard me engaging in discussion about such things!

[Silence.]

19d7     Well, gentlemen of the jury, you gather from your colleagues what is the standing of this report about me; and the other pieces of hearsay about me that the crowds repeat have the same standing too. There is really no substance in these reports. And if you have heard from someone that I try to teach men, and that I make money by teaching – that is false as well; although certainly I think it would be a fine thing if one *were* able to educate men, in the style of Gorgias and Prodicus of Ceos and Hippias of Elis.[3] Each of these teachers has what it takes to go around the cities and win over the young aristocrats – who, after all, could associate for free with anyone they wanted to. But Gorgias, Prodicus and the others persuade them to associate with themselves, pay money for the privilege, and be grateful for it too!

20a2     What is more, there is another wise man here, Euenus of Paros, who I have heard is visiting us. Going out one day, I bumped into Callias son of Hipponicus – a man who has spent more money on the sophists than everyone else put together. Since he has two sons, I questioned him like this: 'Callias,' I said, 'if your sons were two colts or two calves, we would be able to find someone to put in charge of them, and engage his services. He would be a horse-trainer, or a cattle farmer; and he would make them creatures which possessed the virtue appropriate to their nature in the highest degree.

20b2     'But given that your sons are not colts or calves, but men, who do you think you should put in charge of them? Who knows about that sort of virtue – the kind appropriate to humans, virtue in living in a society? Since you have the sons, I am sure you have considered the question! So is there such a teacher, or isn't there?' – 'Certainly there is,' said he. – 'Who is he?' I asked. 'What city is he from? and what is his rate for teaching?' – 'Euenus of Paros,' he said; 'and his course costs five minae.' At this, gentlemen, I exclaimed at Euenus' good fortune. To have this skill of teaching human virtue (if he really does have it) – and to teach it at such a bargain price too! Well, if I had Euenus' skill, I too would pride myself on it, and think myself a remarkably fine person. But the fact is, gentlemen, that I don't have that skill.

20c5    Here perhaps one of you might retort: 'Then, Socrates, what *is* it that you do? How did all these "slanders" arise? Surely your occupation cannot be just as unexceptionable as everyone else's, when it has given rise to so much rumour and talk, which would not have happened had you not behaved quite unlike most people. So tell us what you *do* do, or else we may jump to unfortunate conclusions about you!' This retort seems to me to be a just one. So I will try to demonstrate to you what exactly it is that has brought me notoriety and slander.

20d5    Listen, then. Perhaps what I say will seem like a joke to some of you: but be assured that I shall tell you the whole truth. For, men of Athens, I have gained this notoriety of mine for nothing other than a sort of wisdom. What do I mean – 'wisdom'? I mean that wisdom which is, perhaps, the only true human wisdom. As far as *that* goes, it may well be that I really am a wise man. As for the men I have just been mentioning – Gorgias, Prodicus, Hippias, Euenus: they may be wise in some way of wisdom which is, very likely, superhuman, or – I don't know what to say about it; for I myself don't understand it. And anyone who says I do is lying, and speaks to slander me.

20e4    Athenians, I hope you won't shout me down if you think that what I will now say is too much to swallow. For what I shall say is not my own testimony: no, I shall refer you to an authority whom you are bound to respect. As a witness to my wisdom – if it is wisdom – and to its peculiar quality, I shall call the god Apollo, whose oracle is at Delphi.

21a1　　I expect Chaerephon is known to you. He was a friend of mine from his youth, and of the democratic interest in politics; he was among the democrats who were recently exiled, and he returned to Athens with the rest of the democratic faction.[4] I expect you also know how enthusiastic he was in whatever he undertook. Well, one time he went to Delphi, and actually dared to ask the oracle the following question –
[Commotion.][5]

21a6　　– Please, gentlemen – I asked you not to shout me down! The question he asked Apollo's priestess was: 'Is there anyone wiser than Socrates?'; to which she replied that no one was.[6] (His brother here will testify to the truth of this for you, since Chaerephon himself has died.)

21b3　　Please remember why I am telling you this: it is because I am trying to demonstrate to you how the slanders against me began. – Well, when I heard this story, I said to myself, 'What on earth does Apollo mean? What is his riddle? If I do have any wisdom, great or small, I am quite unaware of it! So whatever can he mean by pronouncing me the wisest human? For he can hardly be speaking falsely: that would be unfitting for him.'

21b8　　For a long time I was perplexed about the oracle's meaning. In the end I set myself, most hesitantly, to inquire into it; in the following way. I went to see someone whom everyone said was wise, with the idea that from his case – if from anyone's – I would disprove the oracle. To the answer it had given, I would reply: 'Here is someone wiser than me – you said I was wiser than him!' There is no need for me to say who he was, gentlemen – though it was in looking at one of the statesmen of this city that I had this uncomfortable experience.[7] But when I examined this man and engaged in logical argument with him, I reached the conclusion that, although he appeared wise to many other men, and above all to himself, in reality he was not wise. So then I tried to demonstrate to him that he just thought he was wise, and, really, he wasn't. But the result was that I made an enemy of him, and of many others of those present too. So I left him: 'I *am* wiser than *this* man,' I said to myself. 'For quite possibly neither of us knows anything at all about being honourable and good. But he imagines he knows when he doesn't, whereas I don't imagine that – for really I don't know. So at any rate I am wiser than he is in this small way: when I don't know something, I don't have the illusion that I do know it.'

21d9     From him, I went on to someone else who was said to be even wiser than the first man. But I reached just the same conclusion as before, and as a result made an enemy of him and of many more others too. After that I went from one person to another on the same errand – fully aware, and grieved and frightened about it, that I was making enemies. Yet I believed I had to put the business of god absolutely first; therefore I had to seek out the meaning of the Delphic utterance, by going to see every single person with a reputation for any sort of knowledge. And by the Dog, men of Athens! Since I must tell you the truth, here's what I truly experienced in my investigations, made in obedience to god: the most highly regarded for wisdom seemed to me not far from being the ones who lacked it most, whereas others of poorer reputation were actually more deserving of the name.

22a5     So next I must tell you of these wanderings of mine: wanderings like those of a Hercules performing his labours, which I underwent to establish to my satisfaction that the oracle was irrefutably true. After the politicians, I went to see the poets – the tragedians, the dithyrambists, and the others – thinking that here I would catch myself in the act of knowing less than someone else. So I took in hand what seemed to me to be these poets' most carefully thought-out productions, and I questioned them on what these works meant, so that I might learn something from them too. And – well, I am embarrassed to tell you the truth, gentlemen justices, but it must be told: you might say that pretty well anyone present could have explained those poems better than the very men who wrote them. I soon recognised that the thing about the poets was that they too did not do what they did by wisdom. Instead they did it by some sort of natural instinct: by inspiration. For poets are like prophets or soothsayers, who also say many fine things – without having any idea what they are talking about. Yes, I realised that this is how it is with the poets too; and at the same time I also noticed that their poetic gifts made them think – again, mistakenly – that they were the wisest of men in other things besides poetry as well. So I left the poets behind too, thinking that I had the same advantage over them as I had over the politicians.

22d1      Last of all, then, I went to see the craftsmen. For I was well aware in myself that I knew more or less nothing at all; but I was sure I would find out that they were men of wide and splendid knowledge. Nor was I mistaken in this: they knew things I didn't know, and in that respect, they were wiser than me. But, men of Athens, I found that our noble technicians had the same weakness as the poets. Because they were good at exercising their own specific skills, each of them imagined he was also as wise as could be in everything else, even in the greatest of other matters. And this presumption on their part – since it was false – brought into question their apparent wisdom in other respects.

It made me ask myself the question that the oracle
might have asked me: whether I would choose to be
exactly as I am, neither wise in their way nor ignorant
in their way, or rather to have both their sort of
wisdom, and their sort of ignorance. I answered my
own and the oracle's question by saying that I was
better off just as I am.

23a1        Men of Athens, it is this inquiry of mine which has
made me so harshly and fiercely resented. And it is this
inquiry which has aroused so much slander of my
name – including the unwelcome title of Wise Man.[8]
For whenever I argue someone else into the floor, the
audience assume that *I* must be wise about whatever
the subject-matter in question may be. But, gentlemen,
it is probably nearer the truth to say that it is Apollo
who is wise, not me; and that what he meant by his
oracular utterance was simply that human wisdom is
worth little or nothing. Evidently he was not really
speaking about me in particular; he was just using my
name to make me an example of human wisdom. It is
as if he had said: 'Humans, the wisest man among you
is the one who recognises – like Socrates – that, in
23b4        truth, he is worthless where wisdom is concerned.'

# 2. PHAEDO 115A–118A

## ✦

## THE DEATH OF SOCRATES

115a1   'Listen, Simmias, Cebes, and the rest of you,' said Socrates: 'you will all go down this road too when your time comes. But as for me, "Fate calls to me e'en now", as a tragedian might put it, and it is almost the hour for my final bath – since it seems better that I should bathe before I take the poison, so that I save the slavewomen here the trouble of washing my corpse.'

115b1   'Very well, Socrates,' replied Crito; 'but do you have any special requests for me or these others here? Anything we can do for your children, or about anything else, that would be most pleasing to you?'

115b3   'Only what I always ask, Crito,' he replied, 'nothing new. If you just pursue your own true interest, then whatever you may do, you will be doing what is pleasing to yourselves, and to me and mine; if you will do that, there's no need to commit yourselves to anything special now. Whereas if you have no regard for your own interest, and are not prepared to follow the path of life that we have traced for ourselves in our discussions, not just now but in our earlier talks too – in that case you will do nothing more that is any good, no matter what weighty and emphatic promises you make now.'

115c2   'Well,' said Crito, 'we will try to live like that, Socrates – with all our hearts. But how shall we bury you?'

  'However you like,' replied Socrates – 'if indeed you catch me, and I don't escape you.' He laughed composedly as he said it, and fixed his eyes on us:

'Gentlemen,' he said, 'I can't persuade Crito that *I* am this Socrates here who is now parading all his arguments as he converses with you: Crito thinks that I am the Socrates whom he will shortly see as a dead body, and so he wants to know how to bury me. All along I have made a great argument of the claim that, when I have drunk the poison, *I* will no longer be with you, and that I shall disappear from here, and depart to the delights of the blessed ones; but Crito, I think, believes that my argument was a mere distraction – just whistling in the wind to keep your spirits up, and mine too.'

115d5 'So,' said he, 'you must pay my bail to Crito, though in the opposite sense to the bail he paid into court for me at my trial. For his bail was to guarantee that I would stay until my trial was complete; but yours is to guarantee that I won't stay when I die, but will disappear and depart. This should make it easier for Crito to bear, and ensure that he will not be utterly distraught when he sees my body being burnt or buried, imagining that it's me who is suffering these indignities. We don't want him saying at the funeral that he is preparing *Socrates* for burial, or carrying *Socrates* to the grave, or putting *Socrates* in the ground. For you know quite well, my worthy Crito, that improper forms of speech like these are not just verbal solecisms; they hurt the soul too. So you must be of good heart, and acknowledge that it is only my body that you are burying. And you can bury *that* in whatever way you think is best and most suitable.'

116a1 With these words Socrates stood up and went off into some side-room to have his bath; Crito followed Socrates, but told the rest of us to wait. So we waited, discussing and considering among ourselves what Socrates had said, or going over and over, in our minds, the greatness of the disaster that had befallen

us. For we felt that we were being deprived of someone
who in his own strange way was like a father to us, and
that we would pass through the rest of our lives as
orphans.

116b1     After Socrates' bath his children were brought to
him – he had two very young sons and one older boy –
together with his female relatives. He talked to them
with only Crito there, and gave them such instructions
as he wished. Then he sent his family away, and came
back to us.[9]

By now it was almost sunset – for Socrates had spent
a long time in the other room. He came in and sat
down, clean from his washing, and we did not have
long after his return to talk before the representative of
the Eleven[10] came in to attend to Socrates' execution.

116c1     'Socrates,' he said, 'at least I won't have to watch in
disgust, as I do with the others, while you scream abuse
and curses at me when I tell you, on my masters' orders,
to drink the poison. No, I have discovered you, during
your imprisonment here, to be a quite different sort of
man. You are the noblest, the gentlest, and the best man
of all who have ever come to this place; and by now I
know very well that you have no hard thoughts for me,
but for others – for you know who is responsible for
your death. But now, you know what the message is
that I bring: so farewell, Socrates, and try to bear what
you must as well as you can.'

116d1     The man turned his back on Socrates and walked
away, but he was in tears. Socrates looked up towards
him, and replied, 'And farewell to you too: we will do
what you ask us to. How polite the man is!' (he added,
to us;) 'All the time I have been in prison he has been
coming to see me; we have talked quite a lot. He has
been the best of men, and now he is generous enough
to weep for me. But come, Crito, let us do what he
asks. Somebody bring me the poison, if it is ready; and
if it isn't, then get the attendant to prepare it.'

116e1    'But Socrates,' protested Crito, 'the sunlight is still on the mountain tops, so I don't think the sun has gone down yet. Moreover I know of other prisoners who left it very late after the order of execution was announced to them: they had full meals and drank good wine, and spent time with some of the people they still wanted to see. So there is no hurry – you don't have to die just yet.'

116e7    'The people you mean do right, Crito,' replied Socrates, 'for they think they have something to gain by it. But I would be wrong to do the same. For I don't see any point in my drinking it a few minutes later rather than a few minutes earlier. I shall just feel ridiculous if I scramble to remain alive – if I spare myself when there is nothing left to spare myself for. No, do what I say and don't divert me.'

117a4    So Crito complied, nodding to the slave-boy who was standing by. The boy left, and after some delay returned, bringing with him the man who was to give the poison to Socrates, which he brought in, prepared in a cup. Socrates looked at the executioner and said, 'Well, my good fellow, you know about these things. What is the method?'

117a9    'All you need do,' replied the executioner, 'is drink it and then walk around the cell until you begin to feel a heaviness in your legs. Then you lie down. If you do this, the poison will do the rest.' And he handed the cup to Socrates, who took it, and asked him – quite cheerfully, without a tremor, without losing control of his expression or going pale, but with his usual bull's-eye stare straight at the man – 'What do you say about this drink? May I make a libation to one of the gods before I drink it down? Is it permitted, or not?'

'Well, Socrates,' the executioner replied, 'we prepare only the exact amount of poison that we think is needed.'

117c1    'I see,' replied Socrates. 'Still, it is surely not just permitted, but a duty, to pray to the gods that my removal from this place to the other world may be a propitious one. So that is my prayer. Amen!' And at once he raised the cup, and – quite easily, almost as if it tasted good – drank all the poison down till the cup was empty.

117c4    As for us, up till then most of us had been able to keep ourselves in good order and restrain our tears; but when we saw him drinking it down, saw the cup empty, we no longer could. Despite myself, my tears welled up in such floods that I threw my cloak around my head and wept – for myself: for I was not crying at his ill fortune, but at my own in losing such a man and such a friend. Crito had been beaten before I was, and had left the room because he could not hold back his crying; but Apollodorus had been weeping all along, and now cried out aloud so that he reduced everyone in the room to tears: except for Socrates himself.

117d7    'Why, what a way to behave, you extraordinary people!' he remarked: 'this was not the least of my reasons for sending away my womenfolk – to prevent this sort of palaver. As I understand it, we should die with no ill-omened speeches. So be quiet, and keep up your spirits.' And these words put us to shame, so that we restrained our weeping.

117e2    But Socrates walked around his cell until he said that his legs were getting heavy, and then lay down on his back, as the executioner had told him to. Straight away the executioner placed his hand on Socrates' body; then after waiting a while, he examined his feet and his legs; then he squeezed Socrates' foot hard, and asked him if he could feel it. Socrates said not. Then the man did the same with Socrates' calves; and so on up Socrates' legs, to show us that he was growing cold and numb. Soon the executioner placed his hand on Socrates again, and told us that, when the numbness got as far as the heart, Socrates would be gone.[11]

118a4    Already by now the chill had reached Socrates' stomach, and Socrates had covered his face with his cloak; but then he moved the cloak away, and spoke for the last time. 'Crito,' he said, 'we owe a cock to the god of healing. So make the payment. Don't forget it.'

'I will,' said Crito; 'but think what else you would ask us.'

Socrates made no further answer to Crito, but after letting a little time pass he stirred, and the executioner uncovered his face once more: Socrates' eyes were no longer moving. And when Crito saw, he closed Socrates' eyes and mouth.

And this, Echecrates, was how the death of our friend happened: the death, as we would say, of the best man that we have ever met, and the wisest and the
118a10 most just as well.

## NOTES

1. One of Socrates' three prosecutors at his trial in 399 BC. As will be clear from readings 1 and 2, Socrates was convicted and executed.
2. See Aristophanes, *Clouds*, ll. 220 ff.
3. Names of famous sophists. For Gorgias' allies Polus and Callicles, see readings 16–18; for Prodicus and Hippias 15.
4. Socrates alludes to the events of 400–399 BC at Athens, during which the short-lived but bloodthirsty junta of the Thirty Tyrants was followed by the restoration of democratic government a few months before his trial.
5. Evidently Socrates' story about the oracle is already widely known, and resented, in his audience.
6. According to Origen, *contra Celsum* 7.6, the exact words of the oracle were these two lines of verse:
   Sophocles is wise, Euripides is wiser,
   of all mankind Socrates is wisest.
7. Socrates' hints about the identities of these distinguished victims of his argumentative skill seem deliberately provocative. Perhaps, as comparison with *Protagoras* 319e (in reading 11) and *Alcibiades I* 118b–e suggests, he even had figures like the great Pericles in mind.
8. *Sophos* both (a) as a name which Socrates does not think he deserves, and (b) as a near equivalent of 'wise guy'.

9. Socrates' priorities in his last hours are striking to a modern eye. Compare Plato's attitude to the family in the *Republic*, and Diotima's words at *Symposium* 208e–209c.
10. The ruling body in Athens at the time.
11. For a famous parody of this passage, cf. Shakespeare, *Henry V*, II. iii.

# PART I
✦✦
# THE SEARCH FOR A
# SOCRATIC ETHICS

# 3. MENO 80A–C

## ⇥⇤

## MENO DESCRIBES SOCRATES

80a1   MENO. Socrates, even before I met you I was warned that you yourself are a confused person, and that all you do to others is perplex them too. And even now I can feel you casting your spell on me: dosing me with weird potions, singing me queer incantations, till I find myself brim-full with bewilderment. Indeed if I have to be comic about it, Socrates, I think you're just like one of those sting-rays that you find in the sea. (You even look like one.) Anyone who comes upon a sting-ray is stung into numbness if they touch it; and you seem to have done something like that to me. Quite seriously I tell you that I have lost all sensation both in my thought and in my speech: I'm frozen, I have no answer for you. Ten thousand times before now I have made long and fluent speeches about virtue before huge audiences: and how well I spoke, too – as I thought at the time! Yet here I am, stuck, without a single word to say about what virtue is. I think you're very sensible to decide not to take ship and leave Athens,[1] or go on tour. For if you went to some other city, and subjected people to this sort of treatment as a foreigner – why, you'd be lynched for witchcraft.

80b7   SOCRATES. Meno, you're a shameless con-man, and you nearly conned me.

MENO. Whatever do you mean, Socrates?

SOCRATES. I know why it is you make your little speech!

MENO. And why is it, according to you?

80c3   SOCRATES. You want me to reply with a similar flattering image about you.[2] I know it for a fact: all

you beautiful people love images – presumably because they serve your turn, since evidently beautiful
objects have beautiful images. But I will make no
images of you, Meno. As for myself – I am only like
the sting-ray if sting-rays can sting *themselves* numb as
well as other people: not otherwise. For I don't cause
others perplexity while being above all perplexities
myself. Far from it: it is because I am so much more
perplexed than others, that I make them perplexed

80c10   too . . .

# 4. THEAETETUS 148c–151d

✦✦

## SOCRATES DESCRIBES HIMSELF

148c3  SOCRATES. Do you think it a small thing, Theaetetus, to find out what knowledge is? Isn't it a task for minds that are, in every sense of the word, at their peak?

THEAETETUS. By Zeus, yes it is: indeed I'd say it was a task for the most superior minds of all.

148d1  SOCRATES. So you should have some confidence in your own abilities – and you should assume, too, that Theodorus' mathematical method[3] is on to something. Now apply yourself to our questions with exclusive devotion; in particular, apply yourself to finding a definition that tells us what knowledge might be.

THEAETETUS. Well, if it's only application we need, Socrates, I'm sure the truth will come to light.

SOCRATES. Come, then: you have just given us a perfect model answer about the square and cube roots of numbers. So try to imitate that answer which you gave: just as you found one class which, despite their variety, contained them all, so try to express all the various sorts of knowledge in a single definition.

148e1  THEAETETUS. Let me tell you, Socrates, that I, having heard by word of mouth about your research,[4] have tried to solve that problem often enough in the past. But I cannot even convince myself that I have any adequate definition of knowledge; nor am I able to find anyone else who can give an answer in the manner that you require. Yet this is not a question I can comfortably leave alone.

SOCRATES. Why, my dear Theaetetus – your discomfort is due to labour pains; and that means that you are not intellectually barren, but pregnant with something.

THEAETETUS. I don't know about that, Socrates; I merely say what I have felt.

149a1   SOCRATES. But, you ridiculous man – surely you have heard that I am a midwife's son? The son of that muscular, noble lady, Phaenarete?[5]

THEAETETUS. Yes, I've heard that before.

SOCRATES. Have you also heard that I practise the same craft of midwifery?

THEAETETUS. No – that I haven't heard!

SOCRATES. But it's true, I assure you. However, don't let on to anyone else, Theaetetus: for I practise my craft in secret. Other people don't report this fact about me because they don't realise it; what they say is that I am an utterly absurd being, who brings other men into perplexity. And this, no doubt, you *have* heard?

149b1   THEAETETUS. I certainly have.

SOCRATES. Shall I tell you why they say this?

THEAETETUS. Please do!

SOCRATES. Well, think about the whole character of midwifery – then you'll see what I mean more easily. For I dare say you know that no midwife ever attends at anyone else's labour while she herself is still conceiving and bearing children; the only active midwives are those past child-bearing age.

THEAETETUS. That's true.

149b8   SOCRATES. They say that Artemis herself is the cause of this; for she, childless as she is, has chosen childbirth as her care. Now Artemis did not give it to the totally barren to be midwives; for human nature is too weak to acquire a skill in matters of which it has absolutely no experience. Instead, she assigned midwifery to those who have become too old to bear children, honouring them for their likeness to herself.

THEAETETUS. No doubt.

SOCRATES. Now doesn't this seem both likely and necessary: that midwives should be better than anyone else at diagnosing who's pregnant and who isn't?

THEAETETUS. Yes, certainly.

149d1 SOCRATES. And aren't midwives the ones who can provide drugs or spells with the power to increase the pains of labour, or to make them less severe? Don't they bring even difficult labours to birth – or induce miscarriages if they think that is necessary?

THEAETETUS. They do, yes.

SOCRATES. Again, have you noticed this fact about them? It is midwives who are most skilled in assigning marriage-partners to one another, since they are the ones who have full wisdom about which woman should have intercourse with which man to produce the best children.[6]

THEAETETUS. No – I had no idea about that.

149e1 SOCRATES. Well, I tell you – they have more wisdom about this than they do about mere umbilicus-cutting. Why, think about it: don't you believe that it is all part of a single skill to tend and harvest the fruits of the earth, and also to recognise which shoot or seed should go in which sort of soil?

THEAETETUS. Yes, that's all part of one skill.

SOCRATES. Well, my friend, in the case of gynaecology, do you think that there is one skill concerning the selection of the right sort of woman for child-bearing, and another for the delivery of the child?

THEAETETUS. It is unlikely, I suppose.

150a1 SOCRATES. Indeed it is. But because of our unjust and unmethodical way of uniting the man and the woman – frankly, 'pimping' is the word – midwives in our society avoid even preliminary match-making; for they are women who deserve reverence, but they fear that any such involvement would bring on them the accusation of pimping. Yet I should say that it is only the true midwife who deserves the name 'match-maker'.

THEAETETUS. Evidently so.

150a8  SOCRATES. So you see how important is the role of the midwife; yet theirs is a lesser work than mine. It is not the way with women that they should sometimes produce sham and sometimes real children, in such a way that it is difficult to tell the shams and the real children apart. For if women *did* do this, then the main and most valuable part of the midwife's work would be just this distinguishing real children from shams. Wouldn't it?

THEAETETUS. Yes.

150b5  SOCRATES. Well, my art of midwifery is just like the women midwives' art, in every respect except these three. First, I practise midwifery on men, not on women; second, it is minds in labour, not bodies, that I attend to. But third is the greatest thing of all about my midwife's art: it can apply all sorts of tests to determine whether my pupil's intelligence is giving birth to a sham and a lie, or to a true and noble offspring.

150c2  Of course, in some other ways I am just like the women midwives. For I am barren and sterile in wisdom, and the charge with which the common people have long indicted me, that I ask questions of others, but find no answers of my own to those questions because I have no wisdom – that indictment is true. But the reason why it is true is this: the god forces me to act as a midwife, but has prevented me from giving birth myself. So I am no Wise Man; nor can I claim that any great philosophical discoveries are the offspring of my mind.

150d1  But just look at those who associate with me! At first some of them seem entirely ignorant; but as our association continues all of them, or at least all those whom god permits, give forth most miraculously – not only in their own eyes, but in others' too. Manifestly, this happens not because they learn anything from me, but because they find and bring forth great numbers of noble truths from within *themselves*. However, the delivery itself *is* my responsibility, under god: as I can prove.

150e1    For many of my patients have not understood my role in their learning. They have disregarded me, thinking that they had managed everything themselves. Such cases have decided – either on their own or at the prompting of others – to leave me before they are ready to leave. But having once left, they have, ever since, brought forth only botchings and abortions, because of the wickedness of their associates; as for the children which I helped them to give birth to, they have destroyed them by their negligence. They have had more regard for their false and sham offspring than for their real children, and in the end they have been found ignorant both in others' eyes and in their own. One such case was Aristides the son of Lysimachus; there have been plenty of others.[7] When these people come back to me, begging for my company and doing all sorts of things to get it, my guardian spirit forbids me to keep company with some of them; though not with others – and then they once more start to give forth.

151a4    So those who associate with me experience just the same as women giving birth. Far more than them, indeed, they feel the pains of labour and are filled with perplexity, both day and night. This is the sort of labour pain which my art of midwifery can bring on or abate; so that is what they undergo.

151b1    (Of course, Theaetetus, I find that some of them are not exactly pregnant, and so, as I realise, are in no need of *me*. In such cases I am quite happy to play the matchmaker, and (with god's help) I guess – with pretty good results – from whose company such people might profit. I have referred many such cases to Prodicus, and to many other distinguished savants too.)[8]

151b8    Now, my fine Theaetetus, I have drawn this subject out at such length because I suspect that you have conceived something or other within you, and are in the pains of labour. So present yourself to me – to the son of a midwife, and someone who is himself somewhat obstetrical – and apply yourself to answering as well as you can the questions I ask you. I will examine each thing that you say, and if I think that it is a sham child and not a true one, I will discreetly remove it from you and expose it.[9] If I do that, do not rage at me, as mothers rage if they lose their first child. For many before now, my gifted friend, have felt so extraordinarily angry towards me that they were ready to snap at me because I exposed some nonsense or other of theirs. They couldn't believe that I had done this out of good will. They have no conception of the fact that no god is malicious to human beings, and that neither do I act like this out of malice: but it is my duty never to go along with a sham or conceal the truth.

151d3    So, Theaetetus, begin the inquiry again from the beginning. What exactly is knowledge? Try to tell me. But never say that you are unable to; for if god chooses, and if he gives you the strength, you will
151d6    be able to.

# 5. MENO 71D–74A

## ❧

# THE SEARCH FOR DEFINITIONS (I)

71d4   SOCRATES. No, Meno – never mind Gorgias, who after all is not here. Please just tell me yourself what, in heaven's name, you say virtue is. Speak out, and don't begrudge me an answer. If you and Gorgias turn out to have this knowledge, that will show up my remark, that I have never met anyone who did know what virtue is, as a mistake on my part – as lucky a mistake as I could possibly hope to make.

71e1   MENO. But, Socrates, it's not hard to say what virtue is. If you want the virtue of a man first, that's easy. The virtue of a man consists in being man enough to do what the city needs – and so to do it that his friends are benefited by it and his enemies harmed; also in making sure that no such harm comes to himself.[10] Or if you want the virtue of a woman, that's not hard to express either. What she has to do is keep house well, looking after its contents and being obedient to her husband. The virtue of a child is another thing, and it is different again depending on whether one talks of the virtue of a boy or a girl. Again there is a particular sort of virtue for an old man, for a free man, or a slave – whichever you wish to discuss. There are any number of other varieties of virtue too; so it's hardly a problem to say what the definition of virtue is. There is a specific virtue for each sort of activity and age, for each of us, in whatever we do. And, I assume, the same is true of vice.

72a5   SOCRATES. I do seem to be having the most remarkable luck today, Meno; for I was only after one virtue, but, to judge by your description, I have found a whole swarm of virtues. But – sticking with this image of the swarm – suppose I asked you about the real nature of a bee: about what a bee truly is. And suppose you replied that there are all sorts of different kinds of bees. Then how would you answer me if I went on to ask this? 'But are they all sorts of different and various kinds *inasmuch as they are bees*? Or do they not differ at all in that respect? Aren't they different only in other respects – like their beauty or size, or some other respect such as that?' Tell me – what would you say if you were asked this question?

MENO. Well, my reply would be that, inasmuch as they are bees, they don't differ at all from each other.

72c1    SOCRATES. So suppose I then asked you this question. 'Well then, tell me this: that respect in which the bees don't differ from each other at all, but are all the same – what is it, in your view?' Presumably you would have some answer to that?

MENO. Yes, I would.

SOCRATES. Then do the same with the virtues. Even if they are of all sorts of different kinds, they must all have some one form in common, which is what makes them all virtues, and which we will presumably do well to fix our sight on if we want to give a clear answer to the question 'What is virtue?'. Do you understand what I mean?

72d2    MENO. Well, I think I do; but I don't yet grasp what you are asking me as well as I'd like to.

SOCRATES. Do you think it is only where virtue is concerned that there is one sort for a man, another for a woman, and so on? Or is the same true of health and size and strength? Do you think that there is one sort of health for a man, and another for a woman? Or is there the one form of health in all these cases, whatever sort of health may be in question – masculine, feminine or whatever?

72e2    MENO. I think there is just one sort of health for a man and for a woman.

SOCRATES. Then isn't the same true of size and strength? If a woman is strong, isn't it the same form, the same strength, that makes her strong, as makes a man strong? What I mean by 'the same' is this: that there is no difference between a man's strength and a woman's strength, inasmuch as they are both cases of *strength*. Or do you think there is some difference?

MENO. No, I don't.

73a1 SOCRATES. So will a child's virtue differ from an old man's virtue, or a woman's from a man's, inasmuch as all these are cases of *virtue*?

MENO. Somehow, Socrates, I think that this time the case is no longer the same as the others.

SOCRATES. But why not? Didn't you say that a man's virtue is to manage a city well, and a woman's to manage a household well?

MENO. I did, yes.

SOCRATES. Can one manage anything at all well – city or household or anything else – if one does not manage it temperately and justly?

73b1 MENO. Of course not.

SOCRATES. But whoever manages what they manage temperately and justly, will do so because of their temperance, and because of their justice.

MENO. Obviously.

SOCRATES. So both women and men, if they are to be good women and men, need to display the same qualities: justice and temperance.

MENO. Apparently so.

SOCRATES. What about a child or an old man? How could there possibly be a good child, or a good old man, who was intemperate or unjust?

MENO. There couldn't, of course.

SOCRATES. So they need to be temperate and just?

MENO. Yes.

73c1 SOCRATES. Therefore all humans are good in the same

sense; for they become good when they acquire the same qualities.

MENO. Evidently so.

SOCRATES. Whereas, presumably, if there was not one and the same virtue for all of them, they would not all be good in the same sense.

MENO. No indeed.

SOCRATES. Then since there is one kind of virtue for everybody, try to recollect, and say what Gorgias and yourself hold virtue to be.

MENO. What else would it be but the capacity to rule over other people? – If, at any rate, you are looking for a single formula that fits everyone.

73d2   SOCRATES. Of course that's what I'm looking for. But is a child's virtue the same thing as a slave's? And in either case, is virtue the ability to rule over their masters? Do you think that anyone who rules remains a slave?

MENO. No, I don't think that at all, Socrates.

SOCRATES. No, my excellent friend – it hardly seems plausible, doesn't it? But then consider this point too. You say that virtue is 'being capable of rule'; but shouldn't we amend this to 'being capable of *just rather than unjust* rule'?

MENO. Yes, I think we should. After all, Socrates, justice is virtue.

73e1   SOCRATES. Do you mean virtue, Meno? Or *a* virtue?

MENO. What do you mean?

SOCRATES. Just what I would mean in any other case. For example, if you like: if I was talking about roundness, I would say that it was *a* shape, not *shape* without any qualification. And the reason why I would speak this way is because there are other shapes besides roundness.

MENO. Yes, and that would be right; in just the same way I would say that there are other virtues too besides justice.

74a1    SOCRATES. What are they? Do tell me – just as I will tell you what other shapes there are besides roundness, if you ask me to. Likewise, you tell me what other virtues there are besides justice.

MENO. Well, courage looks like a virtue to me; so does temperance; so do wisdom and splendour, and many other qualities too.

SOCRATES. But, Meno, the same thing has happened to us again! Once more – albeit in a different manner from before – we have found many virtues when we were only after one. But the one virtue which is the
74a10   same through all these virtues – that we cannot find.

# 6. THEAETETUS 145E–147C

## ➤◄

## THE SEARCH FOR DEFINITIONS (II)

145e6 SOCRATES. Well, but this is the reason for my perplexity, the question that I can't properly get a grip on in my mind: 'What, in fact, is knowledge?' Do we have any account about that?

[146a1–c7]

THEAETETUS. Well – the things that one might learn from Theodorus are kinds of knowledge: geometry and the other examples you went through just now. Also cobbling and the other manual labourers' crafts. All of these are nothing other than knowledge; each of these is nothing other than a kind of knowledge.

146d2 SOCRATES. Nobly said, my friend. Generously, too: you were asked for one thing and you give us lots of things, you were asked for something simple and you give us the whole gamut.

THEAETETUS. What are you talking about, Socrates?

SOCRATES. Quite possibly I'm talking nonsense; but I'll tell you what I think I'm talking about. When you say 'cobbling', what you mean is just knowledge about workmanship regarding shoes, isn't it?

THEAETETUS. Just that, yes.

146e1 SOCRATES. And when you say 'joinery', don't you just mean knowledge about how to make things out of wood?

THEAETETUS. That's right.

SOCRATES. So all you're doing is defining what each of these is knowledge *about*.

THEAETETUS. Yes.

SOCRATES. But that wasn't the question, Theaetetus.

The question was not 'What is knowledge about?' or 'How many kinds of knowledge are there?' We weren't wanting to make a list of kinds of knowledge. We wanted to know *how knowledge itself is to be defined*. So, am I talking nonsense?

THEAETETUS. No, I think you're quite right.

147a1 SOCRATES. Consider this, too. Suppose someone asked us about how to define one of those banal things which are always to hand, like clay: 'What is clay?' Wouldn't it be ridiculous to reply to him that 'Clay is defined as that which is potters' clay and that which is oven-makers' clay and that which is brick-makers' clay'?

THEAETETUS. I suppose so.

SOCRATES. Yes: for two reasons. First, we are apparently assuming that the questioner will understand the word 'clay' in our answer, apart from qualifications like 'that which is statuaries'', or any other craftsmen's, which we might affix. But do you think that anyone can understand the meaning of the name of something, without understanding what the thing itself is?

147b2 THEAETETUS. Not at all.

SOCRATES. But then the person who does not understand 'knowledge' cannot understand 'knowledge *about shoes*'.

THEAETETUS. No.

SOCRATES. Nor, indeed, can he who is ignorant of knowledge understand cobbling, or any other craft.

THEAETETUS. That's right.

SOCRATES. So if someone asks you 'What is knowledge?', it is a ridiculous reply just to give the name of some craft. For this reply mentions knowledge *about* something – which is not what was in question.

147c2 THEAETETUS. Apparently so.

SOCRATES. Second, this sort of answer is interminably

roundabout when it could have been brief and commonplace. For example with the clay question, one could presumably have given some such banal and simple answer as 'Clay is earth mixed with moisture' –

147c7   and let the question of *whose* clay look out for itself.

# 7. CRITO 48B–53A

## OBEDIENCE TO THE STATE

48b4    SOCRATES. Have another look at this view which we have formed, to see whether it has stayed put for us or not. I mean our view that it is not being alive that matters most, but living *well*.

CRITO. Yes – that opinion has stayed put.

SOCRATES. What about our opinion that 'living well' means 'living honourably and justly'? Is that still in place, or has it shifted?

CRITO. No, it's still in place.

48b9    SOCRATES. Then if we agree on these points, it follows that what we ought to examine now is this question: 'Is it just for me to try to get out of here without the Athenians' permission, or isn't it?' If it does appear to be just, then we shall try to escape; but if it doesn't, we shall let the attempt alone.

48c2      Now concerning the arguments you have mentioned, Crito,[11] in favour of trying to escape – about the money you say can be provided for bribes and so forth, about what people will think, and who will bring my children up. The truth is that these are the vulgar multitude's arguments – the arguments of the very people who are in such a hurry to sentence people to death, and would bring them back from the dead with equally ill-considered haste, if only they could. But our own argument has proved to us that we should consider nothing else except the question that we have just been discussing. Namely: 'Would it be *just* to pay money and favours to these men who can release me from this prison, and so to escape or be made to escape? Or would it really be unjust to do any of these things?'

48d3    If we decide that it would be unjust to act in these ways, then there will be no need to explore the question whether I will have to die if I stay here and do nothing – nor the question whether I should suffer anything rather than do what is unjust.

CRITO. I'm sure this argument's all very fine, Socrates: but please, think about what we ought to do.

48d8    SOCRATES. Let us look at that question together, my good Crito: and if you by any chance have anything to say against what I shall say, then say it, and I will agree. But if you haven't, then, my dear friend, do stop repeating the same argument to me – that I must escape from here even though the Athenians do not wish it. For it is very important to me to act as I shall act with your agreement, and not against your advice. So see whether you think that the first steps of our argument have been adequately performed; and now try to answer what I shall ask you, by speaking your real views as sincerely as possible.

49a1    CRITO. Well, I'll try.

SOCRATES. Shall we say that we should never willingly do what is unjust under any circumstances? Or should we do what is unjust under some circumstances, but not under others? Is it always true that it is neither good nor honourable to do what is unjust, as we have agreed in so many previous discussions? All those conclusions which we have achieved together up till now – have they all been thrown away in these last few days? We men who have grown so old in our earnest discussions together, Crito – have we failed from the beginning to see that we are no more than children?

49b2    If anything is true, isn't it that previously settled doctrine of ours – no matter what the multitude might think, and no matter if, because of it, we had to put up with something worse even than these sufferings? The doctrine was: that in any case and in all circumstances,

injustice turns out to be an evil and a cause of shame to
the unjust person. Do we agree to that, or don't we?

CRITO. We agree to it.

SOCRATES. Then on no occasion should we act unjustly.

CRITO. No, we shouldn't.

SOCRATES. Nor, indeed, should we return injustice
when injustice is done to us, as the multitude believe; for we should *never* act unjustly.

49c1   CRITO. Apparently not.

SOCRATES. In fact, Crito, should one ever do any sort
of harm?

CRITO. I suppose not, Socrates.

SOCRATES. So then, can it be just, as the multitude
claim it is, for someone who has suffered harm from
someone else to pay his enemy out by harming him
back? Or is that unjust?

CRITO. Unjust.

SOCRATES. So, evidently, there is no difference between
doing a harm to a man and doing him an injustice.

CRITO. You're right.

SOCRATES. Then it is not right either to return injustice
for injustice or to do harm to anyone, no matter what
we may have suffered at their hands.

49d1   Still, Crito, when you say Yes to this, be sure you
haven't agreed to something you don't really believe.
For I know that only a few people believe this now –
and the same will be true in the future. But those who
accept this view have no common ground for debate
with those who do not; when they look at one
another's deliberations, they are bound to despise
each other. So you too must consider very carefully
indeed whether you share my view, and whether it
seems right to you as well. If you do think it right, then
let us begin to deliberate from this first principle: that
it is never the part of someone whose character is right
to act unjustly, or to return injustice for injustice; nor

should someone who has suffered harm seek to defend himself by returning harm for harm.

49e1    Or do you dissent, and refuse to share this first principle? It has long seemed right, and it still seems right, to me. But if by chance you have some other opinion, then tell me and teach it to me. If on the other hand you still remain constant in the views we agreed on in our earlier discussions, then let me tell you what follows.

CRITO. No, I am constant still, and I share your view. So tell me.

SOCRATES. Indeed I will tell you what follows; or rather ask it of you. What follows is the question whether someone who has agreed to do something that is not unjust, should do it; or may he deceive the other party?

CRITO. No, he should do it.

50a1    SOCRATES. Then observe the consequence. If we leave here without the City's agreement, aren't there people to whom we are doing harm – and they the very ones to whom we should least of all do harm? Also, if we do that, are we remaining constant to the standards of justice which we agreed – or are we deserting them?

CRITO. I have no way of answering your question, Socrates: I really don't understand it.

50a5    SOCRATES. Then look at it like this. Suppose I was just about to cut and run from this prison – or whatever else you would like to call this action we're considering, if not cutting and running – and the laws and common good of the City should come and block my path. They might ask me this:

50a8    'Tell us, Socrates, whatever are you thinking of? In this action you have undertaken, what can your intention be, except to do everything you can to destroy us laws, and indeed the whole of the City? Or do you think that a City can go on existing, and avoid being overturned, when the laws that have been made in it have no binding power at all, but are rendered invalid and brought to naught by private citizens?'

50b4     What shall I say, Crito, to answer this accusation – and others like it? For there are plenty of good arguments that an orator, or indeed anyone else, could find to defend this legal principle which is now being annulled – the legal principle that provides that the decisions handed down by the courts shall be binding. Am I to reply to the laws that it is the City which has done an injustice to me, in passing an incorrect verdict on my case? Shall we say this? If not, what else?

50c2     CRITO. Yes, by Zeus – we *shall* say that, Socrates!
        SOCRATES. But what if the laws should reply to me as follows? 'Socrates, did the agreement we made with you allow for this? Or was our agreement that you should abide by whatever verdicts the City hands down?' – and if I were taken aback by this answer, the laws might add this. 'Socrates, don't be surprised at what we say; give your answer, since you are so used to question-and-answer discussions. Come on, then, what charge do you bring against us and against the City in your attempt to destroy us? To begin with, didn't we bring you to birth? Wasn't it according to us, the laws, that your father took your mother's hand in marriage and fathered you? So tell us – is your quarrel with those laws among us which have to do with marriage? Do you think they are badly designed?'

50d6     'No, I do not,' I would reply.
        'What about the laws touching the upbringing and education of children – according to which you were educated yourself? Those of us which are the laws concerning these matters, did we give your father bad instructions when we told him to give you both a cultural and a physical education?'

50e1     'No, those were good instructions,' I should say.
        'Well then! Since this is how you were born and

nurtured and educated, can you claim, in the first place, that you are not our child and our subordinate – both yourself and your children as well? But if you are, then do you think that the justice that regulates your relationship with us can be the justice of equal partners, so that you imagine that whatever we try to do to you, you can justly do the same back to us?

50e8    'In your relationship with your father, and with your commanders on the occasions when you were under command, that was not the sort of justice that held – the sort where you could requite whatever treatment you received, answering back at harsh words, striking back blow for blow, and so on. So do you think that that sort of justice will hold between yourself and your fatherland with its laws? If we try to do away with you because we think that that is just, do you think it will be open to you to retaliate by trying everything you can do to abolish your fatherland and its laws? Will you say that in doing this you do what is *just*? – You who are truly so zealous for virtue!

51a8    'Or are you so wise, Socrates, that you have forgotten that your fatherland is more valuable, more holy, more sacred, and of greater importance – both to the gods and to all men of any sense – than your own father and mother, and any number of your own ancestors? Have you forgotten that you must revere your fatherland, and show it more obedience and submission when it finds fault with you than you would your own father? Have you forgotten that you must agree to whatever it orders, and do whatever it orders? That you must suffer without complaint whatever your fatherland ordains for you? Whether that is blows or bonds, or wounds or death when the fatherland leads you to war, you have to comply – that is what justice demands: you may not give in, you may not retreat, you are not to leave your station. No: in war, in the court-room, and everywhere else too, you must either do whatever the City and the fatherland commands – or else persuade the City that natural justice requires some other command instead. But it is impiety to do anything to your own father or mother without their consent: it is still more impious, then, so to treat your fatherland.' What shall we say to this, Crito? Do the laws speak the truth, or don't they?

51c5   CRITO. Yes – I think they speak the truth.

SOCRATES. 'Then consider, Socrates' – I suppose the laws would say: 'if we do speak the truth about these questions, then what you are now trying to do against us is not just. For we brought you to birth, nurtured you, educated you, gave you and all your fellow-citizens a share of all the fine things we could give. And yet, despite all this, we also made it clear that if any Athenian put the affairs of the City and us its laws to the test by looking us over, and was not pleased with us, then if he chose to, he had full permission to take his property and go off wherever else he wanted to go. None of us laws is an obstacle to him, none of us forbids him, if someone decides to live in one of Athens' colonies because we and the City do not please him, or to settle as a resident alien in some other city. He can go where he likes and he can take his property too.

51d5   'But suppose some of you remain here in Athens, being fully aware of our normal legal procedures, and of how the state is managed in all other respects. We say that such people as remain have, by that very fact, already given their consent to us the laws; they have consented to do whatever we tell them to. Anyone in this position who refuses to obey the laws is, we say, doing a threefold injustice. First, because we are their parents, and they will not obey us; second, because we are their nurses; and third, because such people have agreed to obey us, but do not obey us, and do not persuade us, either, that we have acted wrongly in some way. And yet we lay ourselves before these people as guidelines – we do not, with mere brute force, impose ourselves on them as government by decree. Rather we give them two choices: "Either convince us that you are right, or else do what we say"; but people like this take neither choice.

52a3      'Socrates, if you carry out the escape you are considering, our claim is that you too will stand indicted by these accusations. Nor will you be the least guilty of these charges among the Athenians; no, you will be one of the most culpable of all.' And if at this point I asked, 'How so?', perhaps they would make the just retort that it so happens that I was one of the most avid of the Athenians to make this agreement with them. They might say this:

52b1      'Socrates, we have decisive proof that you were displeased neither with us the laws nor with the City. For you would not have been so much less keen than all the other Athenians to leave your city, unless you had been more pleased with it than all of them were! You have never been out of the City to consult an oracle, nor indeed anywhere else at all, except when you were on military service. Nor have you made any other journeys away from Athens as other people do; you were never taken with an urge to visit other cities and experience other forms of government. We laws of Athens, and this your city – these were enough for you. That was how emphatically you chose us, agreeing to be a citizen in the way we ordained. And what is more, you fathered children in this city: doesn't that show that you approve of it?

52c2      'Again, even at your trial you could have nominated exile rather than execution as your punishment, if you had chosen – thus achieving with the City's permission what you are now trying to do without its permission. But you made such a display, at the time, of having no grievance about it if you were condemned to death:

you preferred death to flight, you said. But now you do not blush to recall those words, nor do you show any respect for us the laws – no, you are trying to abolish us. You are acting like the basest slave – trying to cut and run, against all the contracts and agreements that you made with us to live as a citizen according to our rule. So, in the first place, answer us this. Is it true or not, our claim that you showed your consent to be a citizen according to our rule, by your actions if not by your words?' – What shall we say to this, Crito? Can we do anything but admit it?

52d8    CRITO. No, we can't, Socrates.

SOCRATES. 'So,' they would say, 'what are you doing now, if not transgressing against all your contracts and agreements made with us? Did you not enter into these without duress, and in full knowledge of what you were doing? Did you not have more than enough time to make up your mind in freedom – seventy years, in fact, in which it was open to you to leave the City, if you did not like the laws, or thought that these agreements we have made were unjust? But you did not prefer to go off to Sparta or Crete, even though you are constantly saying how well governed they are: nor to any other town whatever, Greek or barbarian. No, you are less out of the town of Athens than the lame or the blind are, or any of the others who cannot walk where they will. That is a measure of how far beyond all the other Athenians this city is pleasing to you. So also, quite clearly, must we the laws of Athens be pleasing to you – for how could a city's appeal be separated from that of its laws? So won't you now remain true to what you have agreed? Yes you will, if you take our advice, Socrates; and so you will avoid

53a8    becoming ridiculous by departing from the city.'

# 8. EUTHYPHRO 6D–11E

## ✷✷

## HOLINESS AND THE GODS

6d1   SOCRATES. Euthyphro, my friend, your first reply to my request for a definition of holiness is not sufficiently informative. For all you have said is that *this action here* is holiness: namely your prosecution of your father for murder.

EUTHYPHRO. But that reply was true, Socrates.

SOCRATES. Possibly it was, Euthyphro. But wouldn't you agree that there are lots of other holy things?

EUTHYPHRO. Yes, of course there are.

SOCRATES. Then have you forgotten that this isn't what I asked you to do? I didn't ask you to teach me one or two examples of holiness. I asked you to tell me that very form which is the reason *why* all holy things are holy. After all, you did say that all unholy things are unholy because of a single universal unholiness; and likewise with things that are holy. Do you remember?

EUTHYPHRO. Yes, I do.

SOCRATES. Then instruct me about this universal holiness. Tell me what it is, so that I can aim at it and use it as a paradigm. Then any action which you do or anyone else does, if it is of this sort, I shall say that it is holy; but if it is of some other sort, I shall deny it.

EUTHYPHRO. If you want instruction of that sort, Socrates, I shall provide it.

SOCRATES. But indeed I do want it.

7a1   EUTHYPHRO. Very well: what is dear to the gods is holy, and what is not dear to the gods, is not holy.

SOCRATES. Bravo, Euthyphro! That's just the sort of answer I wanted. As to whether it's right, I can't yet say. But naturally you will demonstrate to me that your statement is true.

EUTHYPHRO. I certainly will.

SOCRATES. Come on then: let us examine what we are saying. What is holy is what the gods love, and the man whom the gods love; what is unholy is what the gods hate, and the man whom the gods hate. And holy and unholy are not the same but opposites. Isn't that our thesis?

EUTHYPHRO. Yes, that's right.

SOCRATES. And you think it's a plausible thesis?

7b1   EUTHYPHRO. Yes, I do, Socrates.

SOCRATES. Haven't we also said,[12] Euthyphro, that the gods have quarrels, that they differ from one another and have feuds among themselves?

EUTHYPHRO. Yes, we did say that.

SOCRATES. But, my fine sir – what are their disagreements about that cause this enmity and anger? Look at it like this. If you and I had a disagreement about numbers, as to which of some pair was the larger, would that sort of disagreement cause enmity and anger between us? Or would we resort to reason about a disagreement of that sort, and so resolve it straight away?

7c1   EUTHYPHRO. Certainly we would.

SOCRATES. Again, if we disagreed about the larger and the smaller, wouldn't we resort to measurement, and so settle that dispute straight away as well?

EUTHYPHRO. Indeed we would.

SOCRATES. Similarly, I think, we could adjudicate a dispute about the heavier and the lighter by using scales?

EUTHYPHRO. Of course we could.

7c6   SOCRATES. Then what sort of disagreement between us could there be that we would *not* be able to bring to some sort of decision, so that it caused us to turn enemies to one another in our anger? Perhaps nothing comes to your mind; so consider a suggestion that I'll make. Perhaps the cases of just and unjust, honourable and dishonourable, good and bad, are problem cases. For isn't it just these sorts of cases which sometimes cause us – you, me and everyone else as well – to turn enemies to one another, because we disagree and cannot reach a satisfactory decision about them?

7d6 EUTHYPHRO. Yes, Socrates: this is the exact sort of disagreement that causes trouble, and these are the problem cases.

SOCRATES. So then, Euthyphro, if the gods disagree about anything, won't it be about this sort of question?

EUTHYPHRO. Yes, it is bound to be.

7e1 SOCRATES. Then, my noble Euthyphro, according to your argument, different gods take different things to be just and unjust, honourable and dishonourable, and good and bad. For presumably they would not have quarrels with one another unless they disagreed about these cases. Isn't that so?

EUTHYPHRO. Yes, you're right.

SOCRATES. So any one group of gods will love those things that they consider honourable, good and just, and hate the opposites of these things.

EUTHYPHRO. Yes, clearly.

7e8 SOCRATES. But then, according to what you say, there are some things that are thought to be just by some of the gods, but unjust by others; for it is their disagreements about these questions that cause their quarrels and their civil wars. Wasn't that what you said?

8a2 EUTHYPHRO. Yes, it was.

SOCRATES. So apparently, the very same things are hated by the gods and are loved by the gods; so the same things are both dear to the gods and hateful to them.

EUTHYPHRO. So it seems.

SOCRATES. And therefore, Euthyphro, by the same

argument, the very same things are both holy and unholy.

EUTHYPHRO. Possibly so.

8a7 SOCRATES. Then, you extraordinary person, you have not yet answered my question! For I didn't ask you for what is both holy and unholy at the same time – as, apparently, whatever is dear to the gods is also hateful to them. If that is right, Euthyphro, it will be nothing remarkable if you make yourself dear to Zeus by seeking to punish your father as you are now doing, but hateful to Cronus and Uranus;[13] or perhaps dear to Hephaestus, but hateful to Hera; and so on in the same sort of way to any other gods who care to take sides about your prosecution of your father.

8b6 EUTHYPHRO. But, Socrates, I don't believe any of the gods would disagree over *this* matter: none of them thinks that anyone who kills someone else unjustly can avoid paying the penalty.

SOCRATES. But then have you ever heard any human, even, claiming that someone who has killed someone else unjustly, or perpetrated any other injustice, can avoid paying the penalty?

8c2 EUTHYPHRO. Why, yes – people are forever making that very claim, above all in the courts. Even men who have committed injustices beyond count will do anything and say anything to escape punishment.

SOCRATES. But, Euthyphro, do they admit that they have done what is unjust, and yet claim that they ought not to be punished, even though they admit their crimes?

EUTHYPHRO. No – they don't do that.

SOCRATES. Then it isn't true that they will do or say *anything*, is it? For, I think, they do not dare to dispute that, *if* they have done something wrong, then they ought to be punished.

8d2 EUTHYPHRO. You're right.

SOCRATES. So they don't dispute the claim that anyone who does what is unjust must pay the penalty. Rather,

I suppose, what they dispute is such questions as 'Who acted unjustly?', 'In doing what?', and 'When?'

EUTHYPHRO. You're right.

SOCRATES. Then doesn't just the same happen to the gods, if indeed they do quarrel about what is just and unjust, as your argument has it, and some of them say that other gods have committed injustices, while those other gods reject the charge? Surely, my extraordinary friend, neither a human nor even a god would dare to deny that a penalty was due to someone who was admitted to have acted unjustly.

8e2 EUTHYPHRO. Yes, by and large I think you're right about that, Socrates.

SOCRATES. So, Euthyphro, I believe that those who dispute about good and bad must be disputing about particular things that have been done, whether they are men who dispute or gods – if the gods really do dispute. What they disagree about is – isn't it? – some particular action: some of them say it was justly done, and others say unjustly.

EUTHYPHRO. Certainly, yes.

9a1 SOCRATES. Come then, my dear Euthyphro: instruct me also, so that I may become wiser. What is your proof that all the gods believe that this slave died unjustly – this murdering slave who was cast in chains by his victim's master, who sent off to the oracle to find out what to do with the murderer; but then the slave died from his chains before an answer could come back? What is your proof that it is right for you, the son of the master in question, to react to this affair by prosecuting your father on a charge of murder? Come on – try to give me a clear demonstration of all this, and show that all the gods think that this action of yours is as right as right could be. If you do prove this adequately to me, I shall never cease from praising your wisdom!

9b4 EUTHYPHRO. But probably it's no small task, Socrates –

even though I certainly could demonstrate the point to you.

SOCRATES. I see – you think I am a slower learner than the jury are. For naturally you will demonstrate to them that such acts as the slave's are unjust, and that all the gods hate them?

EUTHYPHRO. Yes, and very clearly too, Socrates – provided they listen to my speech.

9c1 SOCRATES. Oh, yes, they will listen to it – provided only you appear to speak well. But while you have been talking, I have thought of something else, which I have been considering in my mind. It is this:

'Suppose Euthyphro *did* show me, as clearly as ever he might, that all the gods thought a death like the slave's was an unjust death. What more would I have learnt from Euthyphro about what holiness and un-holiness really are? For, it seems, this act of his father's would be hateful to the gods. But we have just seen that this cannot be how what is holy is distinguished from what is not holy. For what is hateful to the gods, it has turned out, is also dear to the gods.'

9c9 So, Euthyphro, I won't detain you for your proof that your action is right. You are free, if you like, to say that all the gods think that what your father did was unjust, and that they all hate his action. But as for our main argument, isn't the following correction now necessary? We should say that what is unholy is what *all* the gods hate, and that what is holy is what *all* the gods love. But what some gods hate and others love is neither holy nor unholy – or else it is both at once. Are you willing for this to be our new definition of the holy and the unholy?

9d6 EUTHYPHRO. What objection could there be to that, Socrates?

SOCRATES. I have no objections to it myself, Euthyphro – but you must examine it, since it is your own definition. Consider: is it on the basis of this definition that you will find it easiest to show me the rightness of your action, as you promised to?

9e1  EUTHYPHRO. Well, I do accept this definition. I *would* say that the holy is what all the gods love, and that the opposite, what all the gods hate, is the unholy.

SOCRATES. Then shall we examine this statement now, Euthyphro, to see whether it is right? Or shall we let it go, and just take for granted something that is our own opinion and everyone else's too? If someone merely tells us 'This is how things are', do you think we should simply accept what he says? Or should we examine what the speaker means?

EUTHYPHRO. Yes, we should examine it – even though I myself now think that we have got the matter right.

10a1  SOCRATES. Well, my good friend, we'll soon see about that. Consider this question. Is what is holy loved by the gods because it is holy? Or is it holy because it is loved by the gods?

EUTHYPHRO. I don't know what you're talking about, Socrates.

SOCRATES. Then I had better try to express it more clearly. We distinguish being carried and carrying, being led and leading, being seen and seeing. You see that in all these cases the first expression differs from the second? And you see how?

EUTHYPHRO. I think so, yes.

SOCRATES. Well, don't we distinguish in just this way between being loved and loving?

EUTHYPHRO. Of course.

10b1  SOCRATES. So tell me: is something which is carried, carried because someone carries it? Or for some other reason?

EUTHYPHRO. Because someone carries it.

SOCRATES. And what is led, is led because someone leads it? And what is seen, is seen because someone sees it?

EUTHYPHRO. Yes, yes.

SOCRATES. Then it is not because it is seen that someone sees it. The order of explanation is the reverse: it is because someone sees it that it is seen. And it is because someone leads something, or carries it, that it is led or carried: not *vice versa*.

10c1 Is it clear what I mean, Euthyphro? If x becomes y, then it is not because x is in a state of becoming that x becomes y. On the contrary, it is because x becomes y that x is in a state of becoming. And if x undergoes any process, then it is not because x is a thing in process that x undergoes that process. On the contrary, it is because x undergoes that process that x is a thing in process. Do you agree with this?

EUTHYPHRO. Yes, I do.

SOCRATES. So: isn't 'what is loved' either a thing in a state of becoming, or else a thing in some process or other?

EUTHYPHRO. Certainly it is.

SOCRATES. But this case is just like the other ones, isn't it? It is not because it is 'what is loved' that it is loved by those who love it. On the contrary: it is because they love it, that it is 'what is loved'.

EUTHYPHRO. Necessarily.

10d1 SOCRATES. So what shall we say about the holy, Euthyphro? Isn't it, according to your view, what all the gods love?

EUTHYPHRO. Yes.

SOCRATES. Well, do they love it because it is holy, or for some other reason?

EUTHYPHRO. No – for that reason.

SOCRATES. So because it is holy, it is loved? And it is not the case that, because it is loved, it is holy?

EUTHYPHRO. Apparently not.

SOCRATES. But now: it is because the gods love it, that what is dear to the gods is dear to them and loved by them.

10e1 EUTHYPHRO. Of course.

SOCRATES. So what is dear to the gods is not the holy,

as you claim, Euthyphro; nor is the holy what is dear to the gods. The two things are different.

EUTHYPHRO. But why, Socrates?

SOCRATES. Because we agreed that the holy is loved because it is holy, and not holy because it is loved – didn't we?

EUTHYPHRO. Yes.

SOCRATES. But what is dear to the gods, we said, is dear to them for the very reason that they love it: it is not loved because it is dear to the gods.

EUTHYPHRO. You're right.

10e9   SOCRATES. But my dear Euthyphro: suppose what is dear to the gods and what is holy are identical. In that case two consequences follow. First: if what is holy is loved because it is holy, then likewise, what is dear to the gods is loved because it is dear to the gods. And second: if what is dear to the gods is dear to the gods because it is loved by them, then likewise, what is holy is holy because it is loved.[14]

11a3     But, as you can now see, the two cases are opposite to each other, and so must be entirely different. For what is dear to the gods is 'lovable' only in the sense that it *is* loved; whereas what is holy is 'lovable' in the sense that it *deserves to be* loved.[15]

    Euthyphro, I asked you for a definition of the holy; but I rather think that you must have been unwilling to reveal its essence to me. For instead, you just mentioned one of the incidental features of the holy – namely, that it is loved by all the gods. But what it *is*, you still haven't told me. So if you care about the success of our inquiry, don't hide it from me! No, tell me again from the beginning: what is the nature of the holy itself? It doesn't matter whether it is loved by the gods, or whatever else may happen to it; for we shan't disagree about that. But speak it out boldly – what is the holy, and what is the unholy?

11b6   EUTHYPHRO. Why, Socrates, I just don't know how to

tell you what I mean. For somehow it keeps happening that whatever thesis we agree on ends up running rings round us, and will not stay put in the place where we establish it!

11c1 SOCRATES. Yes, Euthyphro, your words behave like the walking statues produced by my forefather Daedalus.[16] If I had spoken your words and made your claims, perhaps you would mock me by saying that my ancestry was the reason why the products of my arguments kept making off, and would not stay wherever they were put. However, the claims are yours; so I must find some other joke. But certainly it's true, as you yourself think, that the claims will not stay put.

11c7 EUTHYPHRO. Actually, Socrates, I don't think our conversation does call for any other joke but that one. I'm not the one who implants this wandering tendency in our arguments, so that they will not stay put. No, you seem to be the Daedalus. As far as I am concerned, the arguments *could* have stayed put, just where they were.

11d5 SOCRATES. In that case, my friend, I think I must have become an even cleverer craftsman than Daedalus – inasmuch as he only made his own handiwork move, whereas, apparently, I make other people's handiwork move as well as my own. Indeed the most ingenious point of all about my skill is that I am an expert in it against my will. For I would far rather that the arguments should stay put, and that they could be established without alteration, than that I should inherit the wisdom of Daedalus – and the riches of

11e4 Tantalus![17]

# 9. REPUBLIC 334B–336A

✦

## JUSTICE TOWARDS ENEMIES

334b8 'By Zeus,' said Polemarchus, 'I don't know any longer what I did mean by what I said about justice. But I do still hold to this view of Simonides':[18] justice means helping your friends and harming your enemies.'

334c1 'When you say friends (or enemies), do you mean those who *appear* to be beneficial to you (or harmful); or those who really are, even if they do not appear to be?'

'Well,' said he, 'it seems likely that a man will count as friends those whom he believes beneficial; and those whom he thinks to be pernicious, he will take for enemies.'

'But don't people make mistakes about this, so that they take to be beneficial many people who are not beneficial, and *vice versa*?'

'Yes, they do.'

'Then aren't good men enemies in such people's eyes? And aren't bad men their "friends"?'

'Certainly, yes.'

'But despite that, it is just for people who are in this situation to help wicked men and harm good men.'

334d1 'Apparently so.'

'But good men are just, and are not of the sort to act unjustly.'

'True.'

'So according to your reasoning, it is just to harm those who do no injustice.'

'Not at all, Socrates,' he said: 'this is to reason like a scoundrel.'

'Then,' I said, 'is it just to harm the unjust, and benefit the just?'

'Yes – that sounds more like it.'

334d8        'But, Polemarchus, it will still turn out that it is just, for all the people who are in error about who is beneficial and harmful, to harm their friends and help their enemies; for such people's friends are scoundrels, and their enemies are good men. And so we shall be saying exactly the opposite of what we decided Simonides meant.'

334e3        'Yes indeed,' admitted Polemarchus, 'that is the consequence. But then let us change our position. Perhaps we were wrong after all in what we said about the friend and the enemy.'

'What did we say, Polemarchus?'

'We said that a friend is someone who *appears* beneficial.'

'How are you proposing to change our position?' I asked.

334e7        'We should say,' he replied, 'that a friend is someone who *both appears and is* beneficial; and that the person who just appears beneficial, but isn't really, appears to be a friend, but isn't really. I make the same proposal about enemies too.'

335a2        'Evidently, by this argument, the friend will be the good man, and the enemy the bad.'

'Yes.'

'So you are telling us to amend our earlier definition of justice – that justice is to do good to the friend and harm to the enemy. You want us to amend this so that it says that it is just to do good to the friend if he is a good man, and harm to the enemy if he is a bad man.'

335b1        'Yes,' said Polemarchus: 'that seems just right to me.'

'But,' I said, 'is it characteristic of a good man to harm anyone at all?'

'Certainly,' he said: 'he ought to harm those who are scoundrels and enemies.'

'Do we make horses better or worse by harming them?'

'Worse.'

'Worse by a decrease in what kind of virtue? The virtue of dogs, or the virtue of horses?'

'Horses.'

'And if we harm dogs, don't they become worse by a decrease in the virtue of dogs, and not that of horses?'

335c1 'Obviously.'

'Well, my friend, shouldn't we say the same about humans? If we harm humans, won't they become worse by a decrease in specifically human virtue?'

'Yes, they certainly will.'

'But isn't *justice* the specifically human virtue?'

'That too is bound to be true.'

'Then, my friend, humans who are harmed are bound to become more unjust as a result.'

'Apparently.'

'But look – is it possible for people who are trained in the arts to make others less skilled in the arts by the use of their training?'

'Of course not.'

'Or is it possible for trained horsemen to make others less skilled on horseback by the use of *their* training?'

'Certainly not.'

335d1 'Then can it really be possible for just people to make others less just by the use of their justice? Or, in general, for good men to make others bad by the use of their virtue?'

'No, that's impossible.'

'Again: heat, I assume, has no tendency to make things cold: that tendency belongs to coldness, heat's opposite.'

'Yes.'

'And dryness has no tendency to make things wet. That tendency belongs to dryness' opposite.'

'Of course.'

'Then neither has goodness any tendency to harm. That tendency belongs to goodness' opposite.'

'Apparently.'

'But the just man is, surely, a good man?'

'Of course he is.'

'Then the just man has no tendency to do harm, Polemarchus, neither to a friend, nor to anyone else. That tendency belongs to his opposite, the unjust man.'

'You seem to be absolutely right about that, Socrates,' said Polemarchus.

335e1      'So if someone said that it is just to give to each his dues, meaning by this that his enemies ought to take harm from the just man and his friends help, then he was no Wise Man[19] who said it. For what he said is not true: as we have seen, it is never just to harm anyone.'

'I agree,' he said.

'So,' I said, 'you and I together will resist anyone who says that it was Simonides who said this, or Bias or Pittacus, or any one of those wise and reverend men.'

'I certainly,' said Polemarchus, 'am ready to join the fray.'

336a1      'Do you know who I think did originate this saying, that it is just to help our friends and harm our enemies?'

'Who?' he asked.

'I think it must have been Periander, or Perdiccas, or Xerxes, or Ismenias of Thebes, or some other fat cat who thought he could get away with anything.'

'You must be right,' he said.

'So anyway,' I said, 'since this has turned out not to be what justice or The Just is, does anyone have any
336a10 other definition for us?'

NOTES

1. Cf. reading 7, and *Apology* 37d1.
2. In fact Meno's image is surely not a flattering one to Socrates.
3. The reference is to Theodorus' and Theaetetus' research project into the defining of mathematical terms. For details see *Theaetetus* 147d–148b.
4. This is Socrates' and Theaetetus' first meeting: *Theaetetus* 144c–d.
5. The name means 'revealer of virtue'.
6. Cf. Plato's eugenics: *Republic* 459 ff.
7. E.g. Alcibiades: see *Symposium*.
8. A veiled insult.
9. A commonplace Greek practice with handicapped babies.
10. Cf. the discussions of harming and being harmed in readings 7, 9 and 16.
11. *Crito* 45a–46a.
12. *Euthyphro* 6b–d.
13. In Greek mythology Cronos was Zeus's father, and Uranus was Cronos' father; both father–son relationships were extremely violent.
14. If 'holy' = 'dear to the gods', then it can make no difference if we substitute either term for the other in any context. But it does make a difference. So these terms are not synonyms.
15. Cf. Moore on Mill, in *Principia Ethica*, ch. 3: ' "Good", Mill tells us, means "desirable" . . . [but] "desirable" does not mean "able to be desired" as "visible" means "able to be seen". The desirable means simply what *ought* to be desired . . .'
16. Cf. reading 27.
17. Which were perpetually just out of Tantalus' reach: cf. our adjective 'tantalising'.
18. Simonides the poet defined justice as 'giving back to each what is owed to him' (*Rep.* 331e); from *Rep.* 332a–b on, Polemarchus interprets this as meaning that help is owed to friends (or good men) and harm to enemies (or bad men).
19. Simonides was often included in the traditional lists of the Seven Sages of Greece, as were the Bias and Pittacus also mentioned here.

# PART II

❖❖

# CAN VIRTUE BE TAUGHT?

# 10. MENO 86c–90a

## ❧

## CAN VIRTUE BE TAUGHT? (I)

86c4   SOCRATES. Then since you and I agree [on the basis of the theory of recollection] that we should inquire into what we don't know about, shall we try together to discover what exactly virtue is?

MENO. Certainly . . . although, Socrates, what I'd really like to consider and hear your views on is the question that I asked at the beginning. That was whether the person who is trying to find out what exactly virtue is, is trying to find out about something that is teachable; or whether virtue is something that comes to men by nature or in some such way as that.

86d2   SOCRATES. Meno, if I had full control not only over myself, but over you too, we wouldn't have begun to look at whether virtue is teachable or not before we had first inquired into what it is. But you will not even try to control yourself – on the grounds, for heaven's sake, that you want to be *free*. Instead you are trying to control me, and succeeding too: so I shall go along with you. For what else can I do?

86e1     So, it seems, we are to discuss the qualities of virtue when we don't know the nature of virtue. Even so, relax your control over me just a little, and allow me to look at the question by the method of hypothesis. [86e3–87c2][1] Consider this hypothesis: *If* virtue is a kind of knowledge, *then* virtue can be taught.

MENO. That must be right.

SOCRATES. Well, haven't we got off lightly! All we need say is: if virtue is of one sort then it is teachable; if it is of another, then it isn't.

MENO. Yes indeed.

SOCRATES. So the next question that we must look at, apparently, is the question whether virtue is knowledge, or something other than knowledge.

87d1    MENO. Yes, I certainly think that's what we must look at next.

SOCRATES. Well, can we deny that virtue is a good thing? Isn't this hypothesis of ours a stable one: that virtue is a good?

MENO. Of course it is.

SOCRATES. So if there is any good which is different and separate from knowledge, then it may easily be true that virtue is not knowledge. But if knowledge is closely involved with every sort of good, then our suspicion that virtue is some sort of knowledge would seem correct.

MENO. So it would.

SOCRATES. Now you agree that it is by virtue that we are good?

MENO. Yes.

87e1    SOCRATES. And if we are good then we are beneficial – for all good things are beneficial, aren't they?

MENO. Yes.

SOCRATES. So, then, virtue is beneficial too?

MENO. It must be, on our premisses.

SOCRATES. Then let us consider, by going over individual cases, what sort of things there are that are beneficial to us. We would say health, and strength, and wealth, no doubt: these and things like them are the sort of things that are beneficial, aren't they?

MENO. Yes.

88a1    SOCRATES. But we also agree that these things can sometimes be harmful. Wouldn't you say so? Or do you hold a different view?

MENO. No, I agree.

SOCRATES. Then let us ask: what is it about these things that makes them beneficial when they are beneficial, and harmful when they are harmful? Isn't the answer that when they are correctly used, they are beneficial; and when they are not, they are harmful?

MENO. Yes, certainly.

SOCRATES. Next let us look at the goods of the soul. Wouldn't you say that these were temperance, justice, courage, teachability, memory, public-spirited generosity, and all that sort of thing?

88b1    MENO. I would.

SOCRATES. Consider then: don't you think that those goods of the soul which are not knowledge, but something else, can sometimes be harmful and sometimes beneficial? Courage, for instance – if courage is not practical wisdom, but only a sort of daring spirit. Doesn't a man come to harm when he is daring but not thoughtful – whereas he is benefited by his daring if it is accompanied by due thought?

MENO. Yes.

SOCRATES. And isn't the same true of temperance and teachability? Don't our submission to discipline and our efforts to learn benefit us when they are accompanied by thought, but harm us if they are not?

88c1    MENO. They certainly do.

SOCRATES. In short, isn't it true that every undertaking or ordeal of our souls brings us to happiness if it is guided by practical wisdom, but to the opposite of happiness if it is not?

MENO. It seems to be.

SOCRATES. So if virtue is one of the conditions of the soul, and if virtue is necessarily beneficial, then virtue must be practical wisdom. After all, all these dispositions of the soul are neither beneficial nor harmful in themselves: they only become harmful or beneficial when practical wisdom or the opposite is present too. So on this argument, virtue must – in so far as it is beneficial – be some sort of practical wisdom.

88d3    MENO. So it seems to me.

SOCRATES. Then what about the other things which we have just mentioned – wealth and so on – as being sometimes good and sometimes harmful? Isn't their case exactly like that of temperance and teachability, where the presence of practical wisdom makes these things beneficial to the interests of the soul, while practical folly makes them harmful? Isn't it likewise true that the soul which correctly uses and directs money and such things makes them beneficial to itself, while the soul which uses them incorrectly makes them harmful?

88e3    MENO. Certainly.

SOCRATES. And the wise soul is the one that directs such things correctly, whereas the foolish one goes astray?

MENO. That's right.

SOCRATES. Then we can draw this verdict from all such cases. The goodness of everything else in a man depends on his soul; and the goodness of his soul depends on his having practical wisdom. Our argument identifies practical wisdom with the beneficial. So shall we say that virtue is the beneficial?

89a3    MENO. Yes, by all means.

SOCRATES. And shall we say that practical wisdom is either the whole or a part of virtue?

MENO. That seems right to me, Socrates.

SOCRATES. But if all this is right, then good men cannot be good by nature.

MENO. Apparently not.

89b1    SOCRATES. No, for if they were good by nature, then I take it this would be the result: presumably some of us would be able to recognise which of our young men were good by nature. And when these youths had been identified, we would arrest them and keep them under lock and key in the citadel. Far better to put them on deposit than any amount of gold! This would prevent anyone interfering with them, and ensure that they could be useful to the state when they came of age.

MENO. Very likely, Socrates.

SOCRATES. So if it is not by nature that the good become good, is it by learning?

89c1 MENO. By now it seems a necessary conclusion. So it's clear from this argument, Socrates, given our hypothesis that if virtue is a kind of knowledge, then virtue can be taught, that since virtue *is* knowledge, it *can* be taught.

SOCRATES. Very probable, by Zeus . . . Still, perhaps our argument was not a sensible one.

MENO. But we've only just said it *was* a sensible one!

SOCRATES. Yes, but it's not enough for it to look sensible just a moment ago; it must look sensible now and in the future too, if there is to be any health in it.

89d1 MENO. Well, I never! What can you have in mind to go making problems, and start doubting that virtue is knowledge?

SOCRATES. I'll tell you, Meno. It's not our hypothesis that *if* virtue is a kind of knowledge then virtue can be taught that I want to take back: that seems sensible. But consider: am I not perhaps justified in doubting whether virtue *is* a kind of knowledge? Tell me this. If anything at all – not just virtue – is teachable, then mustn't there be teachers and learners of that subject?

89e1 MENO. That seems right to me, yes.

SOCRATES. Conversely: if there are neither teachers nor learners of a subject, then it cannot be taught.

MENO. Indeed: but don't you think that there are teachers of virtue?

89e4 SOCRATES. In truth, I have looked again and again to see whether there were any teachers of virtue: I've done everything to find one, and I've failed. Yet I have searched with any number of people, and above all those whom I thought would have most experience in the matter. But look, Meno! Here's Anytus[2] – sitting down with us at just the right moment for us to share 90a1 our inquiry with him . . .

# 11. PROTAGORAS 318A–325C

✦

## CAN VIRTUE BE TAUGHT? (II)

318a2  'Well, Protagoras,' I said, 'it so happens that my friend Hippocrates here has an urge to spend some time under your tuition. So, he says, he would like to know what he will gain from it if he does.'

Protagoras responded straight away, with these words: 'Young sir, if you associate with me, this is what you will gain: the very first day you come, you will go home a better man than you were at the start of the day; and the next day, better again. Every day that you spend with me, you will be making continual progress.'

318b1  When I heard this, I said: 'But, Protagoras, what you predict isn't at all remarkable: it's only to be expected. After all, if anyone taught you anything that you don't happen to know, you would become a better man too – for all your reverend age and wisdom. We didn't mean that: what we meant was this question.

318b5  'Suppose Hippocrates here suddenly underwent a change of urge, and decided that what he wanted instead of a connection with Protagoras was to attend the studio of that young man who has just appeared in our town – Zeuxippus of Heraclea. Suppose he approached Zeuxippus with the same question as he is now approaching you with, and heard from him the same answer as you have given: that "every day he spends in Zeuxippus' company, Hippocrates will become better and will make progress". Hippocrates might then ask Zeuxippus a further question: "Better at what? What sort of progress?" Zeuxippus would say: "Better at *painting*, of course." Or suppose

Hippocrates went to see Orthagoras of Thebes with his question, and heard from him the same answer as you have given. He might then ask Orthagoras the same further question: "In what way will I become better every day by spending time with Orthagoras?" And Orthagoras would say: "Better at *flute-playing*, of course."

318d1     'Protagoras, please give the young man and myself an answer to our question of the same form. If Hippocrates spends time with Protagoras, and goes away a better man on the the very first day he does so, and makes continual progress every day thereafter – *in what way* better? And progress *in what*?'

318d4     'A good question, Socrates,' replied Protagoras when he had heard me out; 'and answering good questions is always a pleasure. Well, Hippocrates will have a quite different experience of education at my hands from what he would have at any other sophist's. For most of them corrupt their pupils; when the young men have already outgrown formal study, they drag them kicking and screaming back into it, and teach them mathematics and astronomy and geometry and music.' (And here Protagoras shot a glance at Hippias.[3]) 'But if he comes to me, he won't learn about anything other than what he wanted to learn about. For what I will teach him is good judgement concerning his own affairs, and how best to order his own household; and as for political matters, I will teach him how to have the greatest power of speech and of deed in his city.'

319a2     'Really!' I said – 'Am I following you right? I think what you are talking of is political science: you are undertaking to make good citizens out of men?'

'That's it exactly,' said Protagoras: 'just that is the promise that I make to my customers.'

319a7     'Why,' I said, 'what a noble achievement that is, Protagoras – if you really have achieved it. To you at least I should say no more and no less than I truly think: but what I truly thought was that *no one* could teach people how to be a good citizen. But you say it can be taught, so who am I to argue? Still, I do have a right to tell you where I got this view that good citizenship cannot be taught – cannot be provided for humans, by humans.

319b3    'I would agree with all the other Greeks that the Athenians are a wise people. But what I observe in our Athenian assemblies is this. When we convene on a question of architecture which confronts the city, we call in architects as advisers on what is to be done; when we convene about a shipbuilding project, we call in the shipbuilders; and likewise with every other kind of business that we think can be taught and learnt. If anyone else tries to be the Assembly's adviser on such questions – anyone who they do not think possesses the relevant sort of technical expertise – they don't accept his advice, no matter how highly regarded or rich or aristocratic he may be. No, on the contrary, they jeer and heckle him until he is so overwhelmed by the uproar that he either abandons the rostrum voluntarily or else is taken down from it by the stewards of the House – perhaps even ejected from the chamber by the order of the Chairmen.

319c9    'This is how they behave regarding matters where they think there is such a thing as expertise. But when they are due to debate some issue concerning the management of the city, just about anyone can get on his feet and advise them about that. Carpenter, blacksmith, cobbler: tinker, sailor, rich man, beggar man, noble, prole – they're all given the same hearing. No one attacks any of them with the sort of charge we heard so much of in the other cases – that here they are trying to advise the city on managing its affairs when they have no qualifications to do so, since no expert has ever taught them political science! The reason why that charge is not pressed is clear: it's that the Athenians don't think that this sort of virtue *can* be taught.

319d9 'This is how things are concerning the common interests of the city; in private life too, our wisest and noblest citizens are unable to transmit the virtue that they possess to others. After all, Pericles, father of these two young men here,[4] gave them a fine and gentlemanly education in every subject for which he found them other tutors. Yet outstanding citizenship, his own speciality, he neither taught them himself nor had them learn from any other teacher. Instead they wander around like a pair of sacred oxen, browsing on the hoof, on the off-chance they might stumble upon real virtue. Or, if you like, take Cleinias, younger brother to Alcibiades here. Pericles was his guardian too; and Pericles feared that Cleinias was being corrupted by Alcibiades, and so took him away from Alcibiades, and put him in care to be brought up by Ariphron. Yet before six months were up Pericles gave it up as a bad job, and handed back Cleinias to Alcibiades, having no further idea about what to do with him.

320b1 'I can think of plenty of other cases of people who were good men themselves, yet never made anyone else any better, relatives or non-relatives. It was these cases, Protagoras, that I had in mind when I formed my view that virtue could not be taught. But when I hear you say that it can, I am not so sure of my view. I'm sure there must be something in what you say, because I consider you to have vast experience and learning, and to be simply the pioneer in certain subjects. So if you have any more cogent way of demonstrating that virtue can be taught, don't say that it is over our heads: put your case to us.'

320c1 'No indeed,' said Protagoras, 'I won't say that, Socrates; but do you want to hear my case put as a story, of the sort an old man like me might tell to young fellows? Or do you want me to make my case by way of straight argument?'

Many in the audience replied by begging him to present his case however he liked.

'Well,' said Protagoras, 'I think it might be more fun if I told you a story.

320d1 'In the beginning there were gods, but no species of mortal creatures. When the destined time came for mortal species to come into being, it was the gods who shaped them inside the earth: compounding them out of earth, and fire, and all the substances that include a mixture of fire and earth.

'When the gods were ready to lead all these creatures forth into the daylight, they commanded the brothers Prometheus and Epimetheus to round off the work by allotting to each the faculties that suited them. Epimetheus begged Prometheus to let him do the allocation – "and you can correct my work," he said, "once I have done it". Prometheus agreed, and Epimetheus went to work.

320e1 'He equipped some creatures with strength but not speed; others he gave speed, but they were the weaker ones. He gave some creatures natural armour; others he gave no natural weapons, but for them he devised some other means of self-preservation. Those creatures which he made small he allowed to have the means of escape by flight or by living underground; the ones which he made big were kept safe just by their size. And so on: Epimetheus dealt out all the faculties in this even-handed way, for the concern in his mind was to ensure that no species should go extinct.

321a3 'Once Epimetheus had given all the species enough resources to ensure that they would not destroy each other, he also made sure they were protected against Zeus's seasons. He cloaked them about with dense pelts and thick hides which would be strong enough to defend them from the winter weather, but able to deal with summer's heat as well, and which when they moulted would provide each of them with a natural and appropriate carpet inside their lairs. He equipped some of them with hooves, others with talons or with hides that would not bleed; and he provided different species with different diets, some eating the flowers of the earth, some the fruits of the trees, and some roots. There were also animals whom he allowed to eat other animals as their food. He made these carnivores so that they only produced a few offspring, whereas the creatures which the carnivores ate produced many offspring, to ensure the survival of their species.

321c1     'Now because Epimetheus was not altogether wise, he did not notice that he had used up all the faculties he had to give out on the dumb animals. The human race he had left over, all unadorned, and he was at a loss as to what he could do with it. It was while this problem was sinking in on his wits that Prometheus showed up to correct his brother's allocations. There were all the other creatures with their fine-tuned faculties, while man, Prometheus saw, was naked, barefoot, and defenceless, with nowhere to lay his head. Yet here already was the day of destiny, on which man too was to emerge from the earth into the daylight!

321c9     'Then Prometheus could see no way of preserving the human species: so he stole from Hephaestus and Athene the gift of wisdom in all the arts together with fire (without which no one could possibly acquire wisdom in the arts, or find it useful)[5] and presented this gift to mankind.

    'This meant that humanity had enough sense to survive. But they still had no political sense, for this lay with Zeus alone. It was as yet beyond Prometheus to make his way into that fastness which is the very house of Zeus, for even Zeus's sentries were fearsome figures. But he did come unseen into the dwelling which Athene and Hephaestus shared as their studio, and stole Hephaestus' craft of fire and Athene's art as well. He gave these to humanity, and that is why humans are able to live in some ease – although, as the story goes, by Epimetheus' error Prometheus later faced the penalties of theft.

322a2    'Since man now had a share in what was proper to the gods, his kinship with the divine meant, first, that he alone among animals recognised that there were gods, and undertook to set up altars and statues of them. Second, human skill soon enabled man to articulate speech and names for things, and to discover buildings, clothes, shoes, and the foods that the earth provides.

322a8    'Thus equipped, men lived in scattered dwellings at first, and there were no cities. This meant that humans were constantly being devoured by the wild animals, since they were weaker than the beasts in every respect. They had enough craftsman's skill to provide them with food, but they had no idea about how to wage war on the wild animals: for as yet they had no political science, of which warfare is a part. So they tried to form associations, and preserve their lives by founding cities. But when they did associate, they were always wronging one another because of their lack of political sense. And so they would be scattered again, and go back to being eaten by wild animals.

322c1    'Then Zeus was afraid for our race, lest it should be altogether wiped out. So he commissioned his messenger Hermes to bring Shame and Justice[6] to humans, that there might be ordered political communities and uniting ties of friendship among men. And Hermes asked Zeus, "In what way should I give Shame and Justice to humans? Should I allot them in the same way as the other arts have been allotted? They were allotted in such a way that one person who has medical skill, or whatever other art, is enough for the needs of many individuals. So shall I distribute

Justice and Shame among humans in the same way? Or shall I allot them to everyone?"

322d1    '"Allot them to everyone," replied Zeus, "and let each have his share. For there can be no communities if only a few people in them share in these gifts, in the same way as only a few share in other gifts. No: set it up as a law with my authority that the person who cannot take his share of Shame and Justice is to be extirpated from the city like a plague."

332d7    'Well, Socrates, this is why the Athenians, and the men of other cities too, think that only a few people should have a share in advising when the argument is about a builder's or any other craftsman's virtue, and will not accept advice from any person outside that élite. So you say: and as I say, they are quite right. But when they meet to take advice on the virtue of the city, which always needs to be promoted by the virtues of justice and temperance, they quite rightly allow every man's opinion, since – if there is to be a city at all – it is proper that every person should have a share of these virtues.

323a3    'So there is your explanation. But lest you should think I am hoodwinking you, consider another proof that all humans really do think that every man has a share in justice and in the other kinds of political virtue. It is this. In the case of the other virtues, as you remark, anyone who says that he is a good flute-player, or claims to have some other skill that he does not really possess, is either ridiculed or condemned, and the men of his household reproach him for his ravings. But in the case of justice and the other kinds of political virtue, if a man who is well known not to be just openly admits his injustice to many other people, they call it raving madness. Yet they would have called it temperance if he had admitted that he knew nothing about flute-playing! People say that everyone should *claim* to be just, whether they are or not, and that not even to make a show of justice would be simple insanity. For they think that, necessarily, no one at all can avoid partaking in justice in one way or another: if they did, they would not be human at all.

323c2 'This much, then, to make the point that all men rightly accept anyone's advice in matters relating to this sort of virtue, because all men think that everyone has a share in justice and temperance. I will now try to demonstrate a further point to you. This is that people do not regard this sort of virtue as natural or instinctive: rather, they think that it is taught, and is acquired by whoever does acquire it by pure application.

323d1 'Take those evils that come to humanity either by nature or by chance. Nobody gets angry with those who have been afflicted by evils of this sort, nor rebukes them, nor lectures them, nor punishes them, for having failed to avoid their predicament. What we do is pity such people. Who would be such a fool as to try using anger or rebuke or whatever to bring about some change in those who are merely ugly, or dwarves, or weaklings? The point is, I take it, that people realise that admirable and unadmirable states of these sorts come about among humans through nature and chance.

323d8 'The case is quite different when it comes to those goods that people think humans acquire through application and training and teaching. If anyone lacks these goods, and has the corresponding evils instead, then they are the ones who endure anger, punishment, and reproof. One of these evils is injustice; then there is impiety, and in brief everything that is contrary to the excellence of the citizen. Every man feels anger and reproach towards anyone who has such vices as these – which just shows that we all treat these vices as resulting from lack of application and teaching.

324a2 'And, Socrates, if you are willing to turn your thoughts to the nature of punishment, then doesn't its power over wrongdoers show you that humans in general consider virtue to be something that can be taught? For no one punishes wrongdoers with the mere fact that they have done wrong in mind, nor just for *that* reason – not unless they are just unthinkingly getting their own back, like savage animals. No; no one who tries to apply punishment in a reasonable way takes revenge for past misdeeds: after all, he cannot undo what has once been done. Rather he punishes with an eye on the future – to make sure that the offender won't do it again, and neither will anyone else who sees him punished. But anyone who punishes with this in mind, must understand that virtue can be taught: for he is punishing to deter.

324c1     'This then is the view of everyone who seeks either private or public redress. But everyone seeks redress from, and the punishment of, those who they think have done wrong: not least the Athenians, your own compatriots, Socrates. Thus if my argument is right, the Athenians too are among those who think that virtue can be acquired and taught.

324c6     'So I think I have given you a sufficient demonstration that the Athenians are right to accept the advice even of the bronze-smith and the cobbler in political affairs; and that they believe that virtue can be taught and acquired. That only leaves us with your third problem – your puzzle about good men. Why is it that the good men all teach their sons every other subject that they can get teachers of, and make them wise men in those ways, and yet don't make their sons even one bit better at their own speciality – being good citizens?

324d8     'On this point, Socrates, I shall address you in straight argument, and not in a story. So ask yourself this. Do you agree that there is any one thing that every citizen must have a share of if there is to be a city at all? Or don't you? This is the question which

determines the solution to your puzzle, and you won't
find the solution anywhere else.

324e3   'Suppose then that there is some such thing, and that
what it is is not the builder's art or the bronze-smith's or
the potter's, but justice, temperance and holiness: that
is, what I shall refer to with one word, as virtue.
Suppose that it is virtue, in this sense, of which all
citizens must have their share, and that it is according to
virtue, and not otherwise, that everything else must be
learnt or performed by whoever wishes to learn or to act
in whatever way. Suppose further that it is the person
who does not share in virtue, whether that person is a
child or a man or a woman, whom we ought to instruct
and punish until they are improved by their punishment: and that anyone who does not respond to this
treatment and correction is to be exiled or executed, as
an incurable case.

325b2   'If all this is right, then what about the good men
who educate their sons in every other way, but not in
virtue? What an extraordinary thing they're doing!
For we have already shown that they think virtue *can*
be taught, both publicly and privately. So do we really
believe that, although virtue can be taught and cher-
ished, good men teach their sons everything else *but*
this – even though the knowledge of all the other
subjects is not a matter of life and death? Do we
really think that they do not teach their sons virtue
with the greatest care of all, when the penalty their
sons will pay for ignorance of and inattention to *this*
subject is death or exile – and not only death but the
confiscation of their properties and the destruction of
their entire families as well? Of course we don't think
that, Socrates. No: they teach and correct their children in virtue continually, from the time when they are
325c8   still little children, to the very ends of their lives.'

# 12. PROTAGORAS 329B–333B

## ⇒⇐

## THE UNITY OF THE VIRTUES

329b8 'Protagoras,' I said, 'you say that virtue can be taught; and if anyone can convince me of that, you can. But try and satisfy me about something that I was surprised at in your speech. You said that Zeus sent Justice and Shame to men; and you repeatedly claimed that justice, temperance, holiness and all such things were like one single unity together: virtue. So now take me through a precise account of these qualities. Tell me whether virtue is one thing, of which justice, temperance and holiness are parts; or whether instead these qualities I have named are all names for exactly the same one thing. This is what I still wish to understand.'

329d2     'But your question is easy to answer, Socrates,' replied Protagoras: 'virtue is one thing, and the qualities you inquire about are parts of virtue.'

'Do you mean parts in the way that the parts of a face are parts – a mouth and a nose and eyes and ears? Or do you mean parts in the way that parts of a block of gold are parts of it – so that there is no difference, except in size, between any one portion of gold and any other: neither between any two parts of the block, nor between any part of the block and the block itself?'

'I believe, Socrates, that it is in the former sense that these qualities are parts of virtue: in the same way as the parts of the face relate to the whole face.'

329e1     'In what way do men partake of these parts of virtue? Do some men have one part and not another, or is it necessarily true that if someone has grasped one of these parts, he has grasped them all?'

'Not at all,' said Protagoras: 'after all, many men are brave but not just, or again just but not wise.'

'So these are parts of virtue too, are they,' I said, 'wisdom and courage?'

330a1 'These most of all,' said Protagoras: 'for wisdom is the most important of all the parts.'

'But each of these parts is distinct from all the others?'

'Yes.'

'Does each of them have its own distinctive ability? Compare the face: the eye is unlike the ears, and so their abilities are different too. It is like that with all the parts of the face: none of them is like any of the other parts, either in its distinctive ability or in any other respect. Is it the same with the parts of virtue: none of them is like any other part, either in its own nature or in what it is distinctively able to do? Clearly they must be if the analogy holds, mustn't they?'

330b3 'Yes, this is how it is, Socrates,' he agreed.

'So none of the other parts of virtue is like knowledge; nor like justice; nor like courage; nor like temperance; nor like holiness.' He agreed. 'Come, then,' I said, 'let us consider together what the quality of each of these parts is like. First let us ask this. Is justice something, or no thing at all? I think it certainly is something: what do you think?'

330c2 'I agree,' he said.

'Well, then, suppose someone asked us this. "Protagoras and Socrates, tell me about this thing you have just mentioned, justice: is justice itself just, or unjust?" I would reply that it's just: how would you cast your vote? The same way as me, or otherwise?'

'The same way,' said Protagoras.

330d1 'So, then, "Justice is the sort of thing to be just", I would say to our questioner. Wouldn't you?'

'Yes,' he said.

'Then suppose he asked us this: "Do you have a use for the name 'holiness'?" We'd say we did, I think.'

'Yes,' said Protagoras.

'Wouldn't you also say that holiness is a thing? We would, wouldn't we?' He agreed to this too. 'Now about this very thing holiness: would you say that it is by nature the sort of thing to be unholy, or holy? I must say I should be displeased with the question here, and I should say "Quiet, man! How could anything else be holy, if holiness itself is not holy?" What would you say, Protagoras? Wouldn't you say the same?'

330e3    'Certainly I would,' he said.

'But suppose that after this he produced yet another question: "Then what did you mean by what you said a little while back? Or did I mishear you? For I thought you said that the parts of virtue were so related to each other that none of them was of the same sort as any other." What I would say to this would be: "Yes, in all other respects you heard aright, except that you are mistaken to think that *I* said this. For Protagoras here gave that answer. I was only the questioner." Then he might say: "Is Socrates telling the truth, Protagoras? You do say that no part of virtue is of the same sort as any other?" How would you answer him?'

331a4    'I'd have to agree that I do.'

'But Protagoras, if we agree to that, how are we to answer him if he comes at us with the following question? "What! Is holiness not the sort of thing to be just, and justice not the sort of thing to be holy? Is justice then the sort of thing to be *not* holy, and is holiness the sort of thing to be *not* just? Indeed, is holiness actually *un*just, and justice actually *un*holy?"[7] How shall we answer him? I myself, speaking in my own defence, would simply say that justice *is* holy, and holiness *is* just; and speaking for you, I would say the same, if you would permit me. For surely justice really is identical with holiness, or as like it as can be; at any rate, justice must be of the same sort as holiness, and holiness of the same sort as justice. But decide whether you are going to stop me saying that, or whether you have the same opinion here.'

331c1 'Well, Socrates,' said Protagoras, 'I don't think it's as simple as that: I don't agree that justice is holy, or that holiness is just: I think there is some distinction to be made about this case. But what does it matter? If you like, we can take it as read that justice is holy, and holiness just.'

'That isn't agreeable to me,' I said: 'my obligation is not to put "If you like" or "If that's what you think" to the test of argument: it is to put Socrates and Protagoras to that test. I mean, I think that the view presently under discussion will be most effectively tested if we remove the "if" from it.'

331d1 'Well,' said he, 'I suppose there must be some sense in which justice is like holiness; there's always some sense in which anything at all is like anything else. There is some way in which white is like black, or hard is like soft, and so with all the other things that seem most certainly opposed to one another. So with the things which we agreed have different abilities and are not of the same sort – namely the parts of the face. There is some way in which the different parts are alike and *are* of the same sort. So by your method, you could equally well show – *if* you liked – that all the face's parts are like each other. But it is unfair to describe things as alike just because they have *some* resemblance, however insignificant that may be. Like- wise, it is unfair to describe things as unalike merely because they have *some* point of dissimilarity.'

331e4 I was taken aback by this answer. 'So,' I said to him, 'you think that the just and the holy are so related that they are only alike in some unimportant way?'

'Not a wholly unimportant way,' he said; 'but not as important as you seem to think.'

332a1    'Well, never mind,' I said: 'since you seem to find my argument about likeness a tiresome one, let's leave it alone, and consider something else that you said. Do you think that "folly" is a name for anything?' (He assented.) 'And isn't wisdom entirely opposite to that thing?'

'Yes, I believe so,' he said.

'Now when men act rightly and beneficially, would you say they are being temperate, or intemperate?'

'Temperate,' he said.

332b1    'So it is because of their temperance that they are temperate?'

'Of course.'

'So those who do not act rightly are both acting foolishly *and* being intemperate in so acting?'

'So it seems to me,' he said.

'Then isn't acting foolishly the opposite of acting temperately?' He agreed. 'But what is done foolishly is done because of one's folly; and what is done temperately is done because of one's temperance.' He assented. 'Now if some deed is the result of strength, isn't it done strongly, whereas if it is the result of weakness, it is done weakly?' He thought so. 'And if something is done with speed, it is done speedily, whereas if it is done with slowness, it is done slowly?' He agreed. 'So if something is done by an agent in manner X, then it is the result of the agent's having the characteristic of Xness; whereas if it is done in the opposite manner, it is the result of his having the opposite characteristic.' He agreed. 'Well, then,' I said, 'is there such a thing as the characteristic of beauty?' He assented. 'And what is the opposite of beauty, if not ugliness?'

332c4    'Nothing else.'

'And is there such a thing as the characteristic of goodness?'

'There is.'

'What is the opposite of goodness if not badness?'

'Nothing else.'

'Next, is there such a thing as high pitch in a voice?' He said there was. 'And there can be no opposite to this except low pitch.' He said not. 'So,' I said, 'doesn't each one of these pairs of opposites itself have one opposite only – and no more?' He went along with this. 'Well,' I said, 'let us tot up what we have agreed so far. We've agreed, haven't we, that to any one thing there is only one opposite, and not more?'

332d3 'We have.'

'And that when actions are done in opposite manners, they result from opposite characteristics?' He assented. 'And that if someone acts foolishly, then he acts in an opposite manner to someone who acts temperately.' He admitted it. 'And what is done in a temperate manner results from the characteristic of temperance, while what is done in a foolish manner results from the characteristic of folly.' He agreed. 'But if something is done in an opposite manner, then it must result from an opposite characteristic?'

332e2 'Yes.'

'And one of these two deeds results from temperance, the other from folly?'

'Yes.'

'The two deeds are done in opposite manners?'

'Certainly.'

'Then they must result from opposite characteristics.'

'Yes.'

'So mustn't folly be the opposite of temperance?'

'Apparently so.'

'Now you recall that earlier we agreed that folly is the opposite of wisdom?' He admitted it. 'And any one thing has only one opposite.'

'Yes.'

333a1 'Then, Protagoras, which of our theses should we give up? Should we abandon the claim that each thing has only one opposite? Or should we give up the argument which said that temperance is a different thing from wisdom, and that both are parts of virtue, different from each other and unlike both in their own natures and in their characteristic abilities, just like the parts of the face? Which of them is it to be? For these theses do not speak quite harmoniously together; they are out of tune and do not fit in with one another. Indeed how could they, if it really is necessarily the case that any one thing has only one opposite and not more, and yet both wisdom and temperance alike seem to be opposites to the single characteristic of folly? – Do I misjudge the situation, Protagoras, or is this our problem?'

Protagoras conceded that such was the position, though very unwillingly. 'But then, mustn't temper-
333b4    ance and wisdom be one and the same thing?'

# 13. PROTAGORAS 349D–351B

## A COUNTER-EXAMPLE TO THE
## UNITY THESIS: COURAGE (I)

349d1   'No, Socrates,' said Protagoras: 'my position really is that all these five characteristics – wisdom, temperance, courage, justice, holiness – are parts of virtue. Four of them are pretty close to each other in nature; but the fifth characteristic, courage, is very widely different from the other four. And here is how you may know I speak the truth: there are lots of people who are altogether unjust, exceedingly unholy, utterly lacking in self-control, and complete fools as well; and yet they are also distinguished for their courage.'

349e1   'Wait!' I said: 'what you say deserves some examination. Do you say that the brave are daring, or would you describe them otherwise?'

'Yes,' said Protagoras: 'indeed, they are characteristically ready for action when others are afraid to act.'

'Well, tell me, Protagoras: would you say that virtue is a beautiful thing? Is it because virtue is so beautiful that you set yourself up as a teacher of virtue?'

'Why, virtue is the most beautiful thing there is,' he replied, 'unless I am quite out of my mind.'

'Well, then: is some part of virtue ugly and another part beautiful? Or is the whole of virtue beautiful?'

'Presumably the whole of virtue is as beautiful as it could possibly be.'

'Do you know of any people who show daring in diving into wells?'

350a2   'Of course I do: you mean professional divers.'

'Do they show this daring because they understand what they are doing? Or for some other reason?'

'Because they understand what they are doing.'

'Then who are the ones who show daring in fighting battles on horseback? Is it the ones who are trained cavalrymen, or those who are not?'

'It's the trained cavalrymen.'

'What about the infantry? Is it the trained infantrymen who show daring, or the others?'

'Yes, yes, it's the trained infantrymen. And in every other case likewise,' said Protagoras, 'if this is what you are after, it's true that those who understand their work are more daring than those who do not; and also true that having once learnt their work, those who understand it are more daring than they themselves were before they understood it.'

350b1    'And yet,' I said, 'you will have seen people who have no understanding of any of these areas being daring in each one of them?'

'I certainly have,' he said, 'and very great daring they showed.'

'But if people are daring in this sort of way, does that make them courageous too?'

'No,' said Protagoras, 'for then courage would be an ugly thing, not a beautiful one, because people like that are just crazy.'

'So then,' I said, 'how do you define who are the courageous? Didn't you claim that the courageous are those who are daring?'

350c1    'I did, and I still do,' he answered.

'But surely,' I said, 'the people who are daring in the sense we have just discussed turn out to be crazy rather than courageous. Again, our discussion of which people are wisest showed that they are also the most truly daring – and so the most courageous. So on this argument, mustn't wisdom be courage?'

350c5    'Socrates,' Protagoras replied, 'you show a poor recall of what I said in my answer to you. For I was asked by you to say whether the courageous are daring; and I said they were. But you didn't ask me whether the daring are courageous; and if you had asked me that, I would have said "Not all of them, no". So you have done nothing to show that my assertion that the courageous are daring was a mistake – as you might perhaps by proving that they are not daring.

350d2    'Then you went on to argue that those who understand their work are more daring than they were before they understood it, and also more daring than others who do not understand it. You think that this shows the identity of courage and wisdom. Would you say that the same argument shows the identity of strength and wisdom? You could begin by asking me whether the strong are powerful; and I would assent. Then you could ask whether those who understand how to wrestle are more powerful than those who do not understand it, and whether they are stronger than they themselves were before they learnt wrestling; and I would assent. Once I had made these admissions, it would be open to you – if you were still using the same standards of "proof" as you currently are – to say that it followed from the premisses I had agreed to that wisdom is strength.

350e5    'At no point in this argument I am imagining would I have admitted that the powerful are strong. What I would have admitted is the different claim that the strong are powerful. Nor would I be agreeing that power and strength are identical. For one of them, power, can arise from understanding, but also from madness and from high spirit; whereas the other, strength, depends on what a person's body is like, and on how he looks after it.

351a3    'Likewise in our actual argument, I don't admit that daring and courage are the same thing. That is why I say that the brave are daring, but that not all the daring are brave. For like power, daring too arises in men from a variety of sources: it can be induced by certain techniques, or it can come from high spirit, or it can arise from madness. But courage depends on what a person's character is like, and on how he looks after his soul.'

351b2

## NOTES

1. In the omitted passage Socrates gives a difficult geometrical example to establish his notion of 'argument by hypothesis'. This means getting the other side to accept a conditional claim ( = a hypothesis), and then proving its antecedent or disproving its consequent. So here the question 'Can virtue be taught?' elicits, not a definition of virtue as Socrates would ideally like, but at least the hypothesis '*If* virtue is a kind of knowledge, *then* virtue can be taught'.

2. An obvious irony: Anytus was to be one of Socrates' prosecutors at his trial.

3. Another sophist present at the discussion. Evidently Protagoras disdains Hippias' methods as Socrates disdains Protagoras'.

4. Pericles' sons Paralus and Xanthippus are both present: *Protagoras* 315a.

5. In more traditional versions of this story, Prometheus stole only fire, not 'fire and wisdom in the arts'; and stole it from Zeus, not Athene and Hephaestus.

6. Shame and Justice, *aido* and *dike*: words which might also be translated as Reverence/Respect/Conscience and Right/Fairness/Balance.

7. Notice the slide from 'is not the sort of thing to be F' to 'is the sort of thing to be not-F' to 'is not-F'.

# PART III

✦✦

# JUSTICE AND PLEASURE

# 14. PROTAGORAS 351B–358D

## PLEASURE AND THE GOOD (I)

351b3 'Do you agree, Protagoras,' I asked, 'that some men live well, and some badly?'

'Yes,' he said.

'Then do you think that a man would be living well who spent his time in pain and distress?' He said not. 'But if he lived a pleasant life and then died, then you would say that he had lived well?'

'I would,' he said.

351c1 'So a pleasant life is good, and an unpleasant life is bad.'

'Yes,' he said, 'provided its pleasures are honourable.'

'What's that, Protagoras? Do you really agree with the multitude that there are some pleasures which are bad, and some pains which are good? I mean, aren't things good just in so far as they are pleasant, and provided nothing different follows from them? And likewise, aren't painful things, just in so far as they are painful, bad things?'

351d1 'I don't know, Socrates,' he replied, 'whether I ought to give a sweeping endorsement of your sweeping generalisation, and reply that all pleasant things are good and all painful things bad. When I consider not just this question, but the whole of the rest of my life, I think it safer to reply that there are some pleasant things that are not good, and some painful things that are not bad (though others are bad); and again that some painful things are neither good nor bad.'

'Presumably what you mean by "pleasant",' I said, 'is things that partake of pleasure, or cause pleasure?'

351e1    'Exactly so.'

'Well then, when I ask whether things are good in so far as they are pleasant, all I am asking is whether pleasure is good.'

'Well,' said Protagoras, ' "let us examine the matter", as you always say. If we think the examination goes as reason directs, and it comes to look as if the pleasant and the good are the same thing, then we shall come to an agreement; but if not, this will be our sticking-point.'

'Well,' I said, 'do you want to direct the inquiry, or shall I take charge?'

'It's your prerogative to take charge,' he said, 'since you raised the problem in the first place.'

352a1    'Very well,' I said. 'Might we shed some light on the problem in this way? – If someone is giving someone else a physical examination, whether general or specific, what he does first is look at the patient's face and hands; but then he says, "Come on, undress: show me your chest and back, or the examination will not be accurate". I want to say something like that about our inquiry. I can see, Protagoras, that your position on the good and the pleasant is as you say. Still I am obliged to make something like this request of you: "Come on, Protagoras, uncover some more of your thought". What is your position on knowledge? Do you take the same view of it that most men do, or some other view? Most people's opinion on knowledge seems to be, roughly, that they do not see it as strong or directive or controlling: they just don't understand it to be anything like that. Rather, their unaccountable view is that it is perfectly common for a man to have knowledge within him which yet fails to be what controls the man. Instead, they say, something else controls him: sometimes anger, sometimes pleasure or pain; occasionally love, and frequently fear. To them knowledge is just like a slave, that can be dragged about by all these other powers!

352c2     'Well, Protagoras – do you think that something like this is the truth about knowledge? Or do you think that knowledge is a beautiful thing, and by its nature capable of ruling over a man, so that if someone *knows* what good and bad are, then nothing at all can force him to do anything other than what his knowledge instructs him to do – wisdom being enough to enable him to conquer all these compulsions?'

352d1     'My view, Socrates,' he said, 'is just the same as yours; why, it would be shameful for me of all people[1] to deny that wisdom and knowledge were the most powerful forces of all in human affairs.'

    'Well said,' I replied, 'and truly too. But you know that, on this matter, the greater part of mankind are not convinced by our view. For they say that many people know what is best but are unwilling to do it even though they could, and instead would rather do something else. All those whom I have asked to explain to me what the cause of this could be have said that men are "overcome by pleasure", or by pain, or by one of the conditions we mentioned just now; it is because they are under the control of one of these that they do what they do.'

352e3     'Well, Socrates,' said Protagoras, 'this is not the only point on which I believe ordinary men do not speak correctly.'[2]

    'Come then,' I said, try with me to persuade the people, and to teach them what exactly is this experience of theirs that they describe as "being overcome by pleasure", and which they cite as the explanation of their not doing what is best even when they know what is best. For probably if we said to them "You're wrong in what you say: it is false that anyone is overcome by pleasure", they would retort by asking us: "Protagoras and Socrates, if this experience is not being overcome by pleasure, then what on earth is it? What do you say it is? Tell us that!"'

353b1     'But Socrates, why need we consider the opinion of the mass of people, who come out with any old idea that happens to strike them?'

    'Because,' I said, 'I think that considering it will give us some aid in our inquiry about courage, and how exactly it is related to the other parts of virtue. If you are still prepared to stick to what we agreed before, that I should direct our inquiry, then you should follow in the direction that seems to me to be best for clarifying our problem. But if you are unwilling, and if it matters to you, then I am happy to let the question go.'

    'No,' said Protagoras, 'quite right: carry on just as you have begun.'

353c1     'To repeat, then,' I said, 'they might ask us this question. "What do you say this experience is, which we call being overcome by pleasure?" This would be my response to them: "Listen, and Protagoras and I will try to tell you. Don't you say that this 'being overcome by pleasure' happens to you in those cases where you know that certain things are wicked, but none the less you do them – as for example so often happens when people are overcome by the pleasures of food and drink and sex?" And they would agree. Then you and I would ask them this further question: "How do you mean it when you say that these things that overcome you are wicked? Is it just that they produce a pleasure at the time, and that each of them is itself pleasant? Or is it that, later on, these pleasures will bring about sickness and poverty and all other such ills? Can it be that, even if such things have no latter effect, but merely cause pleasure at the time, they are none the less evils – just because they teach one to experience a pleasure of some sort?" Surely, Protagoras, we could not suppose that they would give our question any other answer than this: "No, such things are not evil because they bring about

pleasure at the time they occur; they are evil because of
their later effects – illness or whatever".'

353e2    'I certainly think,' Protagoras agreed, 'that most of
them would give this answer.'

   'So don't conditions that cause illnesses cause pains?
And don't conditions that cause poverty cause pains?
Presumably they would concede that they do.' (And
we both agreed to it.) 'On the other hand, what if we
asked them the opposite question? "You people who
claim that some good things are painful, don't you
have in mind such examples as physical exercise,
service in the army, or unpleasant surgical treatments
involving cautery or amputation or drug therapy or
the starving of a fever? Isn't it these cases that you call
good things, but painful?" Would they agree?' (He
thought they would.) ' "Then in what respect" (we
should ask) "do you call them good things? Is it
because at the time of their application they produce
such extremes of agony and distress? Or is it because in
the long run these treatments produce health and
wholeness in the body in some cases, and in other
cases the relief of cities, power over others, and
wealth?" I presume that they would say that this
was the reason' (and Protagoras agreed). ' "So aren't
the things you call painful but good, good only
because they eventually result in pleasures, in relief
from distress, or its prevention? Or can you name any
other end beside pleasure and pain, by reference to
which you may describe these painful experiences as
good?" I believe they would admit there is no other.'

354c2    'Yes, I think they would too,' agreed Protagoras.

   ' "Then don't you pursue pleasure as good, and
shun pain as evil?" ' (He agreed to this.) ' "So you
hold that what is bad is pain, and that what is good is
pleasure. For you only say that any form of enjoyment
is bad when it deprives you of greater pleasures than it
itself involves, or leads to pains which are greater than

the pleasures it involves. If there were some other reason for calling enjoyment a bad thing, some other end which you might have in mind in so speaking, then you would be able to tell us what it was: but you can't." '

354d3    'No, I agree that they can't do that,' said Protagoras.

'Then is it any different with pain? "You call a painful experience a good thing" (we shall say) "only when it releases someone from greater pains than those that it involves, or leads to pleasures which are greater than the pains which it involves. If you had any other end in mind when you said that pain itself was a good thing, you would be able to tell us what that end was: but you can't." '

354e2    'You're right,' agreed Protagoras.

' "Now, gentlemen" ' (I continued my speech) ' "if at this point you are minded to retort by asking what on earth I hope to achieve by saying so much about so many aspects of this question, then" – I should say – "forgive me: but really it is not easy to show the real nature of what you call being overcome by pleasure. That is the first point, and the second is that everything else you might hope to show depends on the first point. But you can still escape from this difficulty, if you can show somehow that there is more to the definition of the good than pleasure, or that what is bad is something other than pain. Isn't it sufficient, in your view, for a man to live out his life without pain? But if it is – and if you cannot specify any further feature of the good and the bad, besides their tendencies towards pleasure and pain – then hear what follows. In that case, I tell you it becomes absurd for you to claim that someone can very frequently know that some bad action *is* bad, and yet do it even though it was open to him not to, because he is led on to it in a daze of pleasure. And equally absurd is your claim that someone can know what is good and yet be unwilling to do it because of the pleasures of the moment which overcome him.

355b4 ' "We will see clearly that both these claims are absurd if we stop using multiple names for the phenomena – 'pleasant' and 'painful', 'good' and 'bad'. Since we have only found *two* realities, let us only use one pair of names at a time to refer to them. Initially we shall refer to them as 'good' and 'bad'; then later on, as 'pleasant' and 'painful' instead.

355c1 ' "Well, then: on these principles, suppose we say that 'a man knows a bad action to be a bad action, but nonetheless does it'. If someone then asks us why, we shall say that it is because he is overcome. 'Overcome by what?' the questioner will say; and now we can no longer reply 'By pleasure', since 'pleasure' has been renamed 'the good'. So when we say in answer to the question that the man is overcome, and are asked 'By what?' – by Zeus, we shall have to reply that he is 'overcome by the good'!

355c8 ' "Now if our questioner is a supercilious man, he will laugh out loud at this: 'What an absurd idea!' he will say – 'that a man should do evil, knowing it to be evil, and under no necessity to do it, *because* he is overcome by the good! Does this happen' – he will ask – 'when the goods in you are insufficient to conquer the evils in you, or when they are sufficient?' 'When they are insufficient,' we shall clearly have to reply – for otherwise there would have been nothing wrong in the action of the person who we said was overcome by pleasure.

355d7 ' " 'But in what sense,' he will ask, 'can goods be insufficient to overcome evils, or evils to overcome goods, except this: that one good or evil in us can be greater in size than another, or one group of goods or evils in us can be more in number than another?' And we shall find no other sense beside this. 'Therefore it is clear' – he will say – 'that when you talk about being overcome, what you mean is the absurdity of accepting a larger evil instead of a lesser good!' " '

355e3      'Yes, we would have to admit that.'

' "Now let us use the other pair of names, 'pleasant' and 'painful', for the same pair of phenomena. Then we will be saying, again absurdly, that 'a man does what is painful (what we previously referred to as bad), knowing that it is painful, but overcome by pleasures' – which were obviously not strong enough to conquer!

356a1      ' "Anyway, what can 'pleasures not strong enough to conquer pains' mean, except there is an excess on the one side and a lack on the other? And that is what happens when pleasures or pains become greater or smaller, more or fewer, more or less vivid. If anyone responds with 'But Socrates, there's a great difference between a present pleasure and a pleasure or pain in the distant future', I shall merely ask 'But is it a difference in anything but degree of pleasure or pain?'

356b1      ' "For there is no other way of distinguishing goods and bads. Like a man who is skilled in measuring weights, put pleasures in the scales together with pains, bearing in mind their distance or proximity; then say which side weighs more. If you are weighing pleasures against other pleasures, choose the larger and the weightier ones; if you are weighing pains against other pains, choose the lesser and the smaller ones. If you are weighing pleasures against pains, then the right choice depends on whether or not the pains are outweighed by some pleasures which follow on them. Are near pains outweighed by distant pleasures, or distant pains by near pleasures? If so, the action to be done is the one which displays these features. But if, in the case of some action, near or distant pleasures are outweighed by near or distant pains, then don't do that action. How could it be otherwise, gentlemen?" I should ask;

and I know that they could not tell me.' Protagoras agreed to this also.

356c3      ' "Then since this is how things stand," I shall say, "tell me this. Do you see how objects of the same size appear larger when they are close to us, but smaller from further away?" "We do," they would say. "Don't thicknesses and numbers behave in the same way? And doesn't the same volume of sound, also, seem greater from nearby, and less from further away?" "Yes," they would say. "Well, if this were what our well-being depended on – our ability to act on and to grasp what was quantitatively larger, and to avoid and not do what was of a small quantity – then what would be our saving guide in life? Would it be our skill of *measuring* how things are? Or would it be the ability which things have to *appear* so and so?

356d5      ' "Surely it is appearance that deceives us, and causes us again and again to mistake the way up for the way down,[3] so that we have to reverse not only our courses of action but also our decisions about which of the same range of pleasures are the large ones and the small ones. Yet a skill in measuring would have made the deceptive appearance powerless, and would have brought composure to the soul by making the truth clear to it and enabling it to remain in that truth, so that its life is not ruined." Given these arguments, wouldn't the people agree with us that it is the skill of measuring goods and bads which saves our lives from ruin; or would they look for some other?'

356e4      'No, they would settle for the skill of measuring,' Protagoras assented.

' "Well then: suppose that what saved our lives from ruin was our ability to choose odd numbers or even numbers, and our knowledge of when we ought to choose a greater number and when a smaller one – considering the size of each number in its own right, whether the quantities in question are near at hand or far away from us. Then what would be the security of our lives? Wouldn't it be knowledge? Specifically, wouldn't it be a knowledge of measuring, since it is a skill of recognising numerical superiorities and inferiorities? And wouldn't it also be a knowledge of counting, since it is concerned with the odd and the even?" Would the people agree with us about this, or not?'

Protagoras thought they would agree.

357a8     ' "Well, gentlemen: it has become evident that the making or breaking of our lives depends on the correct choice of pleasures and pains – of more and less and bigger and smaller and further off and nearer at hand. So isn't it also evident, first, that this examination of the superiorities, inferiorities or equalities of pleasures and pains with one another must be a skill in measurement?" '

357b3     'Of course it must.'

' "And being a skill in measurement, it must be a form of *skill*, and of knowledge." '

'So they will admit.'

357b7     ' "Well, the exact nature of this form of skill and of knowledge is something we can consider some other time.[4] For the present argument which Protagoras and I are required to supply as an answer to your question, it is enough simply to show that it is a form of knowledge which is in question here. For, if you recall, it was once Protagoras and I had agreed that nothing can be stronger than knowledge, which always prevails wherever it is present in people, that you put your question to us. You retorted that there are plenty of times when pleasure overcomes even someone who has knowledge, and it was when we refused to agree that you asked us, 'But if this experience is not being overcome by pleasure, then what on earth is it, and what are you going to say about it? Do tell us!' If we had immediately replied to you that the experience in question is really ignorance, you would have laughed in our faces. But if you laugh at us now, you will also be laughing at yourselves. For you have agreed that it is by lack of knowledge that people who go wrong make their mistakes concerning their choice of pleasures and pains – that is, of goods and bads. Indeed, not only have you admitted that it is lack of knowledge which is in question here: you have also agreed that it is lack of a knowledge *of measuring*.

357e1 ' "Now presumably you realise that an action which is wrongly done in the absence of knowledge must be an action done in ignorance. So being overcome by pleasure is just this – the greatest form of ignorance; an ignorance which Protagoras here says he can cure, as do Prodicus and Hippias. But you, gentlemen, because you think that being overcome by pleasure is something other than ignorance, will neither go to these sophists' schools for ethical ignorance yourselves, nor send along your children. You say that faults of this sort cannot be remedied by teaching, and you are too stingy to give any money to such teachers. And so you do badly, both in your private affairs and in public life."

358a1 'This is how we might have answered the people, Protagoras and I. But, Prodicus and Hippias, let us share our argument with you. So I ask you both, as well as Protagoras, whether you think I have spoken truly or falsely.'

They all thought what I had said was resoundingly true.

– 'So then you agree,' I said, 'that the pleasant is the good and the painful is the bad. And I beg leave to pass over Prodicus' distinctions of names.[5] Whether you call it "the pleasant" or "the delightful" or "the enjoyable" – no matter what manner or sort of name you like to give such things, my fine Prodicus – just answer the question that I mean to ask.'

358b3    Prodicus laughed, and agreed to do so, as did the others.

'Well, gentlemen,' I said, 'consider what follows next. Aren't all actions honourable that aim at living painlessly and pleasantly? And isn't honourable activity good and beneficial?' They agreed. 'Then,' I said, 'if the pleasant is the good, no one who knows (or even just believes) that some other possible action is better than the action that he is about to do, will go ahead and do the less good action, a better one being available. So "being overcome by oneself" is nothing but ignorance, and self-mastery is nothing but wisdom.' They all agreed. 'So is what you mean by ignorance something like this: having a false belief, and being mistaken about matters of great importance?' They agreed to this as well. 'Then there is something else to note,' I said: 'that no one willingly pursues what is evil, or what they consider evil; nor, apparently, is it in human nature for someone to prefer to pursue what he considers to be bad instead of what is good. Moreover, when someone is forced to choose one of two evils, no one will take the larger if the
358d7    smaller is available.'

# 15. PROTAGORAS 358D–361C

## ⇥⇤

## COURAGE (II), AND A CONCLUSION ABOUT TEACHING VIRTUE

358d8 'Well, then,' I said, 'is dread, or fear, a name for anything? If so, do you think it is a name for what I have in mind, Prodicus? I am thinking of a kind of expectation of evil, whether "dread" or "fear" is the name you gentlemen would like to give to this experience.'

358e1 Protagoras and Hippias accepted this definition of dread and fear – but Prodicus remarked that it fitted dread, but not fear.

'It makes no difference, Prodicus,' I said; 'my question is just this. If what we have said up to now [in readings 13 and 14] is true, will anyone be prepared to take a course of action that he is afraid to take, if he can instead choose a course that he does not fear taking? Surely that must be impossible, if what we have agreed on so far is correct. For we have agreed that what someone fears is what he thinks evil. But no one, we saw, takes a course of action that he thinks evil, nor chooses to do it if he can avoid it.' And everyone agreed.

359a1 'Then, Prodicus and Hippias,' I said, 'if all this is granted, Protagoras here needs to defend his earlier answer, and show how it can be right to say what he said. I don't mean what he said right at the beginning [reading 12: 330a1 ff.], when he said that there were five parts of virtue, all unlike each other in kind, and each characteristically able to produce different effects. That isn't what I mean: what I mean is what he said later [reading 13: 349d1]. He said that four of these five parts of virtue were pretty close to each other in nature, but that the fifth characteristic, courage, was very widely different from the other four. And he said I could know he spoke the truth by this sign: "You will find that there are people who are altogether unjust, exceedingly unholy, utterly lacking in self-control, and complete fools as well; and yet they are also distinguished for their courage. So there is your proof that courage is very different from the other parts of virtue."

359b7    'I was quite taken aback by this answer at the time, and I am even more so now that we have gone into matters in such depth. At the time I asked Protagoras whether he thought the brave were daring, and he said "Yes, and ready for action too". Do you remember giving this answer, Protagoras?' He said he did. 'Well, then,' I said, 'come on and tell us: what sort of action do you say the brave are ready for? The same things as cowards?'

359c3    'No,' he said.

'So they are ready for other sorts of action.'

'Yes.'

'So cowards only take courses of action that they feel confident about? Whereas the brave typically take courses of action that they are afraid to perform?'

'That's what people say, Socrates.'

359c9    'Indeed they do,' I rejoined, 'but that's not what I asked. What I want to know is, what sort of actions *you* say the brave are typically ready to do. Is it frightening actions, which they themselves are afraid to do? Or is it actions which they are not afraid to do?'

359d2    'The latter,' said Protagoras: 'your arguments in the last section of our discussion have just shown that the former is impossible.'

'Right again,' I said. 'If that argument was correct, then no one can choose a course of action that he fears to choose. For, as we saw, "being overcome by oneself" is nothing other than ignorance.'[6] He agreed. 'But then everyone alike, cowards and the brave – they all choose those courses of action that they feel confident about. So, by this argument at any rate, cowards and the brave choose the same actions!'

359e1     'Oh, come on, Socrates,' said Protagoras: 'what cowards choose and what the brave choose are diametrically opposite. To give one example, the brave are prepared to face war, whereas cowards are not.'

'Is this preparedness an honourable thing, or a shameful?' I asked.

'Honourable,' said Protagoras.

'But if this preparedness is an honourable thing, then by what we agreed earlier on, it is also a good thing. For we agreed that all honourable actions are good actions.'

'Yes,' said Protagoras, 'and I still maintain we were right.'

360a1     'Quite correct of you,' I said. 'But which people is it that you say are unprepared to face war, where being prepared is honourable and good?'

'The cowards,' he said.

'But if being prepared is what is honourable and good, isn't it also what is pleasant?'

'So at least we have agreed,' he said.

'Then when cowards are unprepared to face war, do they knowingly reject what is more honourable, better, and more pleasant?'

'No,' said Protagoras: 'if we agreed to that, then we would wreck the position that we have agreed on so far.'[7]

'But what about the brave person? Isn't he the one who chooses to face what is more honourable, better, and more pleasant?'

360b1     'I have to agree,' said Protagoras.

'Now as a rule the brave do not fear what it is

shameful to fear, when they experience fear; nor do they show daring where it is shameful to show daring.'

'True,' said Protagoras.

'So if their fear and daring are not shameful, then they must be honourable.' He agreed. 'And if honourable, then good.' He agreed. 'Whereas, by contrast, cowards and impetuous people and madmen do fear what it is shameful to fear; and do show daring where it is shameful to show daring.' He agreed. 'But do they show daring in shameful ways for any other reason than ignorance and lack of understanding?' 'No.'

'Well then, the reason why cowards are cowards – what do you call it? Is it cowardice or courage?'

360c1    'I call it cowardice,' he replied.

'And haven't we seen that the reason why cowards are cowards is their lack of understanding of what they ought to fear?'

'Yes, certainly,' he said.

'It is, then, that lack of understanding that makes them cowards?' He agreed. 'And the reason why cowards are cowards – you agreed that that was cowardice?' He admitted it. 'So won't cowardice be lack of understanding about what to fear and what not to fear?' He nodded. 'But of course,' I said, 'courage is the opposite of cowardice.' He agreed. 'And won't the opposite of this lack of understanding about what to fear and what not to fear, be *wisdom* about what to fear and what not to fear?' He nodded again. 'Now lack of understanding about such things is cowardice.' He nodded – very reluctantly. 'So wisdom about what to fear and what not to fear is courage – the opposite of lack of understanding about these things.'

360d8    Here Protagoras was not even prepared to nod, and simply held his silence. So I asked him, 'Why, Protagoras, won't you affirm or deny what I ask you?'

'You can finish it for yourself,' he said.

'Well,' I said, 'I still have just one question to ask

you: do you still think what you did at the outset, that there are some people who are completely stupid, but none the less courageous?'

360e3     'Apparently, Socrates,' said Protagoras, 'all you care about is winning the argument, with me as your yes-man. So I shall humour you by saying that, given our assumptions, that seems impossible.'

'Honestly, Protagoras,' I said, 'I have not asked you all these questions with any other desire than for an examination of two questions: "What are the inter-relations of our various terms to do with virtue? And what *is* virtue itself?" For I know that if we could just make these issues clear, then our other question would also become as clear as could be – the question you and I have both made such long speeches about, with me saying that virtue can't be taught, and you saying that it can.

361a4     'But in fact, I think that this outcome of our argument which we have just arrived at is accusing us and laughing at us as if it were human. If it had a voice, it would be saying "How ridiculous you are, Socrates and Protagoras! For here are you, Socrates, having insisted in your earlier speeches that virtue can't be taught, and now as keen as mustard to refute yourself by showing that every one of these things – justice, temperance, courage – is *knowledge*. But isn't that the best possible way to make it evident that virtue *is* teachable? If virtue was anything other than knowledge, as Protagoras tried to say it was, then obviously virtue would not be teachable. If it has now proved to be entirely a matter of knowledge, as you are so keen to say it is, then it will be extraordinary if it *can't* be taught. As for Protagoras, on the other hand – he laid it down initially that virtue *was* teachable: but now, on the contrary, he would apparently be happier to show that virtue is virtually anything rather than
361c2 knowledge!"'

# 16. GORGIAS 474C–475E

➤◄

## 'IT IS BETTER TO SUFFER INJUSTICE THAN TO DO INJUSTICE'

474c3 SOCRATES. Polus, do you think that it is worse to do injustice or to suffer injustice?

POLUS. In my view, to suffer injustice is worse.

SOCRATES. Then answer me this: is it an uglier thing to do injustice or to suffer injustice?

POLUS. To do injustice.

SOCRATES. Then isn't it a worse thing, if it is an uglier thing?

POLUS. Not in the least.

SOCRATES. I see: evidently you don't think that the beautiful and the good are the same thing; nor the ugly and the bad.

474d2 POLUS. No, I don't.

SOCRATES. But what about this? Consider all the things that you call beautiful: bodies, colours, shapes, sounds, ways of life. Don't you have some standard in mind each time you call one of these beautiful? For a first example, perhaps you would describe bodies as beautiful because of their usefulness for some purpose that they serve; or perhaps because of some sort of visual pleasure or enjoyment that they cause in those who look at them. Or do you have some other account beside this of what beauty is in bodies?

474e1 POLUS. No, I haven't.

SOCRATES. Well, won't the same account of beauty serve for shapes and colours and so on? Don't you refer to them as beautiful because of some benefit or some pleasure that we get from them – or for both reasons?

POLUS. Yes.

SOCRATES. Isn't it the same with sounds, and with everything to do with music?

POLUS. Yes.

SOCRATES. Again, the case of rules and ways of life is not outside this generalisation either. The beautiful ones are those which either are beneficial or give pleasure: or both.

POLUS. Yes, I think so.

475a1 SOCRATES. Won't the beauty of matters of education be of the same sort?

POLUS. Certainly, yes. Socrates, you are doing a beautiful job of defining the beautiful – by way of what is pleasant and what does us good.

SOCRATES. So I could define the ugly by the opposite terms – by way of what is painful and what does us bad?

POLUS. Of course.

SOCRATES. So whenever two things are beautiful, but one of them is more beautiful, this will either be because it has a superiority in pleasantness over the other, or because it is more beneficial; or for both reasons.

POLUS. Certainly.

SOCRATES. Similarly, whenever two things are ugly, but one of them is uglier, this will be because it has a superiority either in unpleasantness, or in the bad it does; or in both. Mustn't that be true?

475b2 POLUS. Yes.

SOCRATES. Come, then – what did we say just now about doing and suffering injustice? Didn't you say that suffering injustice was worse, but that doing injustice was an uglier thing?

POLUS. I did.

SOCRATES. Then if doing injustice is an uglier thing

than suffering injustice, mustn't it either be more unpleasant than suffering injustice, and so uglier by a superiority in pain; or else uglier by a superiority in the bad it does us; or else both? Isn't this necessary too?

POLUS. Of course.

SOCRATES. Then let us examine first whether doing injustice exceeds suffering injustice in its unpleasantness. Do those who do an injustice feel more pain than those who suffer that injustice?

475c2    POLUS. Of course not, Socrates.

SOCRATES. So doing injustice is not uglier because it is more painful.

POLUS. No indeed.

SOCRATES. If it is not uglier because it is more painful, then it can hardly be uglier for *both* our reasons.

POLUS. Apparently not.

SOCRATES. So it remains that it must be uglier in the other way.

POLUS. Yes.

SOCRATES. That is, by doing us more bad.

POLUS. Evidently.

SOCRATES. But if doing injustice exceeds suffering injustice in *badness*, then it must be *worse* than suffering injustice.

POLUS. Oh, of course it must, Socrates.

475d1    SOCRATES. Now surely, at an earlier point, we saw that the great majority of people agreed, as you agree, that it is an uglier thing to do injustice than to suffer it.

POLUS. Yes.

SOCRATES. But now it has become evident that doing injustice is also worse than suffering injustice.

POLUS. So it seems.

SOCRATES. Then would you really prefer to have *more* of what is worse and what is uglier, than *less* of it?

Please don't begrudge me your answer, Polus. It will do you no harm to reply: so keep your appointment with the argument as if it were with a doctor, and give your answer to my question. Yes or no?

475e1 POLUS. But of course I wouldn't choose more of the worse.

SOCRATES. Would anyone else?

POLUS. I think not – at least, not if this argument is right.

SOCRATES. Then I was right to say that neither I nor you nor anyone else would rather do injustice than

475e4 suffer injustice. For it is *worse* to do injustice.

# 17. GORGIAS 491E–492C

## ✦

## WHY BE TEMPERATE (I)?

491e1   CALLICLES. How naïve you are, Socrates! All you mean
by 'those who are temperate' is 'those who are *dupes*'.

SOCRATES. How could that be right? Nobody could
possibly suppose that that was my meaning.

CALLICLES. But it *is* your meaning, Socrates. For how
can someone possibly have a happy life if they are
anyone else's slave? I shall tell you now, without any of
this hypocrisy, what is noble and just by Nature. It is
this: whoever wants to live in the right way should
allow his desires to become as great as possible, and
should not submit them to any restraint. Then once his
desires are at their greatest, he needs to be man enough
to provide for them by the use of his courage and his
brains, and on every occasion to satisfy whatever
desire he may come to have. Now I believe that, for
the vulgar herd, this life is impossible. That explains
why the men of the herd reproach anyone who lives
like this. As I observed before: they disguise the
impotence of their own natures because it puts them
to shame – and then they dare to call intemperance a
shameful thing, and so achieve mastery over men who
are their natural betters. They themselves are too weak
to achieve the fulfilment of their pleasures; what leads
them to sing the praises of temperance and justice is
merely their own effeminacy.

492b2   But in truth – to those who were princes from the
start, or to those who were men enough by nature to
achieve some kind of rule or kingship or dynastic power
on their own – to people like that, what could be more
contemptible, more pernicious, than *temperance* and

*justice*? If it is open to you to enjoy the good things of life without anyone to hinder you, why should you impose upon yourself the control of herd morality, herd reasoning, herd disapproval? Justice and temperance prevent even a king in his own city from favouring his own friends over his enemies: so how can the 'beauties' of justice and temperance have any effect on his life except to debase it into a wretched struggle?

492c3     No, Socrates, the truth – which you say is what you are after – is this. 'Justice and happiness' means luxury, intemperance, and libertinism, backed up by brute force. All the rest – those man-made conventions which run contrary to Nature – is nothing but a fine
492c8   pretence; it is worthless drivel.

# 18. GORGIAS 493D–497A

## ✥

## PLEASURE AND THE GOOD (II)

493d7    SOCRATES. Consider, Callicles, whether you would agree to this sort of image of the two lives – the temperate, and the intemperate. Suppose each of two men had in him a number of containers or vessels. Both men's vessels are healthily filled up, one with wine, another with honey, a third with milk, and so on for all the vessels: they are all filled up with all sorts of good things, the sources of which, however, are hard to reach and few in number, so that they can only be attained by considerable effort.

493e4      Now the first of the two men, since his vessels are filled, need not top them up with a new influx, and gives them no further thought: his fullness enables him to be at peace. But the other man – he sees as well as the first does that the sources are not impossible to get to, although not easy; but his containers are holed and leaky, and so he is forced to keep on going to refill them, day and night, if he is to avoid suffering the most extreme torments.

494a2      If the two lives are like this, do you really claim that the life of the intemperate man is happier than that of the self-disciplined man? Does my metaphor persuade you at all to concede that the self-disciplined life is better than the intemperate man's life? Or are you not convinced?

     CALLICLES. No, I'm not convinced, Socrates. For the first man in your story, once his vessels are filled up, can have no *further* pleasure. After that, his case is like the one I have just mentioned[8] – the life of a stone. Once he has been filled up, his life will contain neither enjoyment nor pain. A pleasant life, by contrast, consists in experiencing as much influx of pleasures as possible.[9]

494b2   SOCRATES. But where there is a massive influx of pleasures, mustn't there also be a massive *efflux* of pleasures? And to enable this outflowing of pleasures, won't there have to be great big holes in such a man's containers?

CALLICLES. Yes, certainly there will.

SOCRATES. Well, certainly *this* is no corpse's or stone's life. It is more like a gannet's: straight from gobbling to guano. But do tell me: is it such experiences as hunger, and how it feels to eat if you're hungry, that you have in mind?

CALLICLES. Yes, that's what I mean.

494c1   SOCRATES. And thirst, and how it feels to drink if you're thirsty?

CALLICLES. Yes: I mean that, and I mean the having of any other desire; and the power to satisfy one's desires; and the resultant enjoyment that constitutes happy living.

SOCRATES. Well said, you splendid man; do keep going just as you have begun, and be sure to show no embarrassment at your own thesis. But evidently I must not be ashamed of mine, either. So please tell me about this first. A man desires to scratch an itch; no one begrudges him the power to scratch; so he scratches away for the rest of his life. Does *that* constitute happy living?

494d1   CALLICLES. You are as irrelevant as ever, Socrates: this is mere mob oratory.

SOCRATES. Why yes, Callicles: of course it was mere mob oratory that hypnotised Polus and Gorgias, and brought them to a sense of shame; but you are impossible to hypnotise, and you *have* no sense of shame. So brazen-brave you are! Just answer the question.

CALLICLES. Just as you like, then: I say that even the

scratcher would have a pleasant life.

SOCRATES. And if it's pleasant, isn't it happy, too?

CALLICLES. Certainly.

494e1 SOCRATES. But what if it is only the itching of his head that needs relieving? Or only the itching of his – well, shall I go on with these questions? Just consider, Callicles, how you are going to answer, if someone takes this line of questioning to its logical conclusion. Won't the end of all such questionings be to reduce you to living like a whore: to perverseness, shame and wretchedness? Or do you dare say that even pathics are happy – provided they get what they want and no one begrudges them it?

CALLICLES. You should be ashamed of yourself, Socrates, for dragging our discussion down to this level.

494e8 SOCRATES. Why, you distinguished person, am I the one who is dragging it down? Or is it the person who feels so little scruple about saying that whoever enjoys themselves is happy, provided only that they do enjoy themselves: the person who makes no distinction between good and evil pleasures?

495a3 But come, tell me one more time: do you really claim that pleasant and good are the same thing? Or is there some class of pleasures which are *not* good?

CALLICLES. I maintain that they are the same thing: I'd be contradicting my own argument if I said they weren't.

SOCRATES. But Callicles, even if you maintain that, you *still* undermine what you said before[10] – that we should say what we really think. But if you don't say what you really think, you will no longer be worthy to investigate the truth in my company.

495b1 CALLICLES. But *you* don't say what you really think, Socrates!

SOCRATES. If that is so then I am acting wrongly, too: both of us are. But for heaven's sake, look: mightn't

the good be something other than any and every sort
of enjoyment? For if that is the good, then evidently
one consequence will be all these shameful perplexities
we have just discussed: and there are others.

CALLICLES. So you think, Socrates.

SOCRATES. But what do you think, Callicles? That we
really should identify the good with the pleasant?

CALLICLES. Yes.

495c1 SOCRATES. Then are we to discuss this as your sincere
view?

CALLICLES. Absolutely.

SOCRATES. Very well then, if this is what you think,
make this distinction for me. Is there anything you call
knowledge?

CALLICLES. Of course there is.

SOCRATES. Didn't you make the point just now[11] that
there can be a certain kind of courage which goes
together with knowledge?

CALLICLES. I did say that, yes.

SOCRATES. Then what did you mean, if not that
courage and knowledge are two different things?

CALLICLES. Nothing else – just that.

495d1 SOCRATES. Well, is pleasure the same as knowledge, or
different from it?

CALLICLES. Why, you wisest of all men, it is different.

SOCRATES. And courage is different from knowledge?

CALLICLES. Obviously.

SOCRATES. Then let us be sure to make a minute of this:
'Callicles of Acharnia claims that pleasure and the
good are one and the same; and he says that knowledge and courage are not the same as each other, and
not the same as the good either.'

CALLICLES. And shall we add that 'Socrates of Alopece
rejects these claims'? Or does he admit them?

495e1 SOCRATES. No, he rejects them. As, I believe, will
Callicles, once Callicles has come to behold himself
truly. For tell me: don't you think that the condition of

those whose lives are going well is the opposite condition to that of those whose lives are going badly?

CALLICLES. Certainly I do.

SOCRATES. Then if these two conditions are a pair of opposites, doesn't it follow that the same sort of truth must hold of this pair as holds of the pair health and sickness? No one, presumably, can be both healthy and sick at once; nor can he cease to be healthy and to be sick at once.

CALLICLES. What do you mean?

496a1 SOCRATES. Well, take any part of the body you like, and consider that. I believe a man can be sick in his eyes: isn't that called ophthalmia?

CALLICLES. Of course.

SOCRATES. But while a man has ophthalmia, he is not, I take it, healthy in respect of his eyes?

CALLICLES. Not at all, no.

SOCRATES. What about when he loses his ophthalmia? Does he lose the health of his eyes at the same time as he loses the ophthalmia, so that he ends up with neither the health nor the disease?

CALLICLES. No, on the contrary.

SOCRATES. That, I take it, would be a very extraordinary and unaccountable event.

496b1 CALLICLES. Definitely.

SOCRATES. What actually happens, I think, is that he gains the one just in proportion as he loses the other.

CALLICLES. That's right.

SOCRATES. Isn't it the same with the pair of opposites strength and weakness?

CALLICLES. Yes.

SOCRATES. And speed and slowness?

CALLICLES. Yes indeed.

SOCRATES. And so also with good things, with happiness, and with their opposites, evils and wretchedness? In each case, don't we gain the one just in proportion as we lose the other?

CALLICLES. Why, yes, I suppose we do.

496c1 SOCRATES. Then if we find any pair of things which are such that a man loses them and keeps them simultaneously, *that* pair, obviously, cannot be identical with the pair of opposites 'good' and 'bad'. Shall we agree to this claim? Think very hard before you answer.

CALLICLES. I see no problem about agreeing to it.

SOCRATES. Then let us return to what we agreed earlier.[12] Did you say that hunger was pleasant or painful? (I speak of hunger itself.)

CALLICLES. I said it was painful; but I also said that it was pleasant for a man to eat, if he is hungry.

496d1 SOCRATES. I know you did. But hunger in itself – that is painful, yes?

CALLICLES. That's my claim.

SOCRATES. And thirst likewise?

CALLICLES. Just so.

SOCRATES. Well, do I need to ask any more questions, or will you now agree that all lack and all desire is painful?

CALLICLES. I agree, so you needn't ask.

SOCRATES. Very well. But don't you claim precisely that it is pleasant for a man to drink if he is thirsty?

CALLICLES. I certainly do, yes.

SOCRATES. And here, I take it, 'if he is thirsty' means 'if he is in a certain sort of pain'?

496e1 CALLICLES. Yes.

SOCRATES. Whereas drinking, if he is thirsty, is a filling-up of a lack, and a pleasure.

CALLICLES. Yes.

SOCRATES. So, you say, there is enjoyment in the drinking.

CALLICLES. Very much so.

SOCRATES. That is, if he is thirsty there is.

CALLICLES. That's what I said.

SOCRATES. Which means: if he is in pain.

CALLICLES. Yes.

SOCRATES. Then don't you see what follows? When you say someone enjoys drinking if he is thirsty, you are claiming that someone who is in pain is simultaneously enjoying himself. Or do you wish to deny that these things happen simultaneously: are they not at quite the same time? Or do they happen in different places, either in the body or in the soul? Not, as I believe, that it makes any difference. The question is: does this consequence follow or not?

CALLICLES. Yes, it does.

SOCRATES. But now, you claim that it is impossible for someone's life to go both well and badly at the same time.

CALLICLES. Yes, I do claim that.

497a1  SOCRATES. Whereas you have agreed that it *is* possible for someone to feel both pain and enjoyment at the same time.

CALLICLES. Apparently.

SOCRATES. Therefore enjoyment is not the same thing as having a life which is going well, and being in pain is not the same thing as having a life which is going
497a4  badly. So pleasure and the good are *different*.

# 19. REPUBLIC 359B–360D

## ✦✦

## WHY BE JUST? (I: GYGES' RING)

359b5   'The challenge', said Glaucon, 'is that even those whose way of life is just, only live that way against their will – because they are not strong enough to be unjust. We shall see the point most clearly if we conduct the following thought experiment.

359c1   'Let us give full scope to the just man and the unjust man, to do whatever he wants; and then let us suppose that we follow each of them to see where his desire leads him. If we did that, wouldn't we catch the just man red-handed? Wouldn't we find him going after exactly the same things as the unjust man? Yes, we would – because of that desire *to have more* which is in every person's nature, and which naturally makes him pursue the *most possible* as the good: it is only the force of law which diverts this desire into respect for equality between persons.

359c8   'The full scope for action which I am talking about is perhaps best compared to what the just man and the unjust would have, if they had the power that came to Gyges, Lydus' ancestor, in the story. They say that Gyges was a shepherd in the service of the then ruler of Lydia; and one day after a great rain-shower and an earth tremor, the ground gaped open and a chasm appeared in the place where Gyges' flock was. Gyges looked on in astonishment, and then went down into the chasm. There, the story-tellers say, he saw all sorts of wonders: including a hollow horse made out of bronze with small ports in the sides. Gyges looked in through one port, and beheld, inside the bronze horse, a corpse of supernatural size with nothing but a gold

ring on its hand. Well, Gyges took the ring and made
his escape.

359e2      'Now when the customary meeting of the shepherds
came on, the purpose of which was to report month by
month to the king on the state of his flocks, Gyges too
attended, with the ring. And while he was sitting there
with the others, he happened to turn the signet on the
ring towards his palm, in the direction of himself. But
when he did that, he became invisible to all those who
were sitting with him, and they asked one another
"Where's Gyges gone?"! Gyges himself was astonished, and groped once more at the ring; this time
he happened to turn the signet outwards, and changed
back to being visible. Gyges thought about this, and
tried the ring out again, to see if it really had the power
to make him invisible: and he realised that it made him
invisible when he turned the signet inwards, but visible
when he turned it outwards. Once he understood this,
Gyges quickly made sure that he got appointed as one
of the messengers from the shepherds to the king.
Then when he reached the court, he seduced the queen,
and with her help attacked the king, killed him, and
usurped his rule.

360a2      'Well, suppose there were two such rings as this, and
the just man put on one of them and the unjust man
the other. No one, it seems, would prove so adamant
in virtue that he would abide in justice, and have the
hardihood to restrain himself from laying even a finger
on what belongs to others! After all, he could, with
impunity, take whatever he liked from the market-
place itself. He could go into men's houses and have
intercourse with whichever of their wives he fancied.
He could kill anyone he liked, or spring them from
prison; he could do whatever he chose among mortals,
just as if he were a god! But in acting like this, he would
do nothing that the other man would not also do: both
of them would have the same objective.

360c4    'Mightn't it be said that this is a decisive proof that no one is willingly just,[13] but only because they have no choice? Justice is plainly not a good to any *individual*; for whenever someone thinks they are going to be in a position to act unjustly, they *do* act unjustly. Every man holds that, as far as his individual interest goes, injustice is far more profitable than justice. And he is right (or so the person who is issuing this challenge will say). For anyone who came by this sort of power, and then proved unwilling to act unjustly or to get their hands on other people's goods, would be considered most pitifully stupid by those who perceived his behaviour. None the less, they would praise him in front of one another: each person's fear that someone might treat *him* unjustly would cause him to hide what he really thinks of the
360d9  just man.'

>‹

## WHY BE JUST AND TEMPERATE?
### (II: AN ANSWER)

588b1    'Very well,' I said: 'at this point in the argument, let us take up again what was said at the beginning – the statement that brought us to this point. The statement was, I think, that injustice is a profitable thing to the person who is completely unjust, but appears to be just. Wasn't that it?'

'Yes, exactly so.'

'Well,' I said, 'now that we have an agreement about what are the effects respectively of being unjust and of acting justly, let us reason with the proponent of injustice.'

'How?' asked Glaucon.

'Let us make a model of the soul in our argument, so that the defender of injustice may see the real meaning of his claim.'

588c1    'What kind of model?' he asked.

'Something like those creatures of fable in the ancient legends,' I said: 'something like the Chimera and Scylla and Cerberus, and all the other bestiary creatures they tell of, which consist of different species combined together in one body.'

'Yes, I remember the tales they tell,' said Glaucon.

'Then imagine that, in one aspect, our creature is a various and many-headed beast, having the heads of both savage and gentle animals set around its body, and able to transform itself by sprouting the heads of all such animals whatever.'

588d1    'An animal like that,' said Glaucon, 'would need an ingenious sculptor to shape it. Still, it is easier to sculpt in words than in wax or any such medium. So I grant you your animal.'

'Then add that this animal has two other aspects, leonine and human. Add too that the first aspect, the many-headed monster, is by far the largest in size; next in size is the second aspect, the lion.'

'Well, that's easier than the first bit of sculpting; so consider it done,' said Glaucon.

'Now fit these three different aspects together into a unity, as if they had somehow been grafted into one.'

588d8 'They are fitted together,' said Glaucon.

'Next, complete the sculpture by wrapping all the three aspects round with the image of one of them – the man – so that anyone who is not able to look inside our creature, and can only see its outer casing, will take it for a single animal – a human.'

588e2 'Your sculpture has its casing,' said Glaucon.

'Now will a human, thus described, find that injustice is profitable, whereas acting justly is not in his interest? To the person who thinks that he will, let us now point out precisely what his thesis comes to. What he holds is that it profits a man to wine and dine the many-headed monster within, and likewise the lion and everything associated with it, till both are full of strength – while at the same time half-starving the human in him to death, and leaving the human aspect so weak that either of the other two aspects can drag it about[14] in whatever direction they choose to go. He would not have us teach the three aspects to live together and be friends: he would rather leave them to snap and struggle and eat each other up.'

589a4 'Yes,' Glaucon agreed, 'this is what his praise of unjust living means.'

'Conversely, the thesis that justice pays comes to this: that we should say and do whatever will make the human aspect within the human being the strongest of the three aspects, so that that human aspect may take the many-headed brood in hand as a farmer might, nurturing and taming the milder desires, but pruning the growth of the wilder ones. Again, according to this thesis, the human aspect will make an alliance with the lion-like nature within the human being: and together with the lion, the human aspect will care for the interests of all three aspects alike, and will make peace between the lion and the many-headed monster, and between both of them and himself. That will be how the human aspect cares for all these natures.'

589b8     'Yes,' said Glaucon, 'this is exactly what the praise of just living means, too.'

'So from any point of view the person who praises justice is speaking the truth, and the person who praises injustice is a liar. For even the person who recommends justice for its pleasure or its good reputation or its benefits speaks the truth, whereas the person who disparages it is a degenerate, and does not understand what it is that he is disparaging.'

'No,' agreed Glaucon, 'evidently he really doesn't understand justice at all.'

589c7     'So let us then address him with gentle persuasion – for he is not voluntarily misguided – and ask him this. "By heaven, man," we shall say, "mightn't we add that the usual views concerning what is honourable and shameful have come about for precisely these sorts of reasons? Isn't it characteristic of the *honourable* to subjugate the bestial parts of human nature to the human part (we might, perhaps, rather call it the divine part)? And isn't it characteristic of the *shameful* to enslave human nature's gentle part to its savage part?" Will he go along with this, or how will he respond?'

589d4     'If I can persuade him,' said Glaucon, 'he will go along with it.'

'So,' I said, 'if this argument is right, can it be

profitable to anyone to make money by unjust means, when the result of that injustice will be something like this – that at the very moment when he gets the money, the best part of his soul will be sold into slavery to the worst part? Suppose a man made some money by selling his son or daughter into slavery, and to savage, evil men as their masters too. *This* deed would not "profit" him – no matter how much money he made by it. How much less, then, could it possibly profit a man to put mercy aside, and sell the most godlike portion of himself into slavery to his most godless and defiled portion? Won't such a man be a miserable wretch? Won't the money he has taken as a bribe lead him to a more terrible downfall, even, than the necklace that Eriphyle took in exchange for her husband's life?'[15]

590a2     'Let me answer for him,' said Glaucon: 'his downfall will be far worse.'

'And don't you think that intemperate living too has had its bad name so long, because in that sort of life, that terrible thing, that great and polymorphous brood of desires, is allowed more latitude than is proper to it?'

'Clearly so,' said Glaucon.

590b1     'Don't self-will and anger meet with reproach just when they so nourish the lion and the serpent in us as to tune them up to disharmony?'

'Certainly, yes.'

'Luxury and soft effeminacy, on the other hand – aren't they reproached because they loosen and detune the same element until they make cowards of us?'

'Why, yes.'

'What about servility and miserliness? Aren't they reproached when they subjugate that same element – the spirited element[16] – to the mob-like animal? When, from a man's youth up, they accustom the spirited element to contemptuous abuse for the sake of money and the satisfaction of the many-headed monster's insatiate desires – turning that lion into an ape?'

590c1   'Yes – surely,' he said.

'As for 'mechanical" or "manual labour" – why do you think these are terms of abuse? Isn't this the answer? – Because sometimes a person's nature has some sort of weakness in its best aspect, which makes that aspect able only to minister to the broods of desires within him, and not to rule them. And all that such a person is able to learn, is how to serve and obey his passions.'[17]

'Evidently,' he said.

590c8   'So the reason why we say that the natural manual labourer should be the servant of the best person, the man in whom the divine element rules, is not so that the servant may be ruled in such a way as to harm him – as Thrasymachus held was the case with all subjects.[18] No, it is to ensure that this sort of man should have the privilege of being under the same kind of rule as the best sort of man. It is because we think it is best for everyone to be ruled by what is divinely wise. It is best of all if a man has that element within his own nature; but if not, it can be impressed upon him from outside, so that as far as possible we may all be alike and all be friends, since we are steered by the same helmsman. Isn't that the reason?'

590d9   'Yes: and quite right too,' said Glaucon.

# 21. PHILEBUS 45D–52C

## ❧

## MIXED AND UNMIXED PLEASURES; AND ART (I)

45d3    SOCRATES. Tell me, Protarchus, is it in a life of shamelessness or in the temperate life that you see the greater pleasures? By 'greater' I don't mean 'more numerous': I mean 'superior in intensity and degree'. Bring your mind to bear on that question, and then answer.

PROTARCHUS. I understand the question; and my view is that it is hard to make a comparison between the two lives. For I suppose temperate people are always held back by the proverbial adage; that advises them 'Nothing too much', and they concur. By contrast, intemperate and shameless people's lives are in the grip of such exquisitely intense pleasure that it nearly sends them crazy; they become a public reproach.

45e2    SOCRATES. Well said. But if this is really how it is, then it should be clear that it is from some sort of wickedness of soul and body that both the greatest pleasures and the greatest pains arise; it is not from virtue.

PROTARCHUS. True, certainly.

SOCRATES. Then we should pick out some of these greatest pleasures, and consider what sort of characteristics they have to make us call them 'greatest'.

46a1    PROTARCHUS. Of course.

SOCRATES. So consider the pleasures which go with certain pathological conditions: what sort of characteristics do they have?

PROTARCHUS. Which pleasures do you mean?

SOCRATES. I mean those undignified pleasures which

are utterly detested by the anti-hedonist philosophers of whom we spoke.[19]

PROTARCHUS. But which are they?

SOCRATES. I mean things like relieving an itch by scratching it, and that sort of thing – pathological conditions, but they need no other remedy. For, by the gods, what are we to call the experience which comes over us in cases like these? Is it pleasure or pain?

PROTARCHUS. Well, Socrates, it seems to be a bad thing, but of mixed nature.

46b1  SOCRATES. It wasn't Philebus' doctrine of hedonism that led me to bring up this argument; but on the other hand, Protarchus, if we do not look at these sorts of pleasure and their consequences, it seems probable that we will never be able to determine our present point of inquiry.

PROTARCHUS. Then we must consider these pleasures and their relations.

SOCRATES. You mean the pleasures which partake of mixture?

PROTARCHUS. Certainly I do.

SOCRATES. Well, some mixtures have to do with the body, and are in the body; and some are of the soul itself, and are in the soul. Again there are, as we shall find, some pains mixed with pleasures which have to do with both the soul and the body; and these combinations are sometimes called pleasures, and sometimes pains.

46c3  PROTARCHUS. How so?

SOCRATES. Because in all these cases a person has two opposite experiences at once, as some state of body or soul is re-established or else destroyed. So, for example, a person may feel cold, but be getting warm; or he may feel warm, but be getting cold. And then, I think, the person seeks to keep one of the sensations, and lose the other, and this is what the old saying calls 'bitter and sweet mixed together'. For the person finds it difficult to get rid of the unpleasant sensation, and this produces at first discomfort, but later, savage enjoyment.

46d1    PROTARCHUS. Yes – all this that you say is very true.

SOCRATES. Now such mixtures sometimes contain equal degrees of pain and pleasure, and sometimes more of one and less of the other.

PROTARCHUS. Naturally.

SOCRATES. So there are some mixtures where physical pains are greater than physical pleasures: for example itches and tickles of the sort just mentioned are mixtures like this. In other cases the burning and inflamed feeling is internal to the body, and one cannot get through to it by friction or scratching, which only separates out mixtures of pain and pleasure which are on the surface of the body. In such a case we bring our bodies into contact with heat or with its opposite, and by such actions change a perplexing discomfort into an extraordinary pleasure. In other cases again the opposite is true, and internal bodily pleasures are mixed with external bodily pains, and called by either name depending on which of the two preponderates. All these cases happen through the forced separation of what belongs together, or the forced uniting of what belongs apart: that is why pains and pleasures stand alongside each other in these experiences.

47a2    PROTARCHUS. Perfectly true.

SOCRATES. In any case, when there is a greater portion of pleasure than pain mixed into physical experiences of any of these sorts, then the garnish or frisson of pain may tickle the experiencer, creating an enjoyable discomfort in him. Or alternatively, a great and overflowing excess of physical pleasure may tense him up so much, as it were with pain, that sometimes it may actually render him unable to keep still. He may sense all sorts of colours and shapes in the panting delirium which it produces in him; it may even reduce him to meaningless shouting.

47b1    PROTARCHUS. Yes, it's true.

SOCRATES. In such experiences, my friend, a man will say of himself – as will others too – that he is so delighted by these pleasures that he could die. The more intemperate and mindless such a man is, the more avidly he will go on pursuing such pleasures on every possible occasion; he calls such pleasures the greatest things of all, and counts that man happiest who spends as much of his life as possible in experiencing such things.

PROTARCHUS. Yes, Socrates – you have described most convincingly what happens to the majority of people.

47c2    SOCRATES. But, Protarchus, I have spoken only about the pleasures which mingle together purely physical sensations, felt either within the body or at its surface. What about the pleasures in which the soul contributes something opposite to what the body contributes – psychical pain to go with a bodily pleasure, or psychical pleasure to go with a bodily pain, so that the two come together in one mixture? What I remarked before about such mixtures was that when someone is empty, he desires to be filled: he takes pleasure in that expectation, but is pained by his emptiness. Now let me also say what I did not testify to then: that there is just this one sort of mixture of pain and pleasure in all these quite innumerable cases where soul is at odds with body.

47d3    PROTARCHUS. Yes, you may well be perfectly right about that.

SOCRATES. So that only leaves us with one last sort of mixture of pain and pleasure.

PROTARCHUS. Tell me – which is that?

SOCRATES. The kind of mixture which we often say the soul itself undergoes in itself.

PROTARCHUS. What do we call that sort of mixture?

47e1    SOCRATES. Well, wouldn't you say that the following

are all pains which belong to the soul itself: anger, fear, regret, grief, infatuation, jealousy, envy, and so on?

PROTARCHUS. Yes, I would.

SOCRATES. But don't we find that all these emotions are unaccountably mingled with pleasures? Need we recall Homer's wrath, 'Which stirs up even all-wise men to harshness, Sweeter than honey dripping from the comb'?[20] Or the pleasures which are mixed in together with pain in grief and regret?

48a3    PROTARCHUS. No need to recall these; they do indeed come about just as you say, and in no other manner.

SOCRATES. What about those who watch tragedies? Do you recall how they enjoy them and weep at the same time?

PROTARCHUS. Of course.

SOCRATES. And do you see that the state of our souls when we watch comedies too is also a mixture of pain and pleasure?

PROTARCHUS. No – I don't quite see that.

48b1    SOCRATES. Well, truly, Protarchus, the kind of experience that one undergoes when watching comedies is not entirely easy to understand.

PROTARCHUS. No – not for me, anyway.

SOCRATES. But let us all the more take up the question because it is a murky one, so that we will be able to understand the nature of the mixture of pain and pleasure all the more easily in the other cases.

PROTARCHUS. Speak on, then.

SOCRATES. Do you think the word 'envy' which we have just used is a name for a kind of pain of the soul? Or for something else?

PROTARCHUS. No – it is a pain of the soul.

SOCRATES. But surely it will be evident that the person who feels envy, takes pleasure in the evils that befall those around him.

48c1    PROTARCHUS. He certainly does.

SOCRATES. Again, surely ignorance is an evil; and so is the disposition that we often call unimprovable stupidity.

PROTARCHUS. Of course.

SOCRATES. Given these suppositions, ask yourself this. What is the nature of the 'ridiculousness' that makes comedies?

PROTARCHUS. You just tell me!

SOCRATES. Well, briefly, ridiculousness is a kind of badness: it is a name which we use for a character trait. Specifically, it is that kind of badness of character which is opposite to the character trait commended by the inscription over the gate of the Delphic oracle.

PROTARCHUS. Do you mean 'Know Thyself', Socrates?

48d1    SOCRATES. I do. And quite obviously, the opposite of knowing oneself is, as the inscription might have put it, Knowing Thyself Not At All.

PROTARCHUS. Of course.

SOCRATES. Well, Protarchus, please try to divide this trait of self-ignorance into three.[21]

PROTARCHUS. How would you like me to? I fear I'm not the man for the job!

SOCRATES. You're asking me to make the division, for the moment?

PROTARCHUS. Asking – and begging you to as well.

SOCRATES. Very well. If anyone does not know himself, mustn't he necessarily be affected by his ignorance in one of three ways?

PROTARCHUS. Namely?

SOCRATES. The first has to do with possessions such as money: the self-ignorant man in this sense over-estimates how much he can spend, given his actual capital.

48e2    PROTARCHUS. Yes – there are certainly many who suffer from that condition.

SOCRATES. But even more lack self-knowledge in a second way: they imagine themselves taller and more handsome than they really are, and their opinion of their own bodily condition is far wide of the truth.

PROTARCHUS. That certainly happens.

SOCRATES. But, I believe, the greatest number of all lack self-knowledge of the third form: they are mistaken about their own souls, and falsely imagine that they are better than others where virtue is concerned.

PROTARCHUS. Yes: people obviously do make mistakes about that.

49a1 SOCRATES. Now of all the virtues, isn't wisdom the one that the great mass of people – in all their contention and vain imaginings of wisdom – most claim for their own?

PROTARCHUS. Of course.

SOCRATES. But contentiousness, and falsely thinking that one is wise – all such conditions of soul can only be correctly described as evil.

PROTARCHUS. Very true, yes.

SOCRATES. So, Protarchus, if we are to see clearly the puerile nature of envy, and how inappropriately it blends pleasure and pain, we must make a further division in the class of those who do not know their own souls – into two subclasses this time. How, you ask, are we to make this division into two? Well, all those who have this senseless false opinion about themselves can be divided in two just as any group of humans can. For necessarily, some of them are attended by strength and power, and others, I take it, by weakness and ineffectuality.

49b3 PROTARCHUS. Yes – necessarily.

SOCRATES. So that is where you should make the division. People who do not know their own souls, and are so weak and ineffectual that they cannot take their vengeance when they are ridiculed – these are the people whom one could with most justification call ridiculous. Whereas those who do not know their own souls, but are strong and capable of avenging themselves – the most correct name you can give to them is 'dangerous enemies'. For the self-ignorance of the strong is a menacing and shameful thing, and both it and its imitations harm those who are near; but the self-ignorance of the weak is a thing we class as naturally ridiculous.

PROTARCHUS. You're absolutely right. However, I don't yet see what this has to do with the mixing of pleasures and pains.

SOCRATES. Well, take the question of how envy operates first.

PROTARCHUS. Go on.

49d1   SOCRATES. Mightn't envy be an unjust pain and an unjust pleasure?

PROTARCHUS. Yes, it must be that.

SOCRATES. But surely it isn't unjust, and isn't envious either, to be pleased when evils come to our enemies?

PROTARCHUS. Of course not.

SOCRATES. But those occasions when people see evils come to their friends, and are not grieved at it, but pleased – that *is* unjust, isn't it?

PROTARCHUS. Obviously.

SOCRATES. Now we said that ignorance was always an evil to anyone.

PROTARCHUS. Right.

49d9   SOCRATES. Then suppose our friends have a false opinion of their own wisdom or good looks or affluence – the forms of self-ignorance which we have just categorised in three classes, saying that such self-ignorance is ridiculous in the weak but hateful in the powerful. Shouldn't we agree to what I have just argued – that when one of our friends has this trait in a form which is not powerful enough to harm others, then it is ridiculous?

PROTARCHUS. Yes, definitely.

SOCRATES. But haven't we agreed that ignorance itself is an evil?

PROTARCHUS. Yes – a great evil.

SOCRATES. So do we feel pleasure or pain when we laugh at ignorance?

50a1 PROTARCHUS. Clearly we feel pleasure.

SOCRATES. But didn't we say that envy is the cause that brings about pleasure in us when evils come to our friends?

PROTARCHUS. Yes – it must be.

SOCRATES. So the conclusion of the argument is that to laugh at what is ridiculous in our friends is to blend pleasure with pain – because it is mixing pleasure with envy. For we agreed a good while back[22] that envy is a pain in the soul, whereas laughing at things is a pleasure. But on such occasions as we are now considering, we experience *both together*.

PROTARCHUS. True.

50b1 SOCRATES. So now the argument reveals to us that in mourning the dead, in tragedies, and in comedies – not just in the plays, but in all the tragedy and comedy of life itself too – pains and pleasures are mingled together at one time in thousands of different ways.

PROTARCHUS. No one could possibly disagree with that conclusion, Socrates, however argumentative and contrary they were.

SOCRATES. Now we brought forward such feelings as anger and regret and mourning and fear and infatuation and jealousy and envy as cases in which we claimed, as we keep repeating, to be able to find pleasure and pain mixed together. Didn't we?

50c2 PROTARCHUS. Yes.

SOCRATES. Then do we see how everything we have just said applies alike to all three cases, grief and envy and anger?

PROTARCHUS. How could we not see it?

SOCRATES. So aren't there many other cases we could discuss similarly?

PROTARCHUS. Very many, yes.

50c8     SOCRATES. So why do you suppose I made this general
         point about the mixing of pleasure and pain with
         reference to the example of comedy, particularly?
         Why, I took the hardest case, so as to be more
         convincing. For it is easy enough to show that there
         is a mixture of pain and pleasure in the other cases,
         such as fear and infatuation. Also I thought that, if
         you could accept the point in the case of this example
         of comedy, you would let me off having to lengthen
         out the argument to deal with all the other cases. I
         thought you might simply accept this claim: that there
         is a mixture of pain and pleasure in all these experi-
         ences of soul and body, both if each is taken sepa-
         rately, and in the case where they are taken together.
         So tell me – will you let me off discussing the other
         cases, or will you compel me to go on till midnight? I
         believe I have just the formula to inveigle you into
         letting me off. It is: 'I shall be willing to give you an
         account of all these cases *tomorrow*.' What I want to
         do now is steer clear of them, and settle the remaining
         points we need to settle to give Philebus the decision
         which he is asking from us, about whether pleasure is
         the good or not.

50e4     PROTARCHUS. Well said, Socrates: you expound what-
         ever points still need to be settled just as you like.
         SOCRATES. Well, after the mixed pleasures it's only
         natural, indeed in a sense it's inevitable, to go on to the
         unmixed pleasures in their turn.

51a1     PROTARCHUS. Very well.
         SOCRATES. So I shall switch to them, and try to point
         out to both of us what unmixed pleasures are. Some
         people say that all pleasures are just cessations of
         pains. But I absolutely disagree; and I call those very
         people themselves to witness to the fact that some of
         the pleasures they have in mind are only apparent
         and in no way real, while others, however great and
         numerous they may appear, are actually no more than

confused concoctions together of pains with the cessations of the most extreme agonies that any predicament of body and soul can bring.

51b1    PROTARCHUS. But what about the true pleasures, Socrates? Which pleasures might we rightly suppose are true?

SOCRATES. They include all the pleasures which have as their objects what we call beautiful colours and shapes, and most of the pleasures with scents and sounds as their objects. The pure pleasures are those the lack of which is not felt and causes no pain, whereas their fulfilment is perceptible, and gives a pleasure which is undefiled by pain.

PROTARCHUS. But once again, Socrates, which pleasures fit this description?

51c1    SOCRATES. Well, certainly I admit that what I say is not instantly pellucid; so let me try to clarify it. When I speak of the beauty of shapes, I am not gesturing towards what the multitude would assume I mean, for example paintings of living creatures or whatever. Rather, the argument concerns the straight line and the circular line, and the two- and three-dimensional figures which can be made out of these lines using compasses, rulers and set-squares – if you follow me. My point is that such things as these are not beautiful because of their relation to something else, as other things are; rather, they are by nature and eternally beautiful in their own right. They also have their own special pleasures; and these are utterly unlike the pleasures of scratching! And there are colours too which have a beauty, and a pleasure, of this type. Do you understand me, or not?

51d4    PROTARCHUS. I am trying to, Socrates – but you try too, to speak more clearly still.

SOCRATES. I mean those sorts of sounds which are even and clear, emitting a single pure musical note. Such a sound is not beautiful because of its relation to something else, but in its own right; and its natural consequent is a pleasure of the same nature.

PROTARCHUS. Yes, that is so as well.

51e1    SOCRATES. The pure pleasures of smell, it is true, constitute a less divine class than the pure pleasures of sight and sound. However, none of these pleasures involves an admixture of pains as an essential ingredient. And I take any case where *that* is true to be a reprise of the cases of sight and sound – no matter which of our senses is involved, and no matter how. So, if you follow me, here are two forms of unmixed pleasure.

PROTARCHUS. Yes, I follow you.

52a1    SOCRATES. Well, next let us add a third form of unmixed pleasure to these two. This form consists of the pleasures to do with knowledge; provided that those pleasures do not, in our judgement, involve hunger for knowledge, or arise out of hunger pangs for learning?

PROTARCHUS. No, I agree that they don't.

SOCRATES. What about those who are at one time full up with knowledge, but then lose it by forgetting? Don't you espy any pangs of sorrow about knowledge in their case?

PROTARCHUS. Well, not pangs that are essentially about knowledge. But they will feel pangs of sorrow when they reckon up their losses, as will happen if someone who is deprived of knowledge feels grief about it because he had a *use* for that knowledge.

52b2    SOCRATES. Bless you, indeed they will; but all we are talking about at the moment is the feelings natural to the experience of losing knowledge itself, and this is a separate matter from such practical reckoning.

PROTARCHUS. Well, in that case, you are right to say that we never feel pain when we lose our knowledge through forgetting.

SOCRATES. So we may say that these pleasures of

knowledge are unmixed with pain; but they are felt not
at all by the multitude, but only by a very few.

PROTARCHUS. Yes, we have to say that.

52c1   SOCRATES. So now we have done a fitting job of
separating off the pure pleasures from those which
might fairly properly be called the impure pleasures.


NOTES

1. Protagoras particularly, because Protagoras claims that anyone can
   be taught virtue: cf. reading 11.
2. A startling remark coming from Protagoras: cf. reading 36.
3. With a reminiscence of Heracleitus, Fragment DK B 60, Plato
   indicates that (at this stage of his career) he explains 'being overcome' as a purely cognitive failure: being led astray from real goods
   by apparent goods.
4. In fact Plato never develops the 'hedonistic calculus' promised here.
   But he does build an ethical theory around the contrast between
   appearance and reality: cf. readings 31–4.
5. Prodicus was a philosopher of language who delighted in pedanti-
   cally fine distinctions; possibly his rationale was the claim that no
   terms were synonyms.
6. If 'fear of x' means 'expectation of evil from x', and 'greater fear of x
   than of y' means 'expectation of greater evil from x than from y';
   and if 'being overcome by yourself' means choosing what you think
   worse over what you think better; then choosing to do what you find
   very frightening, when less frightening courses of action are open
   to you, is a case of 'being overcome by yourself'. Socrates thinks he
   can show that *no* case of 'being overcome by yourself' can ever
   occur. So whatever people may typically do in cases where they
   exhibit courage, it cannot be that they choose to do what they find
   (most) frightening.
7. I.e., the agreed thesis that no one deliberately chooses the worse
   over the better.
8. *Gorgias* 492e.
9. Compare Hobbes, *Leviathan*, 1.11: 'The felicity of this life consis-
   teth not in the repose of a mind satisfied . . . Nor can a man any
   more live, whose desires are at an end, than he whose senses and
   imagination are at a stand.'
10. *Gorgias* 482e3.
11. *Gorgias* 492a3, in reading 17.

12. *Gorgias* 494c.
13. Plato parodies his own statement (*Protagoras* 345e) that no one willingly does wrong.
14. Cf. *Protagoras* 352c in reading 14.
15. Polyneices bribed Eriphyle with a necklace to induce her husband Amphiaraus to join the disastrous expedition of the 'seven against Thebes'.
16. Cf. reading 23.
17. Cf. Hume, *Treatise* 2.3.3: 'Reason is and ought only to be the slave of the passions, and can pretend to no other office, but to serve and obey them.' Plato would retort that Hume's dictum is perfectly true – of degenerates.
18. *Republic* 343b ff.
19. *Philebus* 44b.
20. Homer, *Iliad* 18.109.
21. This is the 'method of division', which is characteristic of Plato's later philosophy: it also appears in *Phaedrus*, *Sophist* and *Statesman*.
22. *Philebus* 48b.

# PART IV
✦✦
# GOD AND THE SOUL

# 22. PHAEDO 70c–72d

## ✦✦

## THE IMMORTALITY OF THE SOUL (I)

70c3    'Let us approach the question in something like this way,' said Socrates: 'are the souls of dead humans present in Hades, or aren't they? For we all remember the old story that they are there, and came to Hades from here – and what is more, that they will return to this world from that place: they will come back to life from the realm of the dead. If that story is right, and living people do return to life from among those who have died, then clearly our souls must be present there. For presumably they could not come back into the world unless they still existed. If it really was clearly shown by this tale that living people come into the world from no other place than from where the dead are, that would be enough to prove the immortality of the soul. But if this is as yet unproved, then we will need some other argument.'

70d4    'We certainly will,' said Cebes.

   'Well,' said Socrates, 'don't seek this other argument by thinking only about humans; if you want to see the point more easily, think about the other animals and plants as well, and indeed about everything that comes to be. Let us consider all these cases. Don't all these things come to be in no other way than as opposites from their opposites – provided they have opposites? For example, the Beautiful is the opposite of the Ugly, and the Just of the Unjust; and so on in ten thousand other cases. So let us look at this question: Isn't it necessarily true that whatever has an opposite can come to be only from that opposite and from nowhere else? Here is one example: when something becomes bigger, it is presumably necessary that it should come to be bigger from an earlier state in which it was smaller. Isn't it?'

'Yes.'

'And if it becomes smaller, won't it come to be smaller later, having been bigger earlier?'

71a2 'Just so.'

'And doesn't what is weaker come to be out of what is stronger? And what is faster, out of what is slower?'

'Absolutely.'

'What about if something is worse? Mustn't it have become worse from what was better? Or if it is more just, mustn't it have become so from what was less just?'

'Of course.'

'Well then,' he said, 'do we grasp this point sufficiently well – that whatever comes to be like this, is an opposite which comes to be from an opposite?'

'Yes, clearly.'

71a9 'Next, isn't something like this true in all these cases? – Aren't there two processes of coming to be between the two poles of each of these pairs of opposites: from the one into the other, and back from the other into the first? So between a bigger object and a smaller object there is increase and decrease in size – what we call increasing and decreasing.'

71b3 'Yes.'

'Likewise with separation and combination, cooling and heating, and all other such cases: even if we don't have the word for both processes in every case, isn't it, in fact, a necessary truth about all of these cases, that in each case there are two processes, running in opposite directions between the two poles?'

'Of course it is,' said Cebes.

71c1 'Well,' said Socrates, 'is anything the opposite of living in the way that waking is the opposite of sleeping?'

'Of course.'

'What?'

'Being dead.'

'So since they are opposites, won't these two states be generated from each other? And won't two processes of coming to be lie between these two states?'

'Obviously.'

'Very well,' said Socrates: 'let's take these two pairs of states which I have just described to you. I will tell you about the first pair of states, and the two processes that lie between them; you tell me about the second.

'I say, then, that sleeping is one of the states and waking the other. The state of waking comes to be out of sleeping, and the state of sleeping comes to be out of waking; and the two processes that lie between these states are falling asleep and waking up. Do you think that will do?'

71d2      'Obviously it will.'

'Well,' said Socrates, 'tell me something similar about living and being dead. Don't you think that being dead is the opposite of living?'

'Yes, I do.'

'Don't living and being dead come to be out of each other?'

'Yes.'

'What is it that comes to be out of what is living?'

'What is dead.'

'And what is it that comes to be out of what is dead?'

'I am bound to admit,' he said, 'that it's the living.'

'So, Cebes, it is from what is dead that living things, including animals, come to be?'

'Evidently so,' he said.

71e1      'Therefore,' said Socrates, 'our souls are present in Hades.'

'Apparently.'

'Now isn't one of the two processes in this case clear enough to see? I take it we are well aware that dying occurs.'

'We certainly are,' said Cebes.

'Well, what shall we do next? Are we to reject the idea of the opposite process, so that Nature is deformed in this one case? Won't we admit that there must be some opposite process to dying?'

'Let us, by all means,' he said.

'And what is this process?'

'Coming back to life.'

72a1 'Wouldn't this process of coming back to life, if it occurs, be the process whereby those who are dead come to be alive again?'

'Certainly.'

'So we have agreed by this method too,[1] that those who are alive come to be so from the dead, no less than those who are dead come to be so from those who are alive. Since this is so, it seems likely to be enough to prove that the souls of those who are dead are bound to be somewhere – from where they also come back into this world.'

'I think, Socrates,' he said, 'that that must follow from the premises we have accepted.'

72a8 'But look,' Socrates said: 'I think we can also show that it was not unjust to accept those premises: like this. Suppose that there was not this perpetual exchange of opposites into their opposites, as it were going round in a cycle. Suppose that there was no cycle, but always one linear process: one opposite coming to be from the other, carrying directly on without ever turning back or making a curve towards the opposite process. You must see that in the end everything would be in the same state; for the same would have happened to everything, and there would be an end of all coming to be.'

72b7 'What do you mean?' asked Cebes.

'What I mean is nothing difficult to understand,' said Socrates. 'Compare our example. If the process of falling asleep exists, but the opposite state of waking up from sleep is not also granted, then you must see that in the end everything would show up the tale of the mythical sleeper Endymion as a vain story. There would be no chance of *finding* Endymion, because the same as happened to him would have happened to everything else too: everything would be asleep. Again, if everything was in process of combination, and nothing was in the process of separating, then Anaxagoras' diagnosis would soon be accurate: soon 'all things' *would* be 'all together'.[2]

72c5 'In just the same way, my dear Cebes, suppose that everything that has life should undergo the process of dying, and that having once died, all these dead things should remain in that state, and never return to life again. Wouldn't it then be absolutely necessary that there should come a point eventually where *everything* had died, and nothing was alive? For if living things come into being from some other source than the dead, but then die, how can we possibly avoid the result that everything is eventually converted into a state of death?'

72d4 'I don't think we can avoid it, Socrates,' said Cebes.

# 23. REPUBLIC 435E–442E

## ✦

## THE FORMS IN THE SOUL (I); THEIR HARMONY; AND JUSTICE

435e1   'At any rate,' I said, 'aren't we absolutely bound to admit that the same forms or aspects are present in us as in the city? For presumably they could not arise in the city from anywhere else. It would be ridiculous for someone to think that a city does not get its Spiritedness[3] from its individual citizens, whose own Spiritedness is the cause of the city's; as for example Thracians and Scythians, and northern peoples generally, are spirited. The same is true of the Love of Learning, which (it might be said) is what dominates in our part of the world; and of the Love of Money, which one might well attribute to the Carthaginians and the Egyptians.'

436a2   'Quite so,' said Glaucon.

'Then,' I said, 'it is not hard to recognise that this is how things are.'

'No indeed.'

'What is difficult is this question. Do we operate in all these different ways in respect of the same form in us? Or are there three forms operating in three different ways, so that we learn with one of our forms, feel Spirit with a second, and with some third form, desire the pleasures of feeding and coming to be, and whatever is akin to these? Or do we rather operate in each of these ways, whenever we begin to do so, in respect of our whole souls? This is the question that's difficult to determine in a way worth discussing.'

436b3   'I agree,' said Glaucon.

'Here's a way to settle whether these forms are the same or different,' I said.

'How?'

'Well, it is clear that one and the same thing will never do or undergo two opposite things simultaneously, in the same respect, in relation to the same. So if we ever find any two of these forms we have considered thus opposed, we shall know that those two are not one and the same thing, but more than one.'

436c1     'Very good,' he said.

[436c–437b]⁴

437b1     'Well,' I said, 'take the pairs agreement and disagreement, pursuit and aversion, attraction and repulsion. Wouldn't you say that these are pairs of opposites? (Ignore the question whether these processes are active or passive, for it makes no difference.)'

'Yes,' he said, 'these are all opposites.'

437b5     'Well, next,' I said, 'take thirst and hunger and in general every bodily desire, and likewise wanting and deciding. Wouldn't you agree that all these too must fit somewhere into the scheme of the forms or aspects of the soul that we have just mentioned? For example, wouldn't you say that the soul of someone who feels bodily desire *pursues* what he feels desire for? That what he desires should come his way *attracts* him? Or that, in so far as he wants to attain something, his soul *agrees* to that objective just as if it were answering a question, and strains towards bringing it about?'

437c7     'Yes, I would.'

'What about deciding *not* to do something, *not* wanting, *not* desiring? Shan't we class these as the soul's activities of rejection and repulsion – as the opposites of the activities we have just considered?'

437d1     'Of course.'

'If this is agreed, shall we go on to say that there is an aspect of the soul responsible for those bodily desires the clearest examples of which are what we call thirst and hunger?'

'We shall,' said Glaucon.

'Isn't thirst just bodily desire for drink, and hunger for food?'

'Yes.'

437d5    'But shall we say that thirst – considered simply as *thirst* – is a bodily desire felt in the soul for anything *more* than drink? For example, thirst as such is not thirst-for-a-hot-drink, nor a cold one; nor for a big or a small drink. Thirst is not essentially related to any particular *sort* of drink: just to drink. Of course we can change the story, adding that someone might be thirsty *and hot*, and so want a cold drink; or thirsty *and cold*, and so want a hot drink. Or say the thirst is a big one – then it is a thirst for a lot of drink; or a slight one – then it is a thirst for a small drink. But thirst *itself* can never be a bodily desire for anything but its natural object – drink itself. The same goes for hunger and food.'

'Just so,' said Glaucon; 'any desire, in itself, is desire for its natural object, in itself. Desire for a qualified natural object is qualified desire.'

438a1    'So,' I said, 'we mustn't let anyone alarm us by catching us out with the following reply: "No one desires drink or food itself: they desire *good* drink or food. For everyone desires what is good; therefore, if thirst (or whatever) is a desire at all, it must be a desire for good drink (or whatever)."'

'Still,' said Glaucon, 'the person who makes that reply does seem to have a point.'[5]

438b1    'But consider those things which are naturally relative to something else,' I said. 'If they are qualified, then so is what they are naturally relative to; if they are unqualified, then so is what they are naturally relative to.

[438b2–439a8[6]]

'So the soul of a thirsty person, in so far as he is thirsty, wants nothing except to drink. That is what he feels a desire for, and what he strains after.'

439b1    'Clearly so.'

'Therefore if anything ever holds a person back from drinking when he is thirsty, it must be some form in his soul which is different from the aspect which impels him to drink just as an animal is impelled. For we have agreed that the same aspect of him cannot operate in opposite ways in the same respect simultaneously.'

'Yes, we have.'

'And so, I think, it is a poor epigram[7] which says that the archer pushes away his bow at the same time as he pulls it towards him. Rather we should say that one of his hands pushes the bow away, and the other pulls it nearer.'

439c1    'Absolutely.'

'But shouldn't we allow that sometimes people who are thirsty are not willing to drink?'

'Of course we should,' he replied: 'it happens all the time.'

'So what,' I asked, 'are we to say about such people? Shouldn't we say that there is one thing in their souls which tells them to drink, and another which forbids them, which is different from the aspect that tells them to drink, and overcomes that aspect?'

'So it seems to me,' he said.

'Doesn't the aspect which forbids such actions arrive at its prohibitions, when it does arrive at them, by the power of reasoning? Whereas the aspects which lead us on and drag us into these actions come to do so because of our afflictions and our diseases?'

439d2    'Apparently.'

'Then,' I said, 'it is quite reasonable to decide that these aspects are separate and different from one another. We may refer to the aspect wherein someone reasons as the Rational form in the soul; and the aspect wherein he feels lust, hunger and thirst, and the agitations of the other desires, we may call the Irrational, Desiring aspect – the escort of satiations and pleasures.'

'Yes,' he said, 'we might fittingly take that view.'

439e1     'So,' I said, 'we may distinguish these two aspects as different forms present in the soul. But what about the Spirited aspect, wherein we feel high spirit? Is that a third aspect? With which of these two aspects might it share a nature?'

'Perhaps,' he said, 'with the second, the Desiring form of the soul.'

'But,' I said, 'there is this tale I once heard, which I believe to be true. Leontius son of Aglaion was once coming up to Athens from Peiraeus, along the outside of the North Wall, and noticed the corpses lying by the public scaffold. Simultaneously he felt a morbid desire to look at the corpses and a repelling disgust. For a moment he fought the urge and shut his eyes; but soon his urge overcame him, so he opened his eyes and rushed right up to the corpses. "There you are, damn you both!" he said – "take your fill of sightseeing!"'

440a4     'Yes, I've heard that story too,' said Glaucon.

'Well,' I said, 'doesn't this story indicate that anger sometimes fights against our desires, as one force against another?'

'Yes, it does,' he agreed.

440a8     'And,' I added, 'there are plenty of other occasions where we see that someone's desires compel him in a way contrary to reason, so that he berates himself and feels anger at the part of himself that is compelling him. In such people, the Spirited aspect appears like an ally to the Reason in its civil war with Desire. (Although, certainly, that the Spirited aspect should make an alliance with the body's desires, to disobey and do something that the choice of Reason says should *not* be done – that is something that I think no one ever sees, neither in himself nor in another.)'

440c1    'By Zeus, no,' he said.

'Again,' I said, 'when someone admits that he has acted unjustly, isn't it true that, the nobler his character is, the less he is able to feel anger if someone punishes him in a way he considers just – even when he suffers hunger and cold and so on at their behest? Doesn't his soul's Spirited aspect refuse to be provoked against such a man – just as my theory predicts?'

'It's true,' he said.

440c8    'What about when someone thinks he has suffered an injustice? Doesn't the Spirited aspect (in noble characters at least) bubble over with indignation then, allying itself with what it thinks is just? Won't the Spirited aspect endure hunger and cold and every-thing of that sort to overcome the injustice? Won't it refuse to relent until it has either accomplished its purpose, or met its death, or been pacified by the Reason which accompanies it, which calls it off like a shepherd calling off his dog?'

440d4    'Your simile,' he said, 'fits the Spirited form in the soul most accurately – especially as we supposed that the Auxiliaries in our ideal city would be like dogs helping the Rulers – the shepherds of the city, as it were.'

'Yes,' I said, 'you clearly understand what I mean to say. But do you see a further point? We now think the opposite about the Spirited aspect to what we thought a minute ago. For we were supposing that the Spirited aspect was something to do with the Desiring form in us, but we would now say "On the contrary: when there is unrest in the soul, the Spirited aspect adds its forces to those of the Reason."'

440e4    'Certainly,' he said.

'So is the Spirited aspect also separate from Reason? Or is it an aspect of Reason, so that there are not three but two forms present in the soul – Rational and Desiring? Or is the case just like that of the city, which is composed of three classes – Materialistic, Auxiliary, and Executive? Perhaps the Spirited aspect is a third form in the soul, which is an auxiliary to the Rational nature, provided it is not corrupted by a bad upbringing.'

441a3    'It must be a third form,' he said.

'Yes,' I agreed, 'provided we can show that it is something different from the Rational, just as we have already shown that it is different from the Desiring aspect.'

'Well, that's not difficult to show,' he said: 'one can see it even in children. As soon as they come into the world they are brimfull of Spirit; but as for Reason – some of them, I think, never come into their inheritance of that; even the majority of people only become rational late in their lives.'

441b2    'Yes, by Zeus,' I replied, 'that is very well said; and there is also the evidence of animals to demonstrate what you claim. Besides that, we may add what we mentioned earlier – Homer's evidence, where he says that Odysseus "Struck his breast, restraining his heart with this word".[8] For in this line Homer has clearly shown us that the aspect of us which reasons about better and worse is a separate aspect from the part which does not reason, but becomes angry.'

441c3    'You are completely right,' he said.

'Well,' I said, 'we have struggled ashore at last: we have reached a satisfactory agreement that the same classes, all three of them, are to be found both in the city and in each of its inhabitants.'

'We have.'

'Then doesn't it follow at once that the individual must be wise in the same way and in virtue of the same aspect as the city is wise?'

'Why, yes.'

441d1    'And that the city must be brave in the same way and in virtue of the same aspect as the individual is brave? And so on with all the other parts of virtue relating to both city and individual?'

'Yes – necessarily.'

'I believe we also will say that an individual is just in the same sense as we said a city was just.'

'That too is quite inevitable.'

'But we surely can't have forgotten that the city was just when each of the three classes in it performed the function that belonged to it.'

'I'm sure we haven't!' he replied.

'So we must remember this: the just person among us – and the one who performs the function which belongs to him in the state – will be the one in whose soul each of the forms fulfils the function which belongs to that form.'

441e3    'Yes,' he agreed, 'that is what we must remember.'

'Well, isn't it proper to the Reason to rule, since it is wise and has foresight for every other aspect of the soul? And isn't it proper to the Spirited aspect to assist the Reason, and be its ally?'

'Yes, of course.'

'And weren't we right to say$^9$ that it is a mixed education in athletics and the arts which will bring these elements into harmony, by strengthening and nurturing the Reason with beautiful arguments and proofs, and relaxing, appeasing, and softening the Spirited aspect with harmony and rhythm?'

442a2    'We certainly were,' he replied.

'Then when these two forms in the soul have been nurtured like this, and really have learnt to perform their own functions through this education, they together will take charge of the Desiring aspect of the soul, which is the largest part of the soul in each of us, and naturally the greediest for material things. But these two other forms will watch over it, to prevent it from engorging itself on the so-called pleasures of the body until it becomes so large and strong that it will not perform its own function, but tries to enslave and rule over the classes which it is not fit to rule over – thus subverting the very existence of all three classes.'[10]

442b3     'Absolutely,' he agreed.

'And,' I said, 'wouldn't Reason and Spirit together also be best able to ward off external enemies on behalf of the entire soul and the body – the Reason by deliberation, and the Spirited part by fighting, by following its ruler and realising his decisions through its courage?'

'Just so.'

442c1     'In fact, I believe we call any individual *brave* in virtue of this: he is brave if his Spirited aspect preserves in him, through pains and pleasures, the instructions which it has received from the Reason about what is to be feared and what is not.'

'Quite right,' he said.

'And we call him *wise* in virtue of that little part of him which was in charge in him to give these instructions – in virtue of the fact that that part in him possesses knowledge of what is in the interest of each one of the three aspects, and in their common interest taken together.'

'Absolutely.'

442d1     'What about *temperance*? Isn't such a person temperate because of the friendship and harmony of these aspects, when the ruling principle and the two ruled forms all agree that the Reason ought to rule, and there is no rebellion against it?'

'Yes indeed,' he said: 'the virtue of temperance, both in a city and in an individual, is precisely this.'

'Such a person is also *just* in the very way that we have so often described: for each aspect of him performs the function which belongs to it.'[11]

'Yes – that is absolutely bound to be true.'

'So,' I said, 'has our picture of justice blurred in any way, so that it looks to be a different thing in the individual from what we saw it was in the state?'

442e1     'I at any rate,' he replied, 'think it has not.'

➤⬅

## THE IMMORTALITY OF THE
## SOUL (II); AND WHY BE JUST?
## (III: ANOTHER ANSWER)

608c1    'However,' I said, 'we still haven't got on to the most important sort of reward or prize available for virtue.'

'You must mean an extraordinarily great reward,' he said, 'if it is something more than all these other rewards we have discussed.'[12]

'But,' I said, 'how could anything great at all come to be in a short time span? And the whole of the time span from childhood to old age – I believe that is a small thing compared with the whole of time.'

'Tiny? It is nothing!' he answered.

'Well then, do you think that an immortal being should be concerned about such a time span, but not concerned about the whole of time?'

608d2    'I certainly don't,' he replied; 'but what immortal being do you mean?'

'Why,' I said, 'haven't you realised that the soul in us is immortal, and is never destroyed?'

He stared at me in amazement: 'By Zeus,' he said, 'no, I haven't. But you are able to show that it is?'

'Yes – at least if I reason justly,' I replied; 'and, I believe, so can you; it's not a difficult proof.'

'It is to me!' he said. 'So I would love to hear this "proof that isn't difficult" from you.'

'Then you shall,' I replied.

'Speak on,' he said.

608e1    'Is there anything you call good or evil?'

'Yes.'

'Do you conceive them as I do?'

'How's that?'

'Whatever destroys and corrupts is evil; whatever preserves and benefits is good.'

'Yes, that is my conception,' he said.

609a1    'Well, do you say that each thing has its own specific good and evil? For example: ophthalmia is to the eyes as sickness is to the whole body, as mildew is to corn, as rust is to bronze or iron. And so on: in virtually every case each thing has what I mean – its own connatural evil and disease.'

'Yes, that's what I'd say,' he replied.

'When one of these forms of evil comes about in something, doesn't it make that thing bad, and in the end completely dissolve and destroy it?'

'Of course.'

'So it is the natural evil and badness of anything which destroys it. If that does not destroy it, nothing else will. For clearly a thing's natural *good* will never destroy it; nor will what is neither its good nor its evil.'

609b2    'No; how could they?' he replied.

'So suppose we find some existing thing which has an evil that leaves it in a wretched state, and yet is not able to bring about the thing's dissolution and destruction. In that case, won't we know that there can *be* no destruction of the thing in question?'

'That seems likely,' he replied.

'Well,' I said: 'isn't there something that makes the soul evil?'

'There certainly is,' he replied: 'all the things we have just been exploring do that – injustice, intemperance, cowardice, ignorance.'

609c2    'But does any of these vices dissolve and destroy the soul? Make sure that we're not distracted by the idea that if an unjust and thoughtless man is *caught* acting unjustly, then that is a case where he may be destroyed by his injustice – that is, by the badness of his soul.

Rather, consider the question like this. The badness of a body is disease, which wastes it away, dissolves it, brings it to be no longer a body at all. Likewise with each of the examples I have just given. When any of our examples is besieged and then occupied by its own specific evil, it is eventually brought to the state where it no longer exists at all – isn't it?'

609d2        'Yes.'

'Consider the soul in the same way. If injustice and the other sorts of vice are present in the soul, do their siege and occupation of it so destroy and quench the soul that they bring about its death and its separation from the body?'

'No, the vices certainly don't do that,' he said.

'And yet,' I said, 'it would be quite inexplicable for a thing to be destroyed by the badness of something else, when its own badness did not destroy it.'

'Yes.'

609e1        'For notice, Glaucon,' I said, 'that we don't think that the sort of badness proper to foodstuffs, whether that is staleness or mouldiness or whatever, can be what destroys the body. Rather, we think that the badness of foods can bring about a bad state of the body; and then we shall say the body is destroyed *as a result of* eating such foods, but *by* its own badness, which is disease. The badness of foods is one thing, and the badness of the body is another: and we are never going to believe that the body could be destroyed by something else's badness, except in the case where that badness causes the body's own badness.'

610a3        'You're absolutely right,' he said.

'Well,' I said, 'by the same principle, unless the badness of the body can bring about the badness of the soul, we should never believe that the soul is destroyed by something else's badness, in the absence of the soul's own badness. For that would be a case where the badness of one thing destroyed another quite different thing.'

'That's reasonable,' he said.

610b1 'So let us either refute this doctrine, and demonstrate that what we have been saying is wrong; or else, and until it is refuted, let us never say that the soul is brought any nearer to destruction by any fever or other disease, or by the cutting of the throat, or even by the chopping up of the whole body into the smallest bits possible. We should not say that, until someone can prove to us that these bodily ordeals make the soul itself more unjust and unholy. Whether we are speaking of the soul or of anything else, we should not let it be said that something can be destroyed when its own specific evil does not come about in it, and all that happens is that something else's evil comes about in that other thing.'

610c2 'But,' he said, 'no one will ever prove that the souls of those who die are made more unjust by dying!'

'No,' I said. 'But just suppose someone did have the nerve to meet our argument head on, and claim that whoever dies *does* thereby become worse and more unjust – making this claim to avoid being forced to agree that souls are immortal. I imagine we would take the view that, if he were right, then injustice would have to be fatal to the unjust man in the way that a disease is fatal. It would have to be true that those who contracted injustice died of injustice's own inherent lethal properties; so those who had the biggest dose of it would die most quickly, while those who had a smaller dose would die more slowly. What would *not* happen is what actually does happen: that the unjust die because others impose the death sentence on them.'

610d6 'By Zeus,' he said, 'injustice wouldn't be such a terrible thing if it *was* fatal to the person who contracted it, for then it would release him from his evils. In fact I think it is more likely to turn out that injustice does the exact opposite. It kills other people if it gets the chance, but it makes its possessor positively hyperactive – not even able to sleep. That, I take it, is how far it is from being lethal!'

610e5     'Quite right,' I replied. 'For if the soul's own specific evil and badness is not enough to kill or destroy it, then any form of badness which is naturally fitted to destroy something else is hardly going to destroy the soul – or anything else, except whatever that form of badness is naturally fitted to destroy.'

'No, it is hardly likely to do that,' he said.

611a1     'Then since there is not one form of badness by which the soul can be destroyed – neither its own specific form, nor any other form – it is clear that the soul necessarily always exists; and if it always exists,
611a3     then it is immortal.'

## ➤❖

245c5   SOCRATES. Every soul is immortal. For whatever is always capable of change is immortal. Whatever changes something else, or is changed by something else, ceases its life when that changing ceases. But what has a power of changing *itself* never ceases from being changed – for *that* power cannot be exhausted. Rather, it is the thing with the power of changing itself that is the source and principle of change in other things that change. But this principle is not one that could come to be. Because *everything* that comes to be necessarily comes to be from that principle, it itself cannot come to be from anything; if it did, nothing else would be coming to be from a principle.

245d5   Because this principle cannot come to be, it must necessarily be indestructible as well. For if the principle were ever destroyed, then the principle itself could never come to be out of anything at all, and nothing else could ever come to be out of the principle (since everything that comes to be, necessarily comes to be from a principle).

245d9   Thus the principle of all change must be that which changes itself. It is not possible for this to be destroyed or come to be, or the whole heaven and every sort of coming to be would stop dead in confusion; they would never find a way of restarting the processes of change.

245e2   Since the Self-Changing has been seen to be immortal, there will be no embarrassment in saying that this is exactly what the soul is, and its definition. For every body whose changes come to it from outside is soulless; but every body whose changes come to it from inside it, and from itself, is ensouled: that is the nature of the soul. Moreover, if the soul *is* nothing other than the Self-Changing, then the soul must also necessarily be incapable of coming to be and immortal.

246a3     That is sufficient to show the soul's immortality. About what type of thing the soul is, let us say this. To describe its qualities fully would be an altogether divine story, and a long one too: but to compare it to something by simile – that is a story a human can tell, and shorter also. So let us speak in that fashion.

246a8     Let us liken the soul to a composite power: a pair of winged horses, and a charioteer. The gods' horses and charioteers are all good themselves, and of good stock too; but other creatures' horses and charioteers are of various breeds. To begin with us, our ruling part is charioteer to a pair; but though one of his horses is honourable and good, and of good and honourable stock, the other horse is of the opposite kind, as are his forebears, which necessarily makes our chariot difficult and wayward to drive.

246b8     Let us try to say why living beings are distinguished as mortal and immortal. All Soul has as its concern whatever is soulless; Soul paces as watchman across the whole of heaven, appearing in different forms at different times. Soul that is made perfect, with full-fledged wings, rises like a star to make the whole cosmos its household. But Soul that has shed its wings is blown around till it fastens on something solid, and there makes its home, receiving an earthly body. Such a body only seems to have the power of self-change because the soul has it; but the whole combination – a soul and a body frozen together – is called 'alive', and also receives the name 'mortal'.

246c9    No reasonable argument can show that this sort of
         composite is immortal: even though we, who do not
         see god and cannot adequately conceive him, fancy
         that he who is immortally alive has both a soul and a
         body, which are naturally combined for all eternity.
         But let that subject be, and be addressed, just as god
         wills. Let us rather take up the question of how those
         wings which the soul sloughs off can be lost.

246d5    The answer is something like this. The natural
         power of the wing is to carry what is heavy up-
         wards, and cause it to rise to the place where lives
         the whole clan of the gods; so one might say that it is
         the wing, more than any other part of the body, that
         shares in the divine. But what is divine is the Beautiful,
         the Wise, the Good, and everything of this kind; so the
         soul's ability to fly is best nourished and increased by
         these qualities, and most wasted and corrupted by
         their opposites, the Shameful and the Bad.
             [246e–247c$^{13}$]

247c3    As for the place *above* the heaven, no poet from our
         realm has ever sung its praises fittingly, nor ever shall.
         But since we must dare, at least, to speak the truth,
         above all as it is Truth we are speaking about – this is
         what it is like.

247c8    True Being is colourless, has no shape, and cannot
         be touched; it is visible only to Mind, the helmsman of
         the soul; the true sort of knowledge has this Being as
         its subject matter; and it is this that occupies the place
         above the heavens. Now god's understanding is nour-
         ished by Mind and unalloyed knowledge; and the
         understanding of every soul, that is to receive what
         befits a soul, looks on What Is together with god for a
         while. Beholding What Is, contemplating Truth, such
         a soul loves it and is nourished and made well by it –
         until the turning of the Cycle of things brings that soul
         back to its previous position.

247d8    Still, in its turn, the soul gazes on Justice Itself, gazes on Temperance Itself, and gazes on Knowledge. This is not knowledge of the sort that comes to be, or alters somehow as it is found in one or another of the things that we call beings; it is that knowledge which consists in the true essence of What Is. Likewise the soul gazes and feasts upon all the other true Beings; then it descends back to the realm within the heaven, and returns to its own home. And when the soul has come there the charioteer leads his horses to the stall, and feeds them on ambrosia, with nectar to drink.

248a1    Such is the life of the gods. But as for other souls, the best follows god and resembles him. This sort of soul raises the charioteer's head to gaze on the region beyond heaven; but it is borne round and round in the Cycle, and so unsettled by its bucking horses that it can barely see the true Beings. A third sort of soul rises at one moment and sinks again at the next; it is so controlled by its horses that it only sees some of the true Beings, completely missing others. Other sorts of soul again all strain to follow after what is above, but are not able: swamped by this world, they are carried this way and that, running over one another, running into one another, each one striving to get beyond the others. And so an utter confusion comes about, with sweating contention: and many horses are lamed, or their wings broken, by their drivers' incompetence. Then after all this trouble, they give up, without achieving the vision of What Is, and go back to their diet of what merely seems.

248b8    The reason for this urgent quest to see the place of the Field of Truth is this: it is in the grasslands there that the best part of the soul receives its fitting pasture; and the wings of the soul that make it soar are strengthened by that food. Moreover Adrastus, god of destiny, decrees that whatever soul comes to be attendant on god, and glimpses even one of the Truths, is to know no sorrow throughout the rest of that Cycle – while any soul that can manage to look at those Truths without ceasing, shall be free from harm forever.

248c5    But when such a soul can no longer follow god and becomes unable to see those Truths, and because of some chance event comes to forget them, then it is weighed down heavily by the evils which fill it. Such a soul sheds its wings and falls to earth. But its lot is not that it should, at its first birth, appear in a wild beast's nature; the soul that has seen the greatest realities will become nothing less than a man, and a man who is a philosopher or a friend of the beautiful, a man of learning or a great lover. Thereafter at the second birth such a soul becomes a king – law-abiding, warlike, and sovereign; at the third birth, a politician, a manager of the state, or a businessman; at the fourth birth it will be a trainer or healer of the body – some athlete who loves hard labour. At the fifth birth, this soul will have the life of an oracular priest, some fulfiller of rituals; at the sixth birth, the life of a poet or some other man whose business is imitation will befit it; at the seventh, it will be a manual labourer or a farmer; at the eighth, a sophist or rhetorician; lastly, at the ninth birth, this
248e3    soul will become a tyrant.

## THE EXISTENCE OF THE
## DIVINE SOUL

894e2 ATHENIAN. When we see one thing changing another thing, which itself changes a third thing, and so on indefinitely, won't there eventually be some first term to this series?

But if so, how could this first changer of other things itself be something which is moved by something else? That would be impossible.

But suppose a thing that moves *itself* changes something else, and that changes some third thing, and so on until the things that are being changed are multiplied into thousands and tens of thousands. Will there be any first principle of all these movings except the change initiated by the thing which is self-moving?

895a2 CLEINIAS. This is a very fine argument; these claims command assent.

ATHENIAN. Then let us go on to ask the following question – which we shall also answer ourselves. Suppose that everything there is was at rest and was all together – a supposition which most of our physical theorists have been bold enough to make.[14] Which of the ten kinds of motion that we have classified[15] must, necessarily, be the first to come about in this situation? Presumably the answer is: the *self-moving* kind of motion. For that can never be altered by things prior to it, since there *is* no kind of alteration in things prior to it.

895b2 So we shall say that the principle of all the other kinds of movement is self-movement; and that this is the first

kind of movement which comes about in things that
are stationary, and which is present in things that are
moving. By necessity, this is the oldest and most
powerful kind of change of all; whereas what itself
moves other things, but itself is altered by another thing
again, represents a second kind of change.

CLEINIAS. You're absolutely right.

ATHENIAN. Well, now we have reached this point in the
argument, let us ask the following question.

895c1  CLEINIAS. Namely?

ATHENIAN. Suppose that, in some thing which was
made of the elements of earth or water or fire – made
either exclusively of one of them, or of a mixture – we
saw self-movement coming about. What should we say
was happening to such a thing?

CLEINIAS. Aren't you asking me whether we should say
that a thing is *alive* if we find it moving itself?

ATHENIAN. Yes.

CLEINIAS. Well, of course such a thing is alive.

ATHENIAN. But look – don't we make exactly the same
claim about anything in which we see a *soul*? Mustn't
we admit that what is alive is anything with a soul?

CLEINIAS. Yes – that's all being alive is.

895d1  ATHENIAN. But hold on, by Zeus! Wouldn't you
normally say that there are three concepts to grasp
about any thing?

CLEINIAS. What do you mean?

ATHENIAN. One thing is the being itself; the second is
the definition of that being; the third is its name.
Accordingly, aren't there two questions to ask about
anything that is?

CLEINIAS. Which two?

ATHENIAN. One of us may give the name alone, and ask
for the definition; or he may give the definition alone,
and ask for the name.

CLEINIAS. Perhaps what we're now trying to express is
shown by the following example.

ATHENIAN. What example?

895e1   CLEINIAS. Well, evidently we meet with divisions into two, both in mathematics and elsewhere. In mathematics what can be so divided has the name *the even*; and the definition of the even is *what can be divided into two equal parts*.

ATHENIAN. Yes – this is the sort of thing I mean. So isn't it the same thing which we are referring to in either way, whether we give the name when we are asked for the definition, or give the definition when we are asked for the name? Isn't it one and the same existent thing that we refer to by the name 'even' and the definition 'a number divisible into two'?

CLEINIAS. Absolutely, yes.

ATHENIAN. Well then, what is the definition of the being that has the name *soul*? What can we say except what we have just been discussing – the kind of motion that is able to move itself?

896a2   CLEINIAS. So you mean that 'self-movement' is the *definition* of the very same *being* to which we all give the *name* 'soul'?

ATHENIAN. Yes, exactly. If this is right, do we still feel the lack of a proper proof of the claim that the soul is the same thing as the first coming to be and the first movement of everything that is, has come about, and will be, and all the opposites of these? After all, it is now clear that soul is the explanation of all change and all motion in all things.

896b2   CLEINIAS. Yes; it has been most comprehensively proved that soul is the oldest of all things, and has come to be the first principle of motion.

ATHENIAN. Then what about the kind of movement which comes about in one thing by the agency of another, and never provides a source of self-movement to anything? Isn't that kind of movement secondary – or indeed to be ranked as low as you like in the ordering of different kinds of movement? And isn't this the kind of change which is truly natural to a body without a soul?

CLEINIAS. That's correct.

896b9 ATHENIAN. So if we say that the soul has turned out to be prior to the human body, we will have correctly and authoritatively described it, in the truest and most complete way. The body is secondary and comes after the soul, as what is naturally ruled comes after what naturally rules.

896c3 CLEINIAS. Yes, this would be the truest statement.

ATHENIAN. For of course we recall our earlier agreement[16] that, if the soul turned out to be older than the body, then so would the attributes of the soul be older than those of the body.

CLEINIAS. Yes, certainly.

896d1 ATHENIAN. So if soul is prior in its origin to body, then all soul's attributes too – moods, dispositions, wantings, reasonings, true beliefs, concerns, memories: all these will have had a prior origin to any bodily attributes – length, breadth, depth, strength.

CLEINIAS. Necessarily.

ATHENIAN. Next, won't we have to agree that it is the soul which is the cause of good things and of bad, of beautiful things and of ugly, of just and unjust, and of all such opposites? After all, we have supposed that the soul is the cause of everything.

CLEINIAS. Of course.

ATHENIAN. Then if soul governs and inhabits all things, wherever they are moved, mustn't we say that soul governs heaven as well?

896e2 CLEINIAS. Indeed so.

ATHENIAN. One soul, or more than one? 'More,' I shall say, answering on everyone's behalf. At any rate we should certainly not suppose that there are less than two of these souls – namely the soul which brings about beneficial effects, and the soul which is able to bring about the opposite sort of effects.

CLEINIAS. You are absolutely right.

ATHENIAN. So be it, then: it is soul which conducts everything in heaven and earth and sea by its own self-movements. Those movements have these names: wanting, considering, being concerned, deliberating, correct and mistaken belief, being pleased, feeling pain, feeling courage, feeling fear, hating or loving – and all the other things which are related.

897a4     These originating self-movements work through the other movements, which are secondary causes at work in bodies, and conduct them towards growth and decay, separation and combination, and after these towards states of heat or cold, heaviness or lightness, hardness or softness, whiteness or blackness, bitterness or sweetness. In short, these motions move the secondary sorts of movement towards all the states which soul experiences. This is still true whether soul still keeps hold of wisdom as a true divinity, and educates everything into what is right and happy; or else spends its time with folly, and contrives to bring everything into the opposites of what is right and

897b4  happy.

## NOTES

1. For an earlier argument entailing the soul's immortality (though not, in any obvious way, its reincarnation), cf. *Phaedo* 63e–66a. For an argument for reincarnation in the *Phaedo*, see reading 29.
2. Cf. Anaxagoras, DK B1.
3. *To thymoeides* – one of the three forms in the soul which Plato is going to distinguish (terms for all three are marked by capitals). Cf. reading 20.
4. In the omitted passage Plato gives examples of the point.
5. 'The person who makes that reply' seems to be Socrates. Cf. reading 14.
6. In the omitted passage more examples support the point already made (437d–e): the 'principle of correlation'.
7. Heracleitus' epigram: DK B51.
8. Homer, *Odyssey* 20.17; also quoted at *Republic* 390d.
9. *Republic* 411d ff.

10. For the opposite attitude to the pleasures of the 'Desiring aspect' see reading 18.
11. For more on this see reading 20.
12. Cf. reading 20.
13. In the omitted passage Plato describes 'heaven', the place where gods and beatified souls live, in quasi-mythological terms. Notice from what follows that, for him, heaven is not the 'highest' place.
14. Plato is thinking particularly of Anaxagoras' famous claim 'In the the beginning all things were together' (DK B1); but no doubt of other pre-Socratic philosophers (Empedocles, Parmenides, Anaximander?) too.
15. *Laws* 893b–894d.
16. *Laws* 892a ff.

# PART V

✢✢

# KNOWLEDGE AND
# THE FORMS (I)

# 27. MENO 96E–98B

## KNOWLEDGE AND BELIEF

96e1    SOCRATES. Now I look at our inquiry so far, I see something that we shall be ridiculed for failing to notice. It is that human affairs don't have to be guided by *knowledge* to be guided well and aright. It is probably for the same reason that the knowledge of how good men are to be made has eluded us.

MENO. How do you mean, Socrates?

SOCRATES. I mean this. We were right, weren't we, to say that good men must be of some practical *use* – that it could hardly be otherwise?

97a2    MENO. Yes.

SOCRATES. And, I assume, it was fair enough for us to agree that they will be useful to us if they guide our affairs aright?

MENO. Yes.

SOCRATES. But when we agreed that no one could guide human affairs aright unless they were wise – there we seem to have gone wrong.

MENO. How do you mean, 'aright'?

97a9    SOCRATES. I'll tell you. If somone who knew the way to Larisa (or to wherever else you like) led others there by walking to Larisa, he would do it aright and do it well, wouldn't he?

MENO. Certainly.

SOCRATES. What about someone who had a right opinion about what was the way to Larisa, but did not know because he had never been? Wouldn't he lead you the right way too?

MENO. Certainly.

97b4    SOCRATES. So just as long as the second man has right

opinion about what the first man knows about, the
second man will be no worse a guide than the first
man.

MENO. Yes, he will be just as good.

SOCRATES. Therefore true opinion is no worse a guide
than wisdom to rightness of action. This is the point
we have just overlooked in our inquiry about what
kind of thing human excellence is, when we said that
only wisdom leads us to right action. For true opinion
does so too.

MENO. Yes, it seems so.

SOCRATES. So right opinion is no less helpful to us than
knowledge.

97c6    MENO. But they surely differ in this much, Socrates:
that the person who has knowledge should always
hit on the right choice, whereas the person who has
right opinion may hit on it at one time and miss it at
another?

SOCRATES. How can you say that? Won't the person
who *always* has right opinion, *always* choose right, just
so long as he has right opinion at all?

MENO. That seems unavoidable to me. But in that case
I am puzzled, Socrates: why on earth is knowledge
so much more highly valued than right opinion? And
what *is* the difference between the two of them?

97d3    SOCRATES. Can you solve your own puzzlement, or
shall I?

MENO. You should, certainly.

SOCRATES. It is because you have not turned your
attention to the statues of Daedalus[1] . . . Perhaps
there aren't any in Thessaly where you come from.

MENO. What are you getting at?

SOCRATES. This: when the statues of Daedalus are not
kept on a string, they make off and run away. But
when they are tied up, they remain still.

MENO. So?

97e2    SOCRATES. There would not be much value in owning

one of Daedalus' statues if it was not tied on a string. It would be like 'owning' a runaway slave, for the statue would not stay put. But if the statue is on a string, then it is well worth having; such pieces of handicraft are very fine. What am I talking about? True opinions: for so long as true opinions do not shift, they are a fine thing to have, and bring about all sorts of goods for us. But they tend not to last very long; they make their getaway out of our minds so soon that they are of little value, until we bind them with an account of *why* they are true. This account, my friend, is recollection.

98a5    When once the true opinions have been 'tied up' like this, at once they become knowledge, and later they become permanent knowledge. This is why knowledge is more valuable than true belief: and it differs from true belief by being secure.

MENO. By heaven, yes, Socrates – the truth must be something like this.

98b1    SOCRATES. Yet I myself do not speak as someone who knows, but by way of a picture. Still, I don't think I'm speaking in pictures when I say that true opinion is something different from knowledge. I would not claim to know many things; but this is one of the

98b6    few things I would claim to know.

# 28. MENO 80c–86b

## ❧

## RECOLLECTION (I); THE PARADOX OF INQUIRY

80c9   SOCRATES. I don't cause others perplexity by being above all perplexities myself. Far from it: it is because I am so much more perplexed than others, that I make them perplexed too. So it is now with 'virtue'. *I* don't know what it is. Perhaps *you* knew, Meno, before you bumped into me; although by this stage you might as well have lost your knowledge. Still, with your help I want to make a joint attempt to answer the question: 'What exactly is virtue?'

80d5   MENO. But Socrates – how can you try to learn something when you don't know what you're trying to learn? How can you set up one of the things that you're ignorant of as an objective for inquiry? Or even supposing you have the best luck possible, and do actually stumble on your objective – how will you know that you've found it, when what you have found is something you don't know?

80d9   SOCRATES. I understand what sort of point you're making, Meno! Don't you see what a sophistical argument you're advancing? It is this dilemma: 'No one can try to learn anything – not what he knows; and not what he does not know. For he cannot try to learn something that he knows: since he knows it already, he has no occasion to try to learn it. Nor can he try to learn something that he does not know: since he does not know it, he does not know what it is that he is trying to learn.'

81a1   MENO. So you don't think that that's a good argument, Socrates?

SOCRATES. Certainly not!

MENO. But can you say what's wrong with it?

SOCRATES. Yes, I can. For I have heard from wise men and women, concerning divine matters . . .

MENO. What did you hear them say?

SOCRATES. . . . What seemed to me both a true and a beautiful saying.[2]

81a7   MENO. What was it, and who were the speakers?

SOCRATES. The speakers were some of the priests and priestesses who have made it their concern to be able to give a reasoned account of the rites they perform. But Pindar[3] and many other divinely gifted poets say the same too. What they say is as follows – listen and see if you think it is true.

81b3   These priests say that the human soul is immortal: at one time it comes to an end – this is what men call death – and at another it is reborn; but it never ceases to be, and so (they say) we must live our lives as reverently as possible. For we may say, of those by whom

> 'Persephone is paid sin's ancient debts,
> These souls she gives back to the sunlit world,
> Nine years being past; from such grow kings,
> Noble men, splendidly strong, greatly wise;
> By all times that come after they are called
> Heroes most hallowed.'[4]

81c4   Since the soul is immortal and has been reborn so many times, and since it has seen this world and the World of the Dead and everything there is, consequently there is nothing that the soul has not learnt. Therefore it is nothing wonderful if the soul can recall what it knew before, both about virtue and about other things. For all living things are related, and the soul has already learnt everything. So once the soul has recalled just one thing – this recalling is what men mean by *learning* – there is nothing to prevent it from discovering all the other things that it has forgotten as well – if we are only courageous in our quest, and do not grow weary of it. For inquiry and learning is entirely recollection.

81d6     This is why we should not accept the sophistical argument we were discussing. That argument would make us lazy – it is sweet to the ears of the intellectual workshy; whereas the argument I have proposed makes us diligently inquisitive thinkers. It is my belief in the truth of this argument that makes me want to pursue, with your help, our question: What exactly is virtue?

81e2     MENO. Yes, Socrates – but how can you say that we do not learn: that, rather, what we call 'learning' is really recollection? Can't you teach me that this is how it is?
SOCRATES. Like I said,[5] Meno, you're a sly one; you ask me if I can teach you, when I've claimed that there *is* no teaching, but only recollection. You want me to contradict myself at the first step?

82a2     MENO. Heavens – not at all, Socrates. What I said wasn't aimed at that; it was just a manner of speaking. But if you can – well – *show* me that things are as you say, then do.
SOCRATES. It's not easy. Still I want to try, for your sake. So call over one of your retinue – whichever slave you like – so that I may demonstrate the truth by experiment on him.

82b2     MENO. Very well. [To a slave boy:] You – come here.
SOCRATES. He's a Greek, isn't he? and speaks Greek?
MENO. Absolutely – born in the household.
SOCRATES. Pay attention, Meno, and see whether you think he is recollecting or learning from me.
MENO. I'm watching.
SOCRATES. [To the slave, beginning to draw on the sandy ground:] Tell me, boy: do you know that a square is a figure like this one?
SLAVE. Yes.

82c1    SOCRATES. So a square figure is one which has all these four lines equal?

SLAVE. That's right.

SOCRATES. The lines through the middle of the sides, parallel to the sides, are also the same length in a square, aren't they?

SLAVE. Yes.

SOCRATES. Now figures like this can be of different sizes.

SLAVE. True, sir.

SOCRATES. So if this side were two feet long and that side also, what would the area be?

Think of it like this. If this side was two feet long, and that side was one foot long, its area would be two feet times one foot, wouldn't it?

SLAVE. . . . Yes.

82d1    SOCRATES. But both sides are two feet long; so won't it be two feet times two feet?

SLAVE. It will.

SOCRATES. How much is that? Work it out and tell me.

SLAVE. Four feet, Master.

SOCRATES. Now there could be a figure twice the area of this one, which had all its sides equal just like this, couldn't there?

SLAVE. Yes.

SOCRATES. What will that square's area be?

SLAVE. Eight feet.

SOCRATES. Well now, try to tell me: how long are the sides of this square? The sides of the first square were two feet long; so how long are the sides of the square which is double in area?

82e2    SLAVE. Obvious, sir – they will be twice as long.

SOCRATES. Do you see, Meno? I haven't taught him anything; I'm just asking questions, and now he thinks he knows the length of the side of a square with an area of eight feet, doesn't he?

MENO. So he does.

SOCRATES. But does he know it?

MENO. No – he's wrong.

SOCRATES. He's going on the doubling of the area, isn't he?

MENO. Yes.

SOCRATES. Well, watch him now, and he will recollect one thing after another in the proper order. – Tell me, boy: do you really think that doubling the lengths of the lines doubles the area? The area I mean is not that of a rectangle, but that of a square, a figure equal on every side: like this one, only twice as big, with an area of eight feet. Do you still think that doubling the lengths of the lines will give us the square of eight square feet?

83a3  SLAVE. [defiantly] Yes, I do!

SOCRATES. Well, we can double this line by adding another line of the same length, can't we?

SLAVE. That's right.

SOCRATES. You say that a square with all its lines of this doubled length will be eight feet square?

SLAVE. Yes.

83b1  SOCRATES. Well, let's draw this square, with its four doubled-length lines. Your 'eight-foot-square' figure – it will be this one here, won't it?

SLAVE. [still convinced] Yes, that's it.

SOCRATES. Aren't there four squares like this one within your 'eight-foot square', each of which is equal to the *four*-foot-square figure?

SLAVE. Oh . . . Yes.

SOCRATES. So how big is your 'eight-foot-square' figure? Isn't it four times as big as the four-foot square?

SLAVE. I suppose it must be, sir.

SOCRATES. 'Four times as big as' isn't the same as 'double', is it?

SLAVE. It surely isn't.

SOCRATES. 'Double' is twofold, but 'four times' is how many-fold?

SLAVE. Fourfold.

83c1    SOCRATES. So from double-length lines we get a square
which is not twice the area, but four times. From what
length of side will we get a square with an area of eight
feet? From the doubled length of side we get four times
four feet, don't we?

SLAVE. Yes.

SOCRATES. And from the ordinary length of side we get
an area of four feet.

SLAVE. Yes.

SOCRATES. The eight-foot area is twice as much as the
four-foot area, and half as much as the sixteen-foot
area. So won't the eight-foot area be generated by a
length which is between the ordinary and the doubled
lengths of side?

83d2    SLAVE. That seems right to me.

SOCRATES. Good: you answer with what seems right to
you. Tell me, then: the ordinary length was two feet,
and the doubled length was four feet, wasn't it?

SLAVE. Yes.

SOCRATES. So the length of the side of the eight-foot-
square figure must be more than the ordinary length of
two feet, but less than the doubled length of four feet.

SLAVE. It must.

83e1    SOCRATES. So try and say what you think the length
will be.

SLAVE. Three feet.

SOCRATES. Well, if it is to be three feet, then shall we take
the half of this two-foot line, to make a three-foot line?
Here are two feet, and here is a third foot. Likewise,
here is a two-foot line, plus a one-foot line. So this
square is the area you mean.

SLAVE. Yes.

SOCRATES. Now if it is three feet long on this side and
three feet long on that, won't the whole area be three
times three feet?

SLAVE. It appears it will.

SOCRATES. How many feet is three times three feet?

SLAVE. Nine.

SOCRATES. But what was the double area we were looking for?

SLAVE. Eight square feet.

SOCRATES. So we don't get our eight-foot square from the square with a side of three feet, either.

SLAVE. No, we don't.

SOCRATES. Then from what length of side *do* we get it? Try and tell us exactly. If you do not want to calculate it, just show us the line in question.

SLAVE. By Zeus, Master Socrates, I'm sure I don't know.

84a3  SOCRATES. Again you see, Meno, how far the fellow has got by recollecting. At first he didn't know what length of side gives us the eight-foot square – just as he does not know even now. But before, he imagined he did know. He answered me confidently like someone who knew, and he did not think he was at a loss. But now he does think he is at a loss, from this point on; in line with the fact that he does not know, he does not even think he knows.

84b1  MENO. It's true.

SOCRATES. Wouldn't you say he's in a better position, now, about what he doesn't know?

MENO. That also seems true to me.

SOCRATES. So I haven't *harmed* him by leaving him at a loss – by numbing him with my sting-ray's sting?[6]

MENO. I think not.

SOCRATES. Rather, indeed, we seem to have done him a service, helping him to see how things are. Till now he thought that it was easy to say something sensible about the doubled area: namely, that it is generated by a line of doubled length. But now he has lost this 'knowledge', he should be happy to seek for the truth.

84c2  MENO. So it seems.

SOCRATES. Do you think that, in his previous state, he would have tried to find out (or 'learn') what he wrongly thought he knew? Do you think that that would have happened until he had stumbled into this perplexity, realised that he did *not* know – and begun to wish he did?

MENO. I don't believe it would.

SOCRATES. So he gained from being stung by the stingray!

MENO. It looks like it to me.

SOCRATES. Now see how he goes on from this perplexity to find something out by these inquiries, which I am not assisting except by asking him questions – I am not teaching him. But you watch, and see if at any point you can catch me teaching him or explaining things to him, rather than just asking him about his beliefs.

84d3    Tell me then, you. This is a square with an area of four feet, isn't it? Do you understand that?

SLAVE. Yes.

SOCRATES. And this here which we add to it is another square of the same area?

SLAVE. Yes.

SOCRATES. This third square, too, is the same as either of the others – four foot square?

SLAVE. Yes.

SOCRATES. Shall we fill in this vacant space in the corner?

SLAVE. All right.

SOCRATES. Giving us these four squares of equal area?

84e1    SLAVE. Yes.

SOCRATES. Well – how much larger is the area of these four squares together than this, the area of just one of them?

SLAVE. Four times.

SOCRATES. But we wanted to find the square which was twice the area of just one of these four-foot squares, didn't we? Do you remember?

SLAVE. Yes, I do.

SOCRATES. Now look at this line, which goes from one corner of a square to the other corner. Don't such

corner to corner lines cut each of the four-foot squares
in half?

85a1   SLAVE. Yes.

SOCRATES. So now we have four lines of equal length,
enclosing this space?[7]

SLAVE. Yes.

SOCRATES. Now think. What is the area of this space?

SLAVE. I don't understand.

SOCRATES. Hasn't each of these four corner to corner
lines cut off half of each of the four small squares? –
Hasn't it?

SLAVE. . . . Yes.

SOCRATES. So how many halved small squares are in
this space?

SLAVE. Four.

SOCRATES. How many halved small squares are in the
small square?

SLAVE. Two.

SOCRATES. How many twos in four?

SLAVE. Two.

SOCRATES. So, if the small square has an area of four
feet, what is the area of the space inside the corner to
corner lines?

85b2   SLAVE. Eight feet.

SOCRATES. So which line gave us the eight-foot square?

SLAVE. This one.

SOCRATES. The corner to corner line across the four-
foot square?

SLAVE. Yes.

SOCRATES. The experts call it the diagonal. So if we call
it the diagonal, then your opinion – Meno's slave's
opinion – is that the square on the diagonal is twice the
area of any square.

SLAVE. Yes, sir.

SOCRATES. Well, what do you think, Meno? Have you
spotted any opinion which he did not produce in his
answers as his own?

85c1    MENO. No, they were his own opinions.

SOCRATES. Yet as we said before, he did not know the answer.

MENO. That's true.

SOCRATES. Yet these same opinions were there within him, weren't they?

MENO. Yes.

SOCRATES. So then a person may have within him true opinions about matters of which he knows nothing.

MENO. Apparently so.

SOCRATES. And just now those opinions have been aroused in him like dreams. But you can see that, if someone were to put those questions to him again and again in different ways, in the end his knowledge of geometry would be no less exact than any man's!

85d2    MENO. So it seems.

SOCRATES. Won't he understand by recovering the knowledge himself from within himself, with the help of no teacher, but merely of someone who asks him questions?

MENO. Yes.

SOCRATES. This 'recovering the knowledge himself from within himself' – isn't this recollection?

MENO. Exactly so.

SOCRATES. Well, either he gained this knowledge at some time, or else he has always had it.

MENO. Yes.

SOCRATES. But if he has always had it, then he has always been in a state of knowledge. Alternatively, if he gained it at some time, then it cannot have been in this life.[8] Or has someone taught him how to do geometry? For he will be able to do the same things with every part of geometry, and every other part of science too! So is there anyone who has taught him all this? You are the man to know, particularly when he was born and brought up in your household.

85e6    MENO. Well, I do know: no one has ever taught him.

SOCRATES. But does he have these opinions, or doesn't he?

MENO. He certainly seems to have them, Socrates.

SOCRATES. But if he did not acquire them in this life, then isn't it immediately obvious that he must have taken hold of them ('learnt' them) in some other period?

86a2 MENO. Evidently so.

SOCRATES. This must have been the period when he was not a human being.

MENO. Yes.

SOCRATES. Then suppose that there were within him, both when he was a human being and when he was not, these true opinions which can be roused up by questioning and turned into items of knowledge. His soul must always have already known them, mustn't it? For clearly he has always either been a human or not.

MENO. Evidently.

SOCRATES. So if the truth of all things has always been in our souls, then our souls must be immortal. And whatever you do not now happen to know – which means, whatever you do not recollect – you must

86b3 boldly try to find out by recalling it.

# 29. PHAEDO 72E–77B

➤←

## RECOLLECTION (II); THE IMMORTALITY OF THE SOUL (IV)

72e1    CEBES. According to that argument of yours which you are so fond of repeating, Socrates, that our learning is really nothing but recollection – if that's right, then it too seems to entail that we learnt what we now recollect in some previous time. But that is impossible unless our soul existed before it came to be in this human form. So on this argument too the soul appears to be immortal.

73a3    SIMMIAS. But Cebes, what were the proofs of this? Remind me – I don't recollect it very well just now.

CEBES. The best single brief proof is this: when men are questioned about something, if the questioner asks the right questions, they tell him everything just as it is. But if they did not have some knowledge and right reason within them, they would be unable to do this. The evidence that this is so appears most clearly when you confront them with a geometrical drawing or something like that –

73b2    SOCRATES. But if you are not convinced by that argument, Simmias, see if the theory of recollection seems reasonable to you when you consider it this way. – I assume you don't believe that there's any sense in which what we call learning can really be recollection?

SIMMIAS. It's not that I don't believe it: it's just that I need to learn how to do the very thing we're talking about – to recollect. I more or less recollect, and feel persuaded of all this, given what Cebes has begun to say. None the less, I would also like to hear the new argument which you were beginning just now.

73c1 SOCRATES. My argument was this. I suppose we agree that, if anyone remembers something, he must have known it at some earlier time.

SIMMIAS. Yes, certainly.

SOCRATES. Do we also agree to this? Any knowledge is recollection, if it comes about in the right sort of way. Like this, I mean. Suppose someone sees something, or hears it, or grasps it by some other form of perception. But he not only knows it: he also has a mental awareness of something else at the same time, the knowledge of which is not the same as the knowledge of the perceived thing, but different. In such a case wouldn't we say that the man has recollected the thing of which he has the mental awareness?

73d1 SIMMIAS. What do you mean?

SOCRATES. Something like the following. Knowing a man is, I take it, different from knowing his lyre.

SIMMIAS. How could it fail to be?

SOCRATES. But I'm sure you know about people who are in love. When they see the beloved's lyre – or his cloak, or anything else which looks like the things he usually uses – they have this experience: they recognise the lyre, and an image of the young man who owns it comes to their minds. This is recollection. It is just like what so often happens: someone sees Simmias, and they remember Cebes![9] and there must be lots of other such examples.

SIMMIAS. By Zeus, yes – lots.

73e1 SOCRATES. Now isn't that sort of thing a kind of recollection? Especially when it happens regarding things which have been forgotten before it occurs, through inattention and the passage of time?

SIMMIAS. Certainly.

SOCRATES. Well, can't a person who sees a picture of

a horse or a picture of a lyre recollect a man? Can't someone who sees a picture of Simmias recollect Cebes?

SIMMIAS. Certainly.

SOCRATES. Again, someone who sees a picture of Simmias can also recollect Simmias himself?

74a1    SIMMIAS. That's right.

SOCRATES. So doesn't it appear from all these cases that some recollection is caused by what is like, and some by what is unlike, what is recollected?

SIMMIAS. So it appears.

SOCRATES. But when someone has a recollection which arises from things similar to what is recollected, won't something else necessarily happen to him as well? He will consider whether what causes the recollection is in any way deficient of complete similarity to what is recollected.

SIMMIAS. Yes, that is bound to happen.

SOCRATES. Consider next if this is right. We say, don't we, that something exists called Equality? I don't mean the equality of one stick or one stone, or anything like that, to another. I mean something apart from all these instances: The Equal Itself. Shall we say that The Equal Itself is something? Or nothing?

74b1    SIMMIAS. We shall say it is something, by Zeus – and a wonderful thing too.

SOCRATES. Do we know it, in its own nature?

SIMMIAS. We certainly do.

SOCRATES. Where did we get this knowledge of it from? Isn't it from what we have just been speaking of – from seeing that sticks or stones or other such things are equal to each other? Didn't we get our mental awareness of The Equal Itself from such instances, even though it is different from any such instance?

74b6    Or do you think that The Equal Itself *isn't* different from these instances of equality? Look at it like this. Aren't there times when 'equal' sticks and stones appear equal to us in one respect, but unequal in another respect?

SIMMIAS. Yes, this certainly happens.

SOCRATES. Well, was there ever a time when the truly equal ever appeared to you to be unequal? Or Equality to be Inequality?

74c1 SIMMIAS. No, that has never happened, Socrates.

SOCRATES. Therefore those instances of equality are not the same thing as The Equal Itself.

SIMMIAS. Not at all the same thing, I believe.

SOCRATES. All the same, wasn't it from those instances of equality, different as they are from that Equal Itself, that you became aware of The Equal Itself, and arrived at the knowledge of it?

SIMMIAS. Very true.

SOCRATES. And mustn't The Equal Itself be either like its instances, or unlike them?

SIMMIAS. Certainly.

SOCRATES. Not that it makes any difference which. Whenever you see one thing, and arrive at a mental awareness of another thing as a result, that is necessarily a recollection which has occurred – whether the two things are like each other or not.

74d2 SIMMIAS. Yes, indeed it is.

SOCRATES. Well, then: doesn't something like this happen to us with the instances of equality which we meet in sticks, and all the other cases we mentioned? Do they seem equal to us in the same way as What is Equal Itself is equal? In their way of being like The Equal, do they lack anything compared with it, or not?

SIMMIAS. Yes – they lack a great deal by comparison.

74d7 SOCRATES. Then do we agree to this? Suppose someone sees something and is aware in his mind that 'This thing I now see wants to be like some other existing thing, but it is lacking compared with that, and cannot be of the same sort as that; it is inferior to it.' I assume it is necessary that someone who thinks this must, in fact, already have knowledge of the thing to which he compares the thing he sees, saying 'It is like it, but deficient in its qualities'?

74e4    SIMMIAS. Yes, he must.

SOCRATES. So what now? Don't we too experience something like this, concerning instances of equality and The Equal Itself?

SIMMIAS. Absolutely, yes.

SOCRATES. Therefore it is necessary that we already knew The Equal before that time when we first saw instances of equality and became aware that all such things are aiming to be like The Equal, but are deficient in quality.

75a3    SIMMIAS. That is so.

SOCRATES. But we agree this as well, don't we – that we have not gained, and could not possibly gain, our mental awareness of The Equal from anywhere except from seeing, or touching, or from some other sense – and my argument applies equally to all the senses?

SIMMIAS. Yes: the senses are all in the same boat, Socrates, for the purposes of our discussion.

75a9    SOCRATES. Then it is from the senses that we are to learn that everything perceptible, which falls short of true equality, none the less strives towards The Equal Itself? Is that what we should say?

SIMMIAS. Yes.

75b2    SOCRATES. Then before we began to see and hear and perceive in the other ways, we must – *somewhere* – have attained a knowledge of what exactly 'The Equal Itself' is. We must have attained this already, or we could not have gone on to refer things that seem equal to the senses to The Equal Itself – since all 'equal' things long to be like The Equal, but are of a lower kind than it.

75b8    SIMMIAS. You must be right about this, Socrates, given what we have said already.

SOCRATES. Now when we came into the world, we at once saw and heard and had the other senses.

SIMMIAS. Yes, that's right.

75c1 SOCRATES. But didn't we say that we must have attained the knowledge of The Equal Itself before we attained any of these senses?

SIMMIAS. Yes.

SOCRATES. Then apparently it follows that we must have attained the knowledge of The Equal Itself before we came into the world.

SIMMIAS. Yes, that does seem to follow.

75c4 SOCRATES. So if we gained that knowledge before we came into the world, and had it at our coming in, then even before our coming in, and at once when we entered, we knew not only The Equal and The More and The Less, but all such things. (For our present argument is not more particularly about The Equal than it is about The Beautiful Itself, The Good Itself, The Just, and The Holy. As I say, the argument applies to all those things on which our dialectic, by use of the roles of questioner and answerer, has placed the stamp 'What Really Exists'.) – So, it follows that we must have attained the knowledge of all these things before we came into the world.

75d4 SIMMIAS. That's right.

SOCRATES. So unless humans forget it each time they attain this knowledge, it must be that they always come into the world with that knowledge, and have it throughout their lives. For to know is to keep hold of knowledge and not lose it. Isn't that what we mean by forgetting, Simmias: losing knowledge?

SIMMIAS. Absolutely.

SOCRATES. But suppose that we acquired this knowledge before we came into existence and lost it when we entered the world, but then later on recovered this knowledge that we had once previously had, by using our senses on sensible things. Wouldn't what we call 'learning' just be a matter of recovering our own knowledge? And mightn't we rightly call this by the name 'recollection'?

SIMMIAS. Yes indeed.

76a1 SOCRATES. Yes, for it seemed possible that we might perceive something – taking it in by sight or hearing or one of the other senses – and from that perceived object get an idea of something else: some standard that has been forgotten, but which is akin to the thing perceived, whether it is like it or not. So, as I say, there are two alternatives. Either people come into life knowing about these standards, and they all know them throughout their lives. Or else at some later time people recollect them – for those whom we say 'learn' something do nothing other than recollect, and learning *is* recollection.

SIMMIAS. Yes indeed – this is how it is, Socrates.

SOCRATES. So which alternative do you choose, Simmias? Do we come into the world knowing these things, or do we remember at some later time the things we had earlier gained knowledge of?

76b2 SIMMIAS. [Sighing:] At a time like this, Socrates, I am unable to choose.[10]

SOCRATES. [Ignoring the sigh:] What about this, then? You *can* choose – the matter must strike you somehow. Can a person who has knowledge give a rational account of what he knows about, or not?

SIMMIAS. Certainly, Socrates, he must be able to.

SOCRATES. Do you think that everyone can give a rational account of the matters we are discussing?

SIMMIAS. I wish they could; but instead my fear is that this time tomorrow, there won't be a single person left who is able to do it properly.

SOCRATES. [Ignoring this too:] So you don't think that everyone knows about these things?

76c2 SIMMIAS. Far from it.

SOCRATES. So those who do, recollect what they once learnt?

SIMMIAS. They must do.

SOCRATES. When did our souls get their knowledge? It surely can't have been since we became humans.

SIMMIAS. No, it can't.

SOCRATES. So it must have been before that.

SIMMIAS. Yes.

SOCRATES. Which means that our souls existed before we came into the world, before we were in human form, apart from our bodies, and had intelligence.

SIMMIAS. Yes, unless we received this knowledge in the very process of becoming humans – for there's still that interval, Socrates.

76d1 SOCRATES. Well, my friend – if that is the case, what other interval can there be in which we *lose* this knowledge? For as we agreed just now, we do not enter the world in full possession of it. So do you mean that, in the very process of becoming humans, we lose that knowledge at the same time as we gain it? Or are you going to bring in yet another period of time?

SIMMIAS. No, clearly not, Socrates: I failed to see that I was talking nonsense.[11]

76d7 SOCRATES. Then is this how matters stand, Simmias? – These things we talk about so much – The Beautiful, The Good, and every being of this kind: we say that these things exist. We say, too, that we refer back to such a Being everything that comes from the senses. It existed before; now we have found it, is ours; it is to that Being that we compare what we get from the senses. Doesn't it necessarily follow that the soul in us must exist in the same way as these Beings exist, and so must have come into existence before we did, just like them? If these Beings do not exist, we could more profitably have discussed something else. But we have spoken what is true, and there is one and the same proof that these Beings do exist, and that our souls came into existence before we did: disprove one of these claims, and you disprove the other.

76e9   SIMMIAS. I think it is absolutely the same proof, Socrates. Our argument appeals to the beautiful idea that our soul exists before we are born, in the same way as the Being you speak of exists. I myself know nothing so clearly as this – that The Beautiful and The Good and all of these things that you've been speaking of – all such things exist as truly as it is possible to

77a6   exist. It seems to me that your case is fully established.

# 30. PHAEDO 96A–101D

## ❧

## SCIENTIFIC EXPLANATION
## THROUGH THE FORMS

96a4   'When I was a young man, Cebes,' Socrates said, 'I was extremely enthusiastic about that branch of learning that they call "inquiry into the nature of things". I thought it would be a grand achievement to know the causes and explanations of each kind of thing – the reasons why each thing comes to be, and why it is destroyed or persists. Again and again I would go first one way and then the other about questions like these:

96b2   'First, does biological development depend upon a fermentation of some sort arising from The Hot and The Cold (as one theory claimed)?

'Is it the blood in virtue of which we think? Or is it the element of Air? Or Fire?

'Or is it none of these, but rather the brain which provides us with the senses of hearing, sight and smell?

'If so, do memory and opinion arise from these senses?

'If they do, does knowledge arise from memory and opinion when they are settled in a state of unchanging rest?

'And likewise I would research the question of how knowledge perishes, and look at how the heavens and the earth undergo change . . . But in the end I recognised that I was as ill-equipped for these inquiries as anyone could be.

96c3   'I will give you one sufficient demonstration of this fact. It is that I was so thoroughly blinded by my inquiry that I forgot what, beforehand, I and others too had thought I knew quite clearly. About all sorts of subjects, I no longer understood what I had thought I did understand: for example, about the reasons for human growth. Until I took up natural science, I had thought it was plain to anyone that human growth occurs when we eat and drink. The food a man takes in adds flesh to his flesh and bone to his bone, and, in the same way, more bulk of the appropriate sort to each of his bodily materials. And so something that was only a small object becomes a large object: the small man becomes a big man. So I once thought – and doesn't the theory seem an adequate one?'

96d7    'It seems so to me,' said Cebes.

'Well, but listen to what followed. When (for example) some tall man was presented to me standing next to a short man, I believed it was a sufficient explanation to hold that he was taller *by his head*; in the same way, I thought, one horse could be taller than another *by his head*. Again, my belief that ten was greater than eight *by the addition of two* seemed even more evidently true; and likewise my belief that a two-metre line was greater than a one-metre line *by half the two-metre line*.'

96e4    'Well,' said Cebes, 'and what is your present view?'

'By Zeus,' said Socrates, 'I am a long way indeed from thinking that I know what the explanations are for these facts. For I do not even allow myself to claim that, when one and one are added together, it is the unit to which the other unit is added that becomes the two. Or is it the unit which is itself added which becomes two? Or is it that both the units together become two, by the combination of the one with the other?

97a2    'For this is what I find extraordinary: that each of them was *one* when it was separate from the other, and neither was *two* then; but when they came close together, their mere approach to one another was, allegedly, enough to explain their becoming *two*.[12]

204 THE PLATO READER

'Nor indeed can I be persuaded that dividing one into two halves, so that *one* becomes *two*, is to be explained just by reference to the division itself. The case is a mirror-image of the problem of explaining how two comes about from what is one. In that case the explanation was supposed to be that the units were brought close together, and that the one unit was added to the other unit; now it is supposed to be that they have been separated, and that the one unit has been split off from the other unit. But I cannot even any longer convince myself that I understand what makes *one* itself come into being. In fact I don't think I know why anything comes to be, or why it is destroyed or persists, in the sense of those questions in which I used to ask them. Indeed I no longer admit that those questions can be asked at all: what I myself now do is muddle along somehow or other in my own sort of inquiry.

97b8      'For one day I heard someone reading from a book which he told me was by Anaxagoras, propounding the view that what explains everything and arranges everything in the world is *Mind*.[13] I was very taken with this theory of explanation: it seemed to me to be, somehow, entirely fitting that it should be Mind that was the explanation of all things.

97c3      ' "If this theory is right," I thought, "then Mind, in ordering *all* things, will also be ordering *each* thing – which means disposing it in that way which is best for it. Therefore if anyone wants to find the explanation of any particular thing – in what way it comes to be, and is destroyed or persists – he will have to find out what state of affairs is best for that thing, both regarding its persistence and regarding anything else that it may do or have done to it. And so this argument shows that all a man ought to inquire into – not only in this but in other areas of inquiry as well – is what is best and what is most excellent. For if he knows that then he will know what is worst as well, since the knowledge of one is the knowledge of both.''

97d5    'When I had reasoned this out, I was delighted at the thought that I had found in Anaxagoras a teacher of the causes of things according to Mind. I thought that he would begin by telling me whether the earth is flat or round – and then adjoin a complete account of the cause and the necessity of this state of affairs, by telling me about The Best, and the sense in which it was best for the earth to be whatever shape it was. Similarly, I thought, if he held that the earth was in the centre of the universe, then he would offer a complete account of why it was best for the earth to be in that position.

98a1    'In fact I was quite ready to abandon my quest for any further kind of explanation – if Anaxagoras would offer me a clear account of these questions. I was ready, too, to accept the Anaxagorean form of explanation in the case of the sun and the moon and the other celestial bodies – their relative speeds, their seasonal movements, and everything else that happens to them: I was ready to hear in what way exactly it was best for each of them to act and be acted on in the way that they are. For it never occurred to me that someone who claimed that everything is ordered by Mind might be smuggling into his theory any other sort of explanation besides the kind which shows that the actual condition of the things which are to be explained is the best condition for them. And so I thought that Anaxagoras would give an explanation of each thing and of all things at once, and would then give a full account of what was the best for each and the good for all. I would not have swapped this prospect for any money: so, full of enthusiasm, I got hold of Anaxagoras' books and read them as soon as I could, so that I might learn as soon as possible about The Best and The Worst.

98b8    'Well, my friend, my high expectations were violently let down. For as I read on I saw that the fellow made no real use of Mind at all, and did not explain by way of any explanations that could have contributed to a full account of the ordering of things, but by way of all sorts of out-of-place agents – "airs" and "ethers" and "waters" and so on. And then I felt that Anaxagoras' position was like that of a man who admits that Socrates does whatever he does "by Mind" – but tries to give an account of the causes of everything that I am now doing, by speaking in the following sort of way.

98c4          ' "I am sitting here now because, first, my body is composed of bones and tendons, and the bones are tough and separated by joints from one another, whereas the tendons are capable both of tensing and of relaxing, and enclose the bones along with the flesh and the skin, which contains everything else. So since the bones are free to move in their sockets, the contraction and relaxation of the tendons presumably makes me able to bend my limbs as I am bending them now."

98d5          'And this is the explanation of why I am sitting here in my current position? Anaxagoras might just as well say that the "explanation" of why we are talking here is given by such things as our having voices, or by the air and the sounds we are using, or a thousand other supposedly explanatory factors. But he fails to mention the true explanation: which is that it seemed best to the Athenians to condemn me to death, and that therefore I have made my decision to stay here, thinking it more just that I should stand firm and undergo whatever penalty they decree. After all, by Dog, if I did *not* believe it to be more just and more noble to stay here and undergo whatever penalty the city lays down, rather than escaping and making off, I should think that these bones and tendons would be rather nearer to Megara or Boeotia[14] by now. But even then they would have been taken there by a belief about what is best.

99a6  'It is entirely inappropriate to call such accounts as Anaxagoras offers *explanations*. And if someone says that unless I had such organs as bones and tendons and so forth, I could not do what I decided to, then that is true. But to say that I do what I do *because of* these organs – that acting according to Mind means *this*, and not doing what you do through choice of the best – that would be an exceedingly loose way of talking, and a very long-winded one too. For this would prevent us from making the distinction between the question what the real cause of something is, and the question what conditions that cause could not be a cause without.

99b4  'Consequently most people seem to me to be groping blindly in the dark when they apply the misnomers *cause* and *explanation* to what is only the necessary condition of the cause. This is what makes one man put a "vortex" round the earth, as a way of making the earth remain under the heaven, while another supposes that the element Air is the foundation of a plate-shaped earth. What about the power which makes things to be now disposed in the way that is the best possible for them to be disposed? They do not look for this sort of explanation, and they do not understand its divine cogency. They think they can find something else, more godlike and of greater explanatory power than the Good – some all-encompassing Atlas who will hold the world up; in fact, they do not think at all about the Good, though it is that which must unite and encompass everything else.

99c5  'Well, I would be very happy to become a pupil to anyone at all who could teach me what on earth this sort of explanation is to be like. But I have been deprived of all that, since I have not been able either to work it out for myself, or to learn it from anyone else. So, Cebes,' said Socrates, 'would you like me to give you a description of how I have conducted my second voyage in search of a theory of explanation?'

99d5    'Yes indeed,' said Cebes, 'I would love to hear about that.'

'Well, then,' said Socrates, 'after this, I thought that, now I had given up looking directly at particular existents, I had better be careful lest I suffer the very same disaster as can happen to the people who watch the eclipses of the sun so attentively. For, as I have heard, some of them go blind, if they do not follow the eclipses by way of their reflections in water or some such medium. I had something like this danger in my thoughts, and I was afraid lest I should be blinded in the sight of my soul by my concentration on particular things, and my attempts to lay hold of each of them by way of my senses. So I decided that the method I should use was to take refuge in abstract arguments,[15] and to look in them for the truth concerning particular things.

100a1   'Incidentally, it is, perhaps, rather inappropriate for me to compare this new method of mine with an astronomer who looks only at reflections. For if we contrast the person who investigates particular things by theoretical methods with the one who investigates them by practical methods, then I won't at all concede that the theoretical method is an investigation of mere shadows or reflections compared with the practical method. On the contrary.

'But at any rate, it was by turning to that method that I began my voyage. And so in every inquiry I start by taking as read the most powerful definition I can find. Then my attitude to explanations and to every other kind of particular existent is to take to be true whatever I think accords with this definition; and whatever does not accord with it, I take to be untrue. But I should like to explain my view to you more clearly, for I don't think that you understand it at the moment.'

'No, by Zeus,' said Cebes, 'really I don't understand.'

100b1    'But when I speak in this way I don't mean anything new,' said Socrates, 'but merely what I've been constantly saying all along, not just in our earlier talk, but at other times too. For I am now going to try to explain to you the nature of that sort of explanation with which I have been so concerned.

'Let me go back again to those well-worn[16] themes of ours, and make a start from them. Let me suppose that there is something which is Beautiful Itself in its own right, and a Good, and a Big, and so on and so forth. If you grant me this and allow that there are such things, then I believe I shall be able to describe to you what an explanation is – and also to arrive at the conclusion that the soul is immortal.'[17]

100c1    'Carry on, then,' said Cebes. 'Since I grant all this, perhaps you will barely beat me to the conclusion of your argument.'

'Consider, then,' said Socrates, 'whether you agree with me about what follows from these presuppositions. For it seems to me that, if there is anything else at all which is beautiful besides the Beautiful Itself, then its beauty is not explained by anything else but this explanation: "It is beautiful because it participates in the Beautiful Itself". And so likewise with the other cases. Do you agree about this sort of explanation?'

'Yes, I do agree,' he said.

100c8    'For I must admit,' said Socrates, 'that I really don't yet understand those other wise explanations which are offered. I am not even able to recognise them *as* explanations. No, if someone says to me that the reason why something is beautiful is that it has a flourishing colour or appearance, or something else of that sort, I find I have to give up this sort of claim, for all this kind of thing merely confuses me. But what I do keep hold of in my own mind – in my own simple, unaccountable, and no doubt naïve fashion – is just this: that nothing else makes a beautiful thing beautiful unless it is *the Beautiful Itself*, by its appearance in the thing, or its association with it, or its coming together with it in some way or other. (For I do not yet have a firm opinion about how the Beautiful Itself relates to any beautiful thing: yet I am quite sure that it is *by* The Beautiful that all beautiful things become beautiful.) This sort of explanation seems to me to be the most certainly true that I can offer as an answer to anyone else's questions, and to my own too, and I believe that if I hold on to this, then I will never stumble. No, it will certainly be right for me and for anyone else to give this sort of explanation as an answer – that it is by The Beautiful that all beautiful things are beautiful. Do you agree with me?'

100e3     'I do.'

'And isn't it by Bigness that big things are big and bigger things bigger? And isn't it by Smallness that smaller things are smaller?'

'Yes.'

'And if someone said to somebody else that A was bigger than B by a head, and B shorter than A by the same, wouldn't you reject that remark? Wouldn't you testify that you yourself always say only this: that anything which is bigger than some other thing is bigger only by Bigness – that the explanation of its being bigger, is Bigness? And again, that anything which is smaller than some other thing is smaller only by Smallness – that the explanation of its being smaller, is Smallness?

101a5     'For if you agreed that it was by a head that one thing was bigger and another smaller, I believe you would be afraid that someone might bring against you the following two arguments. First: on that account, the explanation of why the bigger thing is bigger is the same as the explanation of why the smaller thing is smaller. Second: this account makes a small thing – the head – the explanation of why a bigger thing is bigger. But that seems monstrous – that a big thing's bigness should be explained by something small! – Aren't these the retorts you would fear?'

101b2     'They certainly are,' said Cebes, laughing.

    'Presumably you would also fear,' said Socrates, 'to say that ten is more than eight by two – that two is the reason why ten exceeds eight – rather than saying that ten is more than eight by *number* – that number is the explanation. And you would not say that a line two feets long is longer than a one-foot line by half – but by size. After all, it would be the same worry as before.'

    'Absolutely.'

101b9     'Well, if one is doubled or divided in two, won't you take care not to say that the explanation of why we now have two is the addition, or the division? Surely you will cry out that you know of no other way for a thing to come into being, except by its sharing in the particular Being of each quality of which it has a share. So with these cases, you can see no other explanation of something's becoming two than its sharing in the Being, Duality. Whatever is to become two must share in that; and whatever is to become one must share in the Being, Unity. So you would leave all these other complications – divisions and additions – on one side – you would leave it to wiser men than yourself to use these terms in their explanations! For your own part, you would start at your own shadow (as the saying is) and be wary of your own inexperience: keeping a grip on our secure hypothesis, you would reply according
101d2  to that.'

# 31. REPUBLIC 475E–480A

➜✦

## KNOWLEDGE, BELIEF AND IGNORANCE

475e2   'So who do you mean by the "true" philosophers, or lovers of wisdom?' asked Glaucon.

'Those,' I said, 'whose favourite spectacle is the truth.'

'Another fine remark,' he replied; 'but what do you mean by it?'

'It's not at all easy to explain to someone else,' I replied; 'but I think you will agree with me on something like the following claim.'

'Namely?'

'That since "beautiful" is the opposite of "ugly", "beautiful" and "ugly" must be two different things.'

476a1   'Yes.'

'Now since they are two things, each of them is a unity.'

'I grant that too.'

'The case is the same concerning the just and unjust, good and bad, and all the Forms. Each of them is one thing in itself, but, by their combination with actions and bodies and other things, they appear all over the place; consequently each of these unities seems to be many things.'

'Fine,' said Glaucon.

476a7   'Well,' I said, 'here is my distinction. On one side we have the lovers of spectacle whom you spoke of just now, and those who admire some practical skill; on the other side are the ones I'm talking about, the only ones whom we can rightly call philosophers.'

'Why do you say that?'

476b2   'Because the lovers of sound and spectacle may

delight in beautiful voices and beautiful colours and beautiful shapes, and in every beautiful thing that the craftsman can make from these; yet their understanding is incapable of seeing or delighting in The Beautiful Itself.'

'True indeed,' said Glaucon.

'As for the other side, won't they be few in number who are able to rise to The Beautiful Itself, and to see it in its own right?'

'Very few, yes.'

476c1      'Then what of the man who believes that there are beautiful things, but does not believe that Beauty Itself exists, and is unable to follow, if someone would lead him towards the knowledge of it? Is he living in a dream-world, or the real world? Consider. Whether they are awake or asleep, isn't someone really in a dream if they think that something which is like something else is not merely *like* it, but *identical with* it?'

'Well,' said Glaucon, 'at any rate I would say that dreaming is something of this sort.'

'What if someone was in the opposite state to this, and believed that there was a real Beautiful Itself, and was able to contemplate both it and the things which participate in it, without confusing it with them or them with it? Do you think his world is a dream-world, or the real world?'

476d3      'No, his world is absolutely real.'

'Then wouldn't we be right to say that his sort of understanding is *knowledge*, since it belongs to someone who knows? Whereas the other man's understanding is *opinion*, since he only has opinions and does not know?'

'Yes, absolutely.'

'Suppose this man who we say only has opinions gets angry with us about it, and resists us, saying that we speak falsely. Have we any way of reconciling him and bringing him round gently – and glossing over the fact that he is not really sane?'

476e2     'I suppose we'd better have something.'

'Consider what we should say to him. Do you want us to ask him a question? Let's say that, if he knows something, then no one begrudges him that knowledge; but we would be pleased to see this knowledge of something demonstrated. "So tell us this" – we shall ask: – "Does someone who knows, know something, or know nothing?" You answer me on his behalf, Glaucon.'

'I will answer,' said Glaucon, 'that someone who knows, knows something, not nothing.'

'Something that is, or something that is not?'

477a1     'Something that is, of course; for how could anything that is not be known?'[18]

'So we're absolutely sure about this doctrine, however many times we review it: *whatever completely Is, is completely knowable*. But what Is Not, is not knowable in any way at all.'

'Yes.'

'Then suppose something was so disposed as to be and not to be at once. Wouldn't it lie in between what purely Is and what altogether Is Not?'

'It would,' said Glaucon.

477a7     'Thus knowledge is concerned with What Is; ignorance, necessarily, with What Is Not. If something lies in between What Is and What Is Not, shouldn't we look for something in between knowledge and ignorance too, to see if there is anything of the same sort as them, but corresponding to what lies in between What Is and What Is Not?'

477b2     'We certainly should.'

'Well, isn't there something that we call belief?'

'Of course there is.'

'Is it a different power from knowledge, or the same power?'

'A different one.'

'Therefore belief is related to one subject-matter and knowledge to another, each according to the particular kind of power that it is.'

'Just so.'

'So isn't knowledge naturally fitted for What Is? Naturally fitted to knowing What Is, *as* it Is? Whereas belief . . . No, I think we'd better make some distinctions first.'

'What distinctions?'

477c1    'About powers. What shall we say? Aren't our powers just those sorts of things in virtue of which we can do whatever we can do, and anything else there is can do what it can do? For instance, sight and hearing are examples of powers – if that helps you understand the class of things I have in mind.'

'Yes, I understand,' said Glaucon.

477c5    'Well, consider my view about powers. The case of powers is unlike many other cases; for I see no particulars like colour or shape that I might appeal to in my own mind, to give me a way of telling the difference between one power and another. So in the case of powers I look to this single criterion:[19] "What is its proper domain, and what is its effect?". That is how I have denominated the various powers. Whatever powers have the same domain and the same effect are, on my view, one and the same power. Whatever powers have different domains and effects, are different powers. What would your classification be?'

477d7    'The same,' said Glaucon.

'Very well, my friend; let us go back to knowledge and belief. Is having knowledge a power? Or would you classify knowledge in some other way?'

477e1    'No, knowledge is in the class of powers,' he said; 'indeed it is the most far-reaching of all powers.'

'What about belief? Shall we classify that as an power, or not?'

'As a power,' he said: 'that in virtue of which we can have beliefs is nothing other than the power, belief.'

'Now not long ago you agreed that knowledge and belief are not the same thing.'

'Yes,' he answered: 'how could anyone of any sense say that what was infallible was the same as what was fallible?'

'Rightly said,' I replied. 'and so it is clear that we have agreed that belief is a different thing from knowledge.'

478a1    'Yes.'

'Therefore each of them is fitted by its nature to different objects, and is able to bring about different things.'

'Yes, necessarily.'

'The power knowledge, I take it, has What Is as its proper domain, and is fitted to knowing What Is, *as* it is.'

'Yes.'

'But the power belief, we say, is fitted only to forming opinions.'

'Yes.'

'Opinions about what? About the same thing as is the object of knowledge, so that one and the same thing will be a possible object both of knowledge and of belief? Or is that impossible?'

'It must be impossible, given what we have already agreed,' said Glaucon. 'For as we have said, different powers are naturally fitted to different objects; and knowledge and belief are both powers, but not one and the same power. These claims rule out the possibility that the objects of knowledge and belief should be identical.'

478b3    'But the object of knowledge is What Is. So mustn't the object of belief be something which is not identical with What Is?'

'It must, yes.'

'So does belief form opinions about What Is Not? Or is it impossible even to have opinions about – never mind knowledge of – What Is Not? Think about it: surely even when someone only has opinions and not knowledge, their opinions must be about something. Or is it possible, after all, that someone should form opinions, but form them *about nothing*?'

'No, that is impossible.'

'So in fact when someone forms an opinion, the opinion is about some one thing.'

'Yes.'

'But What Is Not is not "some one thing". On the contrary, it could most fittingly be described as nothing.'

478c1  'Absolutely.'

'Now of necessity we assigned ignorance to What Is Not, and knowledge to What Is.'

'Rghtly so,' said Glaucon.

'Therefore we can assign belief *neither* to What Is *nor* to What Is Not.'

'Indeed not.'

'So belief is neither knowledge nor ignorance.'

'Apparently not.'

'So is belief some power outside the range from knowledge to ignorance, the objects of which exceed the objects of knowledge in their clarity and distinctness, or the objects of ignorance[20] in their dark confusedness?'

'No, it is neither.'

'So then the objects of belief are more dark and confused than those of knowledge, but also more clear and distinct those of ignorance.'

'Very much so,' said Glaucon.

'Now belief lies within, not outside, the range from knowledge to ignorance.'

478d1  'Yes.'

'So belief is *in between* knowledge and ignorance.'

'Definitely.'

'But didn't we say earlier that if we could find anything which seemed at once to be and not to be, that would be the kind of thing to lie in between what purely Is and what altogether Is Not? Neither knowledge nor ignorance would have this as its domain; it would, again, be the domain of whatever might appear between ignorance and knowledge.'

'Just so.'

'Now what we call belief has appeared in that gap.'

'So it has.'

478e1   'So, it seems, all we need to find now is whatever it is in that domain, which partakes both of Being and of Not Being, but cannot rightly be described as either in the pure sense. If we can find this, then it is this that we can fairly describe as being the object of belief. We will have assigned the two domains at the extremes (Being, Not Being) to the two powers at the extremes (knowledge, ignorance); and the domain in the middle (What Is and Is Not) to the power in the middle (belief). Isn't that so?'

'It is, yes.'

479a1   'Given these assumptions, I will issue a challenge to that profound sage who does not think that there is any Beautiful Itself, or any form at all of Beauty itself which always remains of the same quality and in the same relations – even though he believes in plenty of different "beautifuls". I mean the lover of spectacle, who can find no way to contain his frustration when he hears anyone say that there is *one* Beautiful, *one* Just, and so on. Let him speak, and answer my challenge! For we shall ask him: "My dear sir, is there a single one of these 'beautifuls' which cannot also appear *ugly*? Or is there even one particular case of justice, which cannot also appear to be a case of *injustice*? Or of holiness, which cannot also appear to be a case of unholiness?"'

'But there isn't,' said Glaucon: 'it is bound to

happen that things which are beautiful in one way will seem ugly in another. Likewise with your other questions.'

479b1 'What is more: don't the many things that are twice as much as one thing also appear to be, no less truly, half as much as something else?'

'They do – no less truly.'

'And "big" things, "small" things, "heavy" things, "light" things: are these predicates, on any occasion when we use them of such things, really more applicable than their opposites?'

'No,' he answered: 'on every occasion, each thing will be partly both.'

'Then, for any predicate F that someone may use to describe any particular x, isn't it just as true to say that x *is* F as that x *is not* F?'

479b8 'Such predicates are like the ambiguous puns you hear made at the festivals,' said Glaucon; 'or they are like the children's riddle about the man-and-not-a-man who threw the stone-and-not-a-stone at the bird-and-not-a-bird on the branch-and-not-a-branch[21] – "What did who throw, at what, and what was it on?" they ask. For these predicates too are ambiguous. It is impossible to conceive firmly of any of them either that It Is, or that It Is Not – or even that it *both* Is and Is Not, or *neither* Is nor Is Not.'

479c4 'Then do you have any better suggestion,' I asked, 'about what treatment to give of such predicates, and where to place them in our schema, than to assign to them the position in between Being and What Is Not? For presumably we won't find anything darker and more confused than What Is Not, which will even more truly Not Be than What Is Not. Nor will we find anything clearer and more distinct than What Is, wich will even more truly Be than What Is.'

479d2 'Very true,' said Glaucon.

'So, it seems, we have found that the many opinions

which the common people take for granted, about "beautiful" and all the others – these opinions are all at sea, rolling around somewhere in between What Is Not and What purely Is.'

'Yes, that is our finding.'

'But we agreed earlier, didn't we, that if anything of this sort came to light, we would have to say that it was the object of belief and not of knowledge: that the wanderer adrift in the middle region is captured by the middle power?'

'That was what we said.'

479d9    'So those who gaze on the many "beautifuls", but do not see The Beautiful Itself, and are unable to follow anyone else if they try to lead them towards it; and those who contemplate many cases of justice, but not The Just Itself, and are the same with all the other Forms – we shall say that they have belief about all these things. Yet for all these things that they have belief about, they have *knowledge* of not a single one of them.'

'Yes, we must say this,' said Glaucon.

'What, on the other hand, about those who gaze on the things themselves, Beauty and Justice, which are always alike and unchanging? Won't we say that they have knowledge of these things, not belief?'

479e8    'We're bound to say that, too.'

'Won't we say that they embrace and are in love with the things that knowledge has as its domain, whereas the others are in love with what mere belief or opinion has as its domain? We haven't forgotten, have we, that we said that they were in love with beautiful voices and colours and things like that, whereas they could not tolerate the idea that The Beautiful Itself might even exist?'

480a4    'No, we remember.'

'So it shouldn't jar on their ears if we call them lovers of mere belief rather than philosophers, lovers of wisdom? They won't be too angry with us if we say that?'

'Not if they take my advice,' said Glaucon: 'it is impious to be angry with the truth.'

'As for those who embrace on each occasion What Is – they are philosophers and lovers of wisdom, not of mere belief?'

480a9    'Yes, absolutely so.'

# 32. REPUBLIC 595C–598B

## ✧

## THE FORMS; IMITATION;
## AND ART (II)

595c8 'Glaucon,' I said, 'can you give me a general definition of "imitation"? I don't think I quite grasp what it means, myself.'

'And so you imagine,' he retorted, 'that *I* can tell you!'

'That wouldn't be so absurd,' I said: 'quite often those whose sight is less keen notice things sooner than those who see very clearly.'

596a2 'Indeed they do,' he said. 'But with you here, Socrates, I don't feel able even to try and speak out whatever seems right to me. You examine the question yourself.'

'Then would you be willing to start by looking at the question we always begin with in our inquiries? Which is this: I take it that we are quite used to supposing that, given any number of particular things to which we apply the same name, there is a single Form in each case.[22] Do you understand this?'

'Yes.'

'Well, this time too let's consider a wide variety of examples. Here's one, if you like: there are presumably many beds and tables.'

596b2 'Undeniable.'

'But, I assume, there are only two universals here for all these artefacts: one of Bed, and one of Table.'

'Yes.'

'Now aren't we also in the habit of saying that the bed-maker and the table-maker (and the others likewise) make these artefacts which we use, by fixing their aim on the universals of Bed and Table respectively? Presumably no craftsman makes the universals themselves?'

'No, certainly not.'

'Now tell me what you think the following sort of craftsman ought to be called.'

596c1    'What sort?'

'The sort who makes *everything* – all the things that each one of the other hand-workers makes.'

'A cunning and miraculous man you have in mind.'

'Wait, and soon you will be even surer of that. For this one same hand-worker is not only able to make every sort of artefact; he produces everything else as well – even himself, and heaven and earth besides, with the gods and everything else that lives in the heavens or in Hades under the earth.'

596d1    'This would be an absolutely miraculous sophist!'

'But don't you believe he exists?' I asked. 'Tell me: do you think such a craftsman is an outright impossibility? Or is there a sense in which this maker of all things could come to be – although in another sense he couldn't? Don't you see a sense in which you yourself could be a maker of all these things?'

'What sense would that be?' he asked.

'Why, it's easy,' I said: 'if you got hold of a mirror, and carried it around with you everywhere, you too could quickly make everything everwhere you went. In no time at all you could create the sun, everything in the heavens, the earth, yourself, all the other animals and artefacts, all the plants – and everything else that we mentioned just now.'

596e3    'Yes,' he said, 'I suppose you would be producing *appearances* of these things: but not really the things themselves.'

'Well said,' I replied, 'and you supply the argument with what it needs, too. For, I believe, one of the craftsmen of this sort is *the painter* – isn't he?'

'Of course he is.'

'I suppose you will say that what he makes is not genuine. Yet isn't there is a sense in which even a painter of a bed makes a bed?'

'Yes,' said Glaucon: 'he makes an *appearance* of a bed.'

597a1    'So what of the bed-maker? Didn't you say just now that he does not make the Form, which we say is What The Bed Is, but rather some particular bed?'

'Yes, I did.'

'But if he does not make What Bed Is, then he does not make What Is, but only something which is somehow of the same sort as What Is, although it is not itself What Is. Surely it would turn out to be false to claim that the bed-maker's work (or any other hand-worker's product) is perfectly What Is?'

'Yes, it would – at least according to the experts in this sort of argument.'

'Then let's not be too astonished if the craftsman's bed too should turn to be no more than a dark shadow in comparison with the truth.'

597b1    'No, we won't be.'

'Well,' I said, 'on these presuppositions, are you willing to pursue the question of the definition of the imitative artist?'[23]

'Yes, if you are willing,' he replied.

'Well, don't we find that there are these three sorts of bed? The first is The Bed, which is there in the very nature of things. This, I suppose we would say, is made by god. For who else could make it?'

'No one,' he said.

'The second is the bed which the craftsman makes.'

'Yes.'

'The third sort of bed is the artist's creation, isn't it?'

'So be it.'

'So artist, bed-maker, and god: they are three makers, who have authority over three forms of bed.'

597c1     'Yes, three.'

'Now whether because it was god's will, or whether because there was some necessary reason why god should not make more than one Bed – in either case, god did only make one single That Which Is What Bed Is. Two such Forms, or more than two, were not made by god and never will be.'

'Why not?' asked Glaucon.

'Because,' I said, 'if god made even two Forms of Bed, a third Form of Bed would then have to appear. The first two Forms would share in the third Form – which would mean that the third Form would be the true Form of Bed, and not the other two Forms.'

'You're right,' said Glaucon.

597d1     'God is aware of this danger, and has it in his will to be the true creator of the true Bed, and not merely some particular creator of some particular bed. This, I believe, is the reason why each Form that he creates as a part of the nature of things is naturally unique.'[24]

'So it seems.'

'Then are you willing that we should refer to god as the creator of the *nature* of Bed – or something like that?'

597e1     'Yes, that would be fitting,' said Glaucon, 'if indeed he really created Bed, and all these other realities, in nature itself.'

'How shall we refer to the bed-maker? Isn't he the craftsman who makes the physical bed?'

'Yes.'

'What about the painter? Is he a craftsman and maker of the same sort of thing as the bed-maker?'

'Certainly not.'

'Then how will you refer to him? What does he have to do with beds?'

'I think,' said Glaucon, 'he could most correctly be referred to as the *imitator* of what the craftsman makes.'

'Very well,' I said: 'you say that the imitator of anything is at the third remove from its true nature?'

'I certainly do,' said Glaucon.

'Then this will be true of the tragic poet as well, if indeed he is an imitator. By his birth he will be third in succession to the throne of truth, as will all other imitators.'

'That's probably right.'

598a1    'So we have reached general agreement about imitative artists. Now tell me this about the painter. Do you think, when he tries to imitate, that it is the Thing Itself in nature that he tries to imitate? Or is it the craftsmen's products?'[25]

'The craftsmen's products,' he said.

'Make another distinction for me: does the painter imitate those products as they *are*, or as they *seem*?'

'What do you mean?' he asked.

'I mean this. Suppose a bed – or whatever you like – is seen from the side, or from the front, or from whatever angle. Does the bed then differ from itself? Or does it rather just look different from these angles, although really it isn't?'

'It just looks different: it isn't really different, no matter what perspective you take on it.'

598b1    'Then consider this question. What is the making of all graphic art concerned with? Is it concerned to imitate what the physical object is really like – as it *is*? Or just to imitate the appearance of the physical object – as it *looks*? Is graphic art an imitation of the truth about the physical world? Or just of an image of the physical world?'

'Just of an image,' he said.

'So evidently imitative art really is a long way off from the truth of things. And this explains its facile production of anything and everything. It only apprehends a tiny fraction of whatever it touches – and even

598b8    that is no more than a fleeting impression.'

# 33. REPUBLIC 508A–509B

## ➤✦

## THE IMAGE OF THE SUN

508a3 'Which of the heavenly bodies in the heavens can you cite, as the explanation of the power whose light makes our eyes to see as well as they may? Whose light makes the things we see visible?'

'I'd give just the same answer to that as you or anyone else,' said Glaucon: 'obviously you're asking about the sun.'

'Then the natural relationship of sight to that heavenly body – isn't it as follows?'

'How?'

'Well, the sun is identical neither with sight, nor yet with what sight occurs in – the organ we call the eye.'

508b1 'Of course not.'

'And yet, I think, the eye is the most like the sun in form of all the organs of perception.'

'Yes, far and away.'

'For doesn't the eye actually receive the power of sight as a stewardship delegated to it, which flows into it from the sun?'

'Yes, certainly.'

'Again, the sun is not the same thing as sight; but it is both seen by sight, and the cause of sight.'

'Just so,' said he.

'So here's what I meant when I said I would show you, if not The Good itself, at any rate the begotten child of The Good, which The Good fathered in its own likeness. For the role of The Good in the realm of thought, in its relation to thought and to the objects of thought, is the same as the role of the sun in the realm of sight, in its relation to sight and to the objects of sight.'

508c3     'What do you mean?' he asked. 'Explain this to me
          further.'
              'Well,' I said, 'you know what happens, once some-
          one is no longer directing his eyes towards objects
          whose colours are under the sway of daylight, and
          instead is looking at objects in moonlight or starlight.
          His eyes become dim and imprecise, and almost like
          blind men's eyes, as if there were no pure power of
          sight in them at all.'
              'Yes indeed,' said Glaucon.
508d1     'But when they look at objects which are illuminated
          by sunlight, of course they see clearly, and now the
          pure power of sight does seem to be present in those
          same eyes.'
              'Of course.'
              'Well, apply the same idea to the soul. When the
          soul is fixed firm upon what Truth and What Is
          illuminate, then the soul understands it and has
          knowledge of that, and has evident comprehension.
          But when the soul turns towards what is mixed with
          darkness – what comes to be and passes away – then it
          apprehends only dimly and imprecisely, shifting its
          opinions up and down, and appears to have *no*
          comprehension.'
508e1     'Yes, it does.'
              'So what brings about truth for all the things that
          are known, and gives the power to know them to the
          knower: that is what you may call the universal The
          Good. Think of it as the explanatory cause of knowl-
          edge, and of truth too, in so far as truth is known.
508e4     'Yet, beautiful as both knowledge and truth are, you
          will be nearest the truth if you believe that there is
          something else more beautiful even than either of
          these. Compare light and sight in the other case. It's
          right to think that both of these are like the sun in
          form, but wrong to think that either is identical with
          the sun. Likewise in this case, it's right to think that

both of these are like The Good in form, but wrong to think that either is identical with The Good. For the nature of The Good is still more to be honoured than these.'

509a4    'This is a quite extraordinary beauty that you speak of,' said Glaucon, 'since it can bring about knowledge and truth, and yet is beyond both knowledge and truth in its beauty! For you can't, I suppose, mean that this beauty is the same thing as pleasure?'[26]

'That would be blasphemy,' I replied: 'no, look at this image of The Good in another way.'

509b1    'What way?'

'I think you'll agree that the sun doesn't merely bring it about that visible things are actually seen. It also causes generation, nourishment and growth; even though it is not itself generation.'

'No, it couldn't be.'

'Likewise then we should say, not merely that The Good brings it about that what can be known, is known. We should also say that The Good actually brings about, for the things that can be known, their very natures and their Being; and yet The Good itself is not one of these Beings, but is still higher, beyond Being, outstripping them all both in its majesty and in

509b10  its power.'

# 34. REPUBLIC 514A–519A

✣✢

## THE IMAGE OF THE CAVE; *OR* CAN VIRTUE BE TAUGHT? (III)

514a1 'Next,' I said, 'take the following sort of experience, as an image of the degree to which our nature is educated – or rather uneducated. Imagine people living in some sort of underground, cave-like dwelling. Their cave is open to the light; in the distance, right at the other end of the cave's length, is the entrance to it from outside. But the people have been there since they were children, with chains on their legs and their necks so that they have to stay put, and can only look straight in front of them: because of the fetter, they cannot even turn their heads from side to side.

514b2 'Now imagine the light of a fire, which is burning higher up the cave towards the entrance, some distance from the prisoners and behind them. Between this fire and the prisoners' backs there is a raised path, along which, you see, a little wall has been built – something like a conjuror's partition or screen, which hides the performer himself while he shows his tricks over it.'

'I can picture it all,' said Glaucon.

'Then picture this too: there are men carrying all sorts of contrivances along behind this wall, so that they stick up over it. They are carrying dummies of humans and other living things, made in stone and wood and every other sort of material. Some of these stage-hands are talking, no doubt; others are silent.'

515a3 'What a bizarre picture!' said Glaucon. 'And what bizarre prisoners!'

'But they are just like us,' I replied. 'To begin with –

do you think that people in this situation would even have seen themselves and each other properly? Or just their own shadows, cast by the fire on to the wall of the cave which faces the prisoners?'

'How could they see anything else,' said Glaucon, 'if they are forced to hold their heads still all their lives?'

515b1　　'What about the dummies which are carried back and forth behind the wall? Won't the prisoners see only the shadows of those as well?'

'Yes: what else could they see?'

'And if these prisoners were able to speak to one another in language, don't you think they would take it that their words were names for those same shadows that they see passing in front of them?'

'They'd be bound to,' said Glaucon.

'What if their prison had an echo, too, rebounding off the wall in front of the prisoners whenever one of the stage-hands behind the wall spoke? Do you think the prisoners would believe that the source of the sound was anything other than whichever shadow they could see at the time?'

'By Zeus, no,' he replied.

515c1　　'Then prisoners like these will think that the truth is nothing other than the shadows of dummies.'

'They are absolutely bound to,' said Glaucon.

'Consider what a release from their chains it would be, and what a healing for their deluded minds, if in the course of nature something like the following happened to them. Suppose one of them was unchained, and was immediately made to stand up and turn his head around, to walk about and look up the cave towards the firelight. It would hurt him to do all these things, and the firelight would be so dazzling that it would prevent him from seeing properly the dummies whose shadows he was looking at before. So if someone said this to him: "Up till now, you have been looking at specious rubbish; but now you are a little closer to what is real. Since you have turned to face objects which more truly exist, you are seeing more truly" – what do you think he would say to that?

515d3    'Or what if someone pointed out the dummies as they passed by, and obliged him to answer questions about what each one was? Don't you think that he would be at a loss, and would think that the shadows he had seen before were more real than the dummies now being pointed out to him?'

'He would think they were much more real,' said Glaucon.

515e1    'What if he was made to look at the firelight itself? Wouldn't it hurt his eyes, so that he would turn away and take flight to the things he can see clearly – the shadows? Wouldn't he think that those shadows were really more clear and distinct[27] than the dummies and the firelight that he was shown?'

'Just so,' said Glaucon.

'What if someone dragged him away by force, up the roughnesses and steepnesses of the way out of the cave, and did not let him go until they had dragged him out into the *sun*light? Wouldn't he be in agony, and in a rage at being dragged about so? When he reached the daylight, wouldn't his eyes be so saturated by the sunbeams that he wouldn't be able to see a single thing – even though he is told that *these* things are the real ones?'

516a2    'Certainly he wouldn't be able to see anything at first,' said Glaucon.

'No – I assume he would have to get used to the daylight, if he was going to see the things in the upper world. In the early stages he would find shadows easiest to see properly; after that, the reflections of men and other things in water; only then, the objects themselves. Then it would be easier for him to contemplate the sky at night-time, and to look at the light of the stars and the moon, than to look at the sun and its light during the day.'

516b1    'Of course it would,' said Glaucon.

'But eventually, I believe, he would become able to gaze on the sun itself, and contemplate it, not reflected in water, or appearing in ghostly form in some other setting – but itself, just as it is, in its own proper place.'

'Surely.'

'And once he had seen it, he would reason about the sun. "This," he would say, "is the source of the hours of the day and the seasons of the year, and the steward of all things in the visible world; and it is, somehow or other, the explanation[28] of all the things that we used to see in the cave." '

516c2    'Clearly,' said Glaucon, 'this is what he would come to next.'

'Suppose he recollected his previous habitation, and what was called wisdom in that place, and his fellow-prisoners. Don't you think he would pity them, and consider himself fortunate to have been transformed?'

'He certainly would.'

'Suppose that, among the prisoners at that time, it was a matter of honour and glory, of prizes even, to be the one who was able to pick out with the greatest clarity the dummies as they passed by, and to remember as well as may be the usual relations of "before", "after", or "at the same time" in which different dummies stood to each other, so as to be most skilled at foretelling which dummy would come up next. Do you think that the liberated prisoner would care much about such prizes? Do you think he would be jealous of those lordly characters whom the prisoners held in such honour? Wouldn't he feel about them more like the man in Homer[29] did? –

516d6        Better the lowest slave of a landless man
             On the living earth, than king of all the Dead –

'Wouldn't he endure anything rather than have the sort of beliefs that they have, or live as they do?'

516e1      'Yes,' said Glaucon, 'I think he would: he will prefer any kind of suffering to a life like that.'

'Remember this too,' I said: 'if the liberated prisoner goes back down to the cave and sits down in his usual place, won't his eyes be filled with darkness, since he has only just come from the sunlight?'

'That's bound to happen.'

516e7      'Suppose he is obliged once more to compete with the others, the perpetual prisoners, in the discrimination of shadows, even though his sight is still dim and his eyes have not yet got used to the darkness – for it would take him a long time to readjust. Won't he cut a foolish figure? Won't they say of him that he has come back from his journey into the upper world with ruined eyesight – that this just shows that even trying to get to the upper world is not worth the trouble? Again: if they could find a pretext for arresting and killing the man who was trying to unchain them and lead them into the upper world, wouldn't they do it?'

517a8      'They surely would,' said Glaucon.

'Now,' I said, 'you must fit together this picture I have given you with all the things we said before. Compare the prison-house of the cave to the realm of visual appearance; compare the light of the fire in the cave to the power of the sun. And you won't be far from what I'm trying to say (which is what you want to hear) if you take it that the prisoner's journey to the upper world, and his contemplation of what is up there, stands for the soul's journey up into the intelligible realm.

517b6      'As to whether this story is really true – god knows. But this is how things appear to me – in so far as I see at all. In the realm of the known, what is seen last of all – and with difficulty – is The Universal of The Good. Once that is seen, we can reason about it: it is the explanation of all that is right and beautiful. In the visible realm, The Universal of The Good gives birth to light and the power of light, the sun. In the intelligible realm, The Universal of The Good is itself the power which brings about truth and understanding; and it is what anyone who is to act wisely, either for his own ends or for the public good, must see.'

'So far as I understand you,' said Glaucon, 'I agree.'

517c6    'Come then,' I said: 'agree with me about this too. It is no wonder if those who have come this far do not want to live like mere humans, and instead their souls always long to pass their time in the upper region. Presumably this is natural enough, if things are really as the picture of the cave suggested.'

517d2    'Indeed it is likely,' he said.

'So,' I said, 'you won't think this strange, either: that a man who returns from divine contemplations to human matters should be sadly out of place, and look most absurd while he is still dim-sighted and has not yet got used to the prevailing darkness? Is it strange that he looks absurd when he is obliged to contend, in a law-court[30] or wherever, about the mere shadows of What is Just, or about the dummies of justice that cast the shadows? Is it strange that he looks absurd, when he has to join the hurly-burly about justice natural to a place where shadow-justice and dummy-justice are taken for granted by people who never once look on Justice Itself?'

'No, it's not strange at all.'

518a1    'Any sensible person,' I said, 'would recall that there are two ways of disturbing the operation of an eye, with two different causes: one in the case of eyes which are removed from light to darkness, the other when they are removed from darkness to light. He would realise that exactly the same is true of the soul. So when he saw a soul which was disturbed and unable to make something out, he would not thoughtlessly laugh at it. Rather he would look to see whether this soul had come from a brighter life, and was cast into darkness by not being used to the dark; or whether it had arrived at a clearer understanding from a greater ignorance, and was overwhelmed by the increasing brightness of the light-beams. Likewise he would think the first of these souls happy in its experience and its way of life, and the other pitiful. If he chose to ridicule the second soul, his ridicule would be justified – but it would be ridiculous to ridicule the soul that has come down into the darkness from the light of the upper realm.'

'Yes – that is most justly said,' agreed Glaucon.

518b6    'Then,' I said, 'if this is true, we must take something like this line on education. Education will not be capable of being all that some people[31] boastfully claim it can be. For their view, I believe, is that they can put into a soul knowledge that was not there before, like doctors who put sight into blind eyes.'

518c2    'Yes, they do say that.'

'But what our present argument shows,' I said, 'is this. This inherent power in each person's soul, and the instrument – the understanding – by which each person comes to learn: it is not so much like a blind eye, as like the eye of one of the prisoners we spoke of – an eye that can see, but which cannot be turned from darkness to light unless the whole body is turned. Just likewise, we must reorient the whole soul away from the world of becoming. We must shift the whole scene around, to the point where the soul becomes able to contemplate steadily What Is, and the brightest part of What Is – which we say is The Good.'

518d1    'We do.'

'Perhaps,' I said, 'education is this sort of skill: it is a skill of scene-shifting for the soul, of reorienting it as quickly and effectively as possible. It's not a matter of placing sight in the soul; education deals with souls that have sight already, but are not facing in the right direction or looking where they ought to look.'

'That seems right,' said Glaucon.

'Perhaps too the other types of virtue (as they are called) which are found in the soul are rather like the virtues of the body. For where they do not already exist, they can indeed be brought into being by habit and by application. By contrast, the virtue of thought seems to be of some far more divine nature. Thought never loses (or gains) its power to know; but whether this power is good and beneficial, or else useless and pernicious, depends entirely on its orientation.'

519a1

## NOTES

1. Cf. *Euthyphro* 11c–d in reading 8.
2. Socrates pauses to mark the transition from a lighter to a more solemn mood of conversation, and deliberately obliges Meno to draw his story out of him.
3. Pindar (522–442 BC) is best known for his *Pythians* and *Olympians*, victory odes written in honour of great athletic heroes. Along with Homer and Hesiod, his works were a staple part of a classical Greek's literary education.
4. Plato quotes from one of Pindar's lost funeral dirges where we might quote Wordsworth:

   > Our birth is but a sleep and a forgetting:
   > The Sun that rises with us, our life's Star,
   > Hath had elsewhere its setting,
   > And cometh from afar.
   > (Wordsworth, '*Intimations of Immortality*', 58–61)

5. *Meno* 80b9.
6. Cf. reading 3.
7. In Socrates' diagram, a large square is divided into four smaller squares. He now draws a diagonal line across each of the smaller squares so that the ends of the four diagonal lines meet to form another square, composed of the four triangular halves of the small squares. This last square has the required area of eight square feet.
8. Ordinary houshold slaves received no education in classical Athens.
9. Cebes and Simmias were probably lovers.
10. Recall that Simmas' and Socrates' conversation takes place immediately before Socrates' execution; cf. reading 2.

11. In fact Simmias' objection is not nonsense; it is very close to a damaging objection. Bostock, *Plato's Phaedo*, p. 61: 'Perhaps we simply came into existence . . . with the knowledge already in us, so we have had it all the time that we have existed, but have not existed for ever.' Plato sems to equivocate between 'I have always ( = as long as I have lived) known p' and 'I have known p always ( = throughout eternity)'.

12. How do two ones become one two? This cannot be explained in purely physical terms; what is needed is a conceptual explanation – a theory of the relations of the *concepts* 'one' and 'two'. The theory of Forms is just such an account.

13. Anaxagoras, DK B12.

14. The nearest places where Athenium fugitives from the law could find political asylum.

15. 'Taking refuge in abstract arguments' (*eis tous logous kataphugonta*) is a phrase which became a stick to beat Plato with: cf. Aristotle, *Nicomachean Ethics* 1105b13–15. To judge by his next paragraph, Plato foresaw that this might happen.

16. Curiously, the theory of Forms is never introduced by Plato as appearing for the *first* time.

17. Cf. readings 22, 28 and 29.

18. For problems about 'What Is Not' cf. reading 42.

19. Socrates' criterion may seem more like a *double* criterion than a single one, based as it is on two apparently distinct questions. That he does not take his criterion to be a double one is clear from 478a5 ff.

20. As Plato himself asks at *Theaetetus* 187d ff., what on earth could 'objects of ignorance' be?

21. The answer to the riddle is a eunuch who throws a piece of pumice at a bat hanging from a reed. Epicurus is said to have used this as a counter-example to Plato's own principle that 'Nothing partakes of opposite qualities in the same respect, in the same relation, and at the same time' (*Republic* 436b, in reading 23).

22. The One over Many argument for the Forms.

23. Compare this inquiry into the definition of the imitative artist with earlier Socratic quests for definitions (readings 5, 6 and 8); also the *Sophist*'s quest for a definition of the sophist. (Note Glaucon's description of the imitative artist as 'an absolutely miraculous sophist', 596d1.)

24. Here Plato addresses a danger to the theory of Forms which he has already seen: the Third Man Argument (see reading 35). (Is his blocking move successful?)

25. Another objection anticipated: 'Why not say that art imitates the *Forms*, not the particulars?'
26. Cf. readings 14, 18 and 21.
27. Cf. Descartes, *Meditation* 3.
28. Cf. reading 30.
29. Agamemnon in *Odyssey* ll. 489.
30. An obvious reference to Socrates' trial.
31. E.g. Protagoras in reading 11.

# PART VI

✥

# KNOWLEDGE AND THE FORMS (II)

# 35. PARMENIDES 130B–135C

## ✦

## CRITICISMS OF THE THEORY OF FORMS

130b1   'Socrates,' said Parmenides, 'you have the mettle to be an enthusiastic beginner in arguments. But tell me – are you yourself the originator of this distinction you speak of, between given Forms, apart on the one side, and the things they are Forms of, apart on the other? You think that there is such a thing as Likeness Itself, separate from that likeness which we grasp, and that there is The One, and Manyness, and likewise for all the things which you heard of from Zeno just now?'[1]

  'I certainly do,' said Socrates.

  'And,' said Parmenides, 'do you also think that there are such things as some Form of The Just, in its own right? And of The Beautiful, and The Good, and all such things as these?'

  'Yes,' said Socrates.

130c1   'Then is there a Form of Humanity, apart from us and apart from all of those who are of the same sort as we are – some actual Form of Humanity? And one of Fire, or Water?'

  'In truth, Parmenides,' said Socrates, 'I have often come to perplexity about these cases, as to whether or not one should affirm that there are Forms here as there are in the other cases.'

  'Again, Socrates, what about those cases in which Forms might seem an absurdity – hair, for example, or clay or wax, or anything else which is most humble and lowly in status? Isn't your difficulty whether you should say that there is a separated Form for each one of these, too, which is once more something different from any hair or clay or wax which we can touch?'

130d3      'Not at all,' said Socrates: 'because these things are exactly what they seem; so it would be absurd to think that there is a Form of any of these. Still, I have sometimes been worried by the thought that the same truth might apply to all cases.[2] Then no sooner have I come to a halt in this place than I run away from it again, for fear that at this point I will fall into some ocean-abyss of sheer babble, and perish. So I go back to those things which, as we have just been saying, surely *do* have Forms, and I devote my time to studying them.'

130e1      'Understandable. For you are still young,' said Parmenides, 'and philosophy has not yet gripped you as, I rather think, it soon will: and then you will despise none of these things.[3] But now, because of your inexperience, you are still sensitive to other people's opinions.

'Anyway, tell me this. Do you really believe, as you claim, that such Forms exist, and that other things come to be called after those Forms because they have a share in them? So, for example, things which are like partake of Likeness, things which are big of Bigness, and things which are beautiful and just, of Beauty and Justice?'

131a3      'Yes, certainly,' said Socrates.

'Then does each particular thing which partakes of a given Form, partake of part of that Form, or of all of it? – Or do you think that there is some third way of participating, besides these two?'

'No. How could that be?' said Socrates.

'Then do you think that the whole of the Form – which is after all a single thing – is in each one of the many particulars? Or what do you think?'

'Yes, all of it is in each,' said Socrates: 'and why shouldn't it be, Parmenides?'

131b1      'So while it is one and the same thing, the whole of it is simultaneously present in a variety of things, all separate from each other and the Form. But then the Form itself is separate from the Form!'

'Not so,' said Socrates: 'not at least if the case is like that of night, which is one and the same as itself, and yet is in many different places simultaneously, without being separate from itself. In the same way, any of the Forms could be both a unity and at the same time the same thing in everything.'

'A nice suggestion, Socrates,' said Parmenides, 'that a unity could at the same time be the same thing in many places. It is as if you should throw the same piece of sailcloth over a group of people, and then say that the whole of the one sailcloth was over them all. Do you think you mean something like that?'

131c1     'Possibly,' said Socrates.[4]

'Then would the whole sailcloth be over each person? Or would a different part of it be over each?'

'The latter.'

'Then,' said Parmenides, 'mustn't it likewise be possible to discern parts in the Forms themselves? And won't the things which participate in them, in fact participate only in parts of the Forms? Won't each participating thing no longer participate in the whole Form itself, but only in a part of it?'

'Yes, that looks likely.'

'Then are you willing, Socrates, to say that in our view the one Form is really divided into parts, and yet is still one Form?'

'Not at all,' said Socrates.

131d1     'For consider this,' said Parmenides: 'if you divide up Bigness Itself in this way, and then allow that each particular big thing will be big because of some part of Bigness which is smaller than Bigness Itself – won't that be illogical?'

'It certainly will,' said Socrates.

'Or what about this? Can a particular thing take

as its portion some small part of The Equal, in such a way that the particular will thereby possess a portion of Equality the possession of which will explain the particular's equality to other things – even though that portion of The Equal is less than, and so not equal to, The Equal Itself?'

'No, that is impossible.'

'Or suppose that one of us has a portion of The Small. Then The Small will be bigger than this portion, since it is a portion of The Small. And so The Small itself will be bigger than something; while the particular to which the portion of The Small is added, will be made smaller than it was before by this addition, and not bigger.'

131e1    'Yes,' said Socrates: 'none of which could never happen.'

'Then, Socrates,' asked Parmenides, 'in what way do other things participate in these Forms of yours, if they cannot participate either in parts of them, nor yet in the whole of them?'

'No, by Zeus,' said Socrates, 'I think that is a very hard question to decide.'

'Well, what about this? What is your attitude to this question?'

'Namely?'

132a1    'I think you believe that each Form is a unity on something like these grounds. When you consider many different things that appear big to you, you think, I suppose, that there is a single universal which is common to all the things you see: and so you conclude that there exists the one thing, Bigness.'

'That's right,' said Socrates.

'But what if you were likewise to consider in your soul all the big things, *plus Bigness Itself as well*? Wouldn't there appear a second Big, by means of which, necessarily, all these things including Bigness appear big?'

'Apparently so.'

'So then a second Form of Bigness will appear, alongside Bigness plus those things which participate in Bigness. And then, what is more, a third Form of Bigness will appear, alongside the big things plus Bigness plus the Form of the big things plus Bigness. And so each of your Forms will *not* be a unity any more; in each case the number of Forms will be infinite.'[5]

132b3    'Alternatively, Parmenides,' said Socrates, 'couldn't each of these Forms be a concept?[6] Then none of them would have to exist anywhere except in our souls. In this way each of the Forms might still be a unity, and it would not yet be evident that the Forms are prone to generate the regress just mentioned.'

'Very well,' said Parmenides; 'would each one of these concepts be a thought of nothing?'

'No, that would be impossible,' said Socrates.[7]

'So each concept would be a thought of something?'

'Yes.'

132c1    'Of something that exists, or does not exist?'

'Of something that exists.'

'Each concept, in fact, would be a thought of some one thing that the concept in question considers in its potential relation to all other things. That is, each concept would be a thought of a single real universal.'

'Yes.'

'So then won't this universal, which is conceived by the concept as a unity that is always the same in every relation it has, be a Form?'

'Yes, that too seems inevitable.'

'In which case,' said Parmenides, 'don't you think that the same necessity which obliges you to say that particulars partake of the Forms, also obliges you now to say that each particular thing is made out of concepts, and so that everything, Forms *and* particulars, is thought? For if even particular things are made out of concepts, then how can even particulars be objects of anything but thought?'[8]

132d1    'That wouldn't be reasonable either,' Socrates said. 'However, Parmenides, what now seems most plausible to me is this suggestion about the nature of the Forms. The Forms are there in nature – not just in our minds – existing so to speak as *paradigms*; other things resemble these paradigms, and are likenesses of them. As for the participation of particular things in the Forms, this comes about only in the sense that particulars can *resemble* the Forms, and not in any other sense.'

'But,' said Parmenides, 'if a particular resembles a Form, how can the Form fail to resemble the thing which resembles it – in so far as that thing is made to be a likeness of the Form? Or is there any get-out clause, whereby X could be like Y without Y being like X?'

'No, there isn't.'

'And if X and Y resemble each other, isn't there the strongest possible reason for saying that *it is because they participate in the same Form*?'

132e2    'There must be, yes.'

'And won't the thing that different resembling things resemble by participating in it, be that Form itself?'

'It certainly will.'

'In that case, then, *nothing* can resemble the Form, and the Form can resemble nothing. For otherwise, another Form will appear alongside the Form on each occasion; and if that second Form resembles anything else, then a third Form will also appear. If the Form resembles anything that participates in it, there will never be an end of the coming to be of new Forms!'[9]

133a3    'You're absolutely right.'

'So it can't be by resemblance that other things participate in the Forms; we must find some other way of explaining their participation.'

'So it seems.'

'Well, Socrates,' said Parmenides, 'do you see now how great the problems are that result from separating the Forms off as existents in their own right?'

'Very much so!'

'And yet', he continued, 'I might say that you truly ought to realise that you *don't* yet grasp the scale of the problems that you bring on yourself by persisting in your view that, in the case of each kind of particular, the Form is something separated from it.'

'How do you mean?' asked Socrates.

'Why, there's a whole swarm of objections,' said Parmenides. 'The greatest objection is this. Someone could object that, if the nature of the Forms is what we say it must be, then the Forms *are not proper objects of knowledge at all.* If someone made that objection, no one would be able to disprove it – unless[10] they had wide philosophical experience and were highly gifted, and willing to follow a counter-proof through many wanderings into seemingly irrelevant territory. Without that sort of disputant, the objector would be quite unmoved from his insistence that the Forms are unknowable.'

133c3    'Why so?' asked Socrates.

'Because presumably both you and anyone else, who supposes that to each kind of particular there corresponds a Being existing in its own right, would agree (in the first place) to the claim that none of these Beings exists *in us.*'

'Yes,' said Socrates, 'for if it existed *in us,* how could it exist *in its own right*?'[11]

'True,' agreed Parmenides. 'But now consider those universals which are what they are *in relation to each other.* Such universals will be what they are *only* in these interrelations. Their true nature will not be found in those universals' relations to the particular things around us: that is, to the likenesses of those universals, or whatever else you care to suppose they are, by participation in which we come to have ascribed to us predicates derived from this or that universal.

133d2     'Likewise with the qualities that *can* occur in us, which have the same names as those universals. They are related to each other, but not to the Forms; they belong to themselves, and not to the Forms which share their names with them.'

'What do you mean?' asked Socrates.

'Suppose, for example,' said Parmenides, 'that one of us is someone's master, or someone's slave. Presumably the man who is a slave is not a slave of The Master Itself, nor of What A Master Is. Nor is the man who is a master, a master of The Slave Itself, nor of What A Slave Is. No, both terms of the relation are *humans*: quite simply, one man is master of another. Whereas Mastery Itself is what it is in relation to Slavery Itself; and likewise Slavery Itself is what it is in relation to Mastery Itself.

133e6     'The point is that the kind of slavery or mastery which can be in us has no causal involvement[12] with the Forms Slavery and Mastery; and conversely, those Forms have no causal involvement with us. Rather, as I said, those Forms belong to themselves and relate only to each other; and likewise, the kinds of slavery or mastery which can be in us also belong to themselves and relate only to each other. Do you understand my argument now?'

134a3     'Yes,' said Socrates, 'I see it quite clearly.'

'Well,' said Parmenides, 'wouldn't this also apply to knowledge? What Knowledge Itself Is would be knowledge, not of truth, but of What Truth Itself Is.'

'Certainly.'

'Likewise for each of the various kinds of knowledge. What That Kind Of Knowledge Is would be knowledge, not of the subject matter in question, but of What That Kind Of Subject Matter Is.'

'Yes.'

'Whereas the sort of knowledge that can be in us will be knowledge of the kind of truth that can be in us; and each of the various kinds of knowledge that can be in us will turn out to be knowledge of the relevant subject matter *itself* – not of the *Form* of that subject matter.'

134b2          'Necessarily.'

'Whereas, as you agree, we have not got hold of the Forms themselves, nor is it possible for them to be in us.'

'No.'

'As for these classes of Things That Are themselves, presumably what knows *them* is the Form of Knowledge itself.'

'Yes.'

'But that is something that we have not got hold of.'

'No, we haven't.'

'Then not one of the Forms is known; or at any rate not by us, because we have no share in Knowledge Itself.'

'Apparently not.'

'Therefore The Beautiful Itself, and The Good, and all these things that we take to be universals, are all unknowable to us.'

134c2          'I fear so.'

'Consider another consequence of your doctrine of separation, still more terrible than the last one.'

'What?'

'Presumably you'd say that, if there is any class of Knowledge Itself, then it is a far more perfect sort of knowledge than the sort which can be in us. You'd say the same sort of thing about Beauty, and all the other cases?'

'Yes.'

'And wouldn't you say that, if anything has a share of this Knowledge, then no one is likelier than god to have the most perfect sort of knowledge?'

'Inevitably.'

134d1    'Then can god know about what can be among humans, since he possesses Knowledge Itself?'

'Yes: why ever not?'

'Because we agreed that whatever causal involvement those Forms may in fact have, they have no causal involvement with what can be among humans. Nor do the qualities and relations that can be in us have any causal involvement with those Forms. Each side is related only to itself.'

'Yes, we agreed that.'

'But if what is with god is the most perfect Mastery Itself, and the most perfect Knowledge Itself, then neither can this mastery of the Forms also be a mastery *of us*; nor can this knowledge know *us*, nor any of the things that are to do with us. Moreover, we cannot influence the gods by any power we have,[13] nor can we touch the divine by way of our sort of knowledge. Again, by the same argument, the gods, precisely *because* they are gods, are not our masters; nor do they have any knowledge of human affairs.'

134e8    'But this argument is an absolutely extraordinary one,' said Socrates, 'if it means we are going to deprive god of knowledge!'

'Well,' said Parmenides, 'these problems, and a whole host of others besides, are necessary concomitants of the Forms – if the Forms are universals of things which are real in their own right, and if we define each Form as itself being a Something. This is why your hearers are thrown into perplexity by you, and dispute the very existence of the Forms; adding that, even if they were as real as possible, there would be every reason why they would be unknowable to human nature. Whoever reacts to your theory like this feels that he has a strong case; and as we were saying, he is going to be exceedingly difficult to dissuade from his view. Only a very gifted individual will be able to grasp your doctrine that there is, for each particular thing, a Class and a Being In Its Own Right. It will take an even more wonderful person to find his way through all these teachings so as to be able to instruct someone else to have proper discernment about them!'

135b2      'But I absolutely agree, Parmenides,' said Socrates: 'this is just what I think, too.'

'On the other hand,' said Parmenides, 'if someone is so impressed by all these objections we've considered, and others like them, that he won't allow that there are any Forms of particular things, and refuses to draw up a Form for each type of thing, then his thought will not know where to turn. For he does not allow that *any* abiding and unchanging universal exists in the case of *any* particular thing. But by this move he completely destroys the possibility of any discourse at all[14] – an objection which you seem to be very well aware of.'

135c3      'Yes, you're right,' said Socrates.

'Then what are you going to do about philosophy? Which way will you turn, if all these doctrines are dubious?'

135c6      'I can see no answer to that: at least, not just now.'

# 36. THEAETETUS 170A–171C

><-

## PROTAGORAS REFUTED

170a2   SOCRATES. Isn't Protagoras' position that 'what seems true to someone, *is* true – to that person'?

THEODORUS. Yes.

SOCRATES. Well, Protagoras, we too will give some-one's opinion – or rather everyone's opinion – and say this: there isn't a single person who thinks that there are no matters in which he is wiser than other people, and no matters in which other people are wiser than he is. Consider the greatest dangers we encounter. When people are tempest-tossed by war or sickness or the sea, they trust those who are in charge with absolute faith. The led expect the leaders to provide salvation, even though the only difference between leaders and led is in knowledge. Everywhere you look in human affairs there are men seeking teachers and masters, not just for themselves but for their livestock and their businesses too; everywhere you look there are also men who think they have what it takes to be such teachers and masters. What conclusion can we draw from all these cases – if not that humans, for their part, do believe that there are such things as wisdom and ignorance among them?

170b8   THEODORUS. No other conclusion is possible.

SOCRATES. Don't they think that wisdom is a true conception of things, whereas ignorance is believing what is false?

170c1   THEODORUS. Naturally.

SOCRATES. Then, Protagoras, what use can we have for your thesis? Either we should say that all men always have true beliefs; or we should say that sometimes they have true beliefs, and sometimes false ones. But whichever we say, it will still turn out that men *don't* always have true beliefs, but sometimes true and sometimes false beliefs. For consider this, Theodorus: would any of those in Protagoras' circle be willing to defend the view that no one ever thinks that someone else is ignorant, and has a false belief? Would *you* defend that position?

THEODORUS. No; the position is quite untenable.

170d1 SOCRATES. Yet this is the position to which the argument which says that 'Man is the measure of all things' necessarily leads.

THEODORUS. How so?

SOCRATES. Suppose you make a judgement about something in your own thinking, and reveal your opinion to me. Let's admit, with Protagoras, that such a judgement is true *to you*. What about the rest of us? Can't we become judges of your judgement? Or must our verdict always be that your opinion is right? In fact, for any belief you form, won't ten thousand oppose you every time – holding the opposite view, and thinking and judging that what you think is false?

170e1 THEODORUS. By Zeus, yes – 'ten thousand times ten thousand', as the poet says, who provide me with as much work to do as humans possibly could.

SOCRATES. Then what comes next? Don't you think we should say that in such cases, what you believe is true *to you*, but false *to the ten thousand*?

THEODORUS. It seems we must say that, given the argument.

SOCRATES. But what about Protagoras himself? Either not even he believed that 'Man is the measure of all things' – no more than the great majority of men believe it (for indeed they don't). In which case, that book that he wrote – *Truth* – was truth-to . . . no one at all!

171a1    Or else he did believe his own doctrine, although nobody else agreed with him. In which case, two points are in order. First, you know, his doctrine is more false than true exactly in proportion as it seems false to more people than it seems true to.

THEAETETUS. Necessarily – if his doctrine really isn't true or false without qualification, but is true or false relative to each person's opinion.

SOCRATES. Second, it has this most elegant consequence. Since Protagoras agrees that all people's beliefs are true beliefs, presumably he admits the truth of what those who disagree with him think about his own theory. And their thought is: 'Protagoras' theory is *false*'.

THEODORUS. Yes, exactly.

171b1    SOCRATES. So isn't he conceding that his theory *is* false, since he agrees that those who believe that he is wrong have a true belief?[15]

THEODORUS. Necessarily.

SOCRATES. But his opponents believe that they are not mistaken, don't they?

THEODORUS. Yes.

SOCRATES. Then Protagoras, to go by his book, must also concede the truth of his opponents' belief that they are right!

THEODORUS. So it seems.

SOCRATES. So Protagoras' thesis will be contradicted by everyone – and Protagoras will be the first to contradict it. He will be the first to admit the contrary of his view, when he agrees that the person who says the opposite to Protagoras has a true belief. At that point even Protagoras himself will concede that no stray dog or random passer-by is a 'measure' of any subject at all – until he has learned to understand it.

171c3    THEODORUS. That's right.

SOCRATES. Then since Protagoras' *Truth* is contradicted by everybody, it isn't true-to anyone either. It's not true-to anyone other than Protagoras; it's not

171c5    even true-to Protagoras himself.

# 37. THEAETETUS 181B–183C

## ❧❧

## HERACLEITUS REFUTED

181b9  SOCRATES. Since you are so keen to look at the Heracleitean view, I suppose we'd better. Probably the right way to begin our examination of their Theory of Flux is to ask what kind of change they have in mind when they say that 'Everything is always changing'. I mean something like this: do they say that there is just one form of change? Or do they admit that there are two? If they do, I think they're right – but it's not just my view we want. We want your agreement too, so that we may share whatever difficulties may result from this. So you tell me: do you call it change when something swaps one position for another, or turns round in the same position?

THEODORUS. I do.

181d1  SOCRATES. Then here's one form of change. What about when something stays in the same place but gets old, or turns from white to black or from soft to hard, or is altered in some other sense of alteration? Wouldn't it be right to call this another form of change?

THEODORUS. I think so.

SOCRATES. But really it must be right. So I say there are these two forms of change: alteration, and motion.

THEODORUS. Right.

SOCRATES. Having made this distinction, let's engage in dialogue with those who declare that 'Everything is always changing'. Let us ask them: 'Do you mean that everything is always changing in both senses of change – alteration and motion? Or that, at any time, some things are changing in the one sense, and some in the other?'

181e2   THEODORUS. By Zeus, I don't know what they'd say to
        that . . . I think they'd say 'In both senses'.
        SOCRATES. Yes, Theodorus, they must say that. If they
        don't, their view will be that 'Everything is always
        changing *and not changing*'; and then it will be no more
        correct to assert that everything is always changing
        than to deny it.
        THEODORUS. Absolutely right.
        SOCRATES. Then since things must be changing, and
        since there can be nothing unchanging in anything,
        mustn't everything always be changing in every sense
        of change?

182a2   THEODORUS. It must.
        SOCRATES. Then consider, please, this point in their
        theory. Didn't we say that their view about how heat
        or whiteness or anything like that comes into being
        was something like this? – At the moment of a
        perception of any such thing as heat or whiteness,
        that thing will be in motion between the passive
        element and the active element, in such a way that
        the passive element comes into a state of perceiving
        (though it does not become a perception), while the
        active element becomes such-and-such (though it does
        not become *a* such-and-such*ness*).[16]

182a8       Now perhaps you think that 'such-and-suchness' is a
        verbal monstrosity which you don't understand in any
        general way; so listen to some particular uses. The active
        element does not become the such-and-suchness *heat*, or
        *whiteness*; it becomes such-and-such: hot, or white. And
        so on. I say this because of what we said, as I expect you
        remember, in the earlier part of our discussion: that there
        is nothing at all which exists in its own right, not even the
        active or the passive element. What happens is rather
        that the active and passive elements bring forth, from
        their union with each other, a 'perception' which be-
        comes an act of perceiving something, and a 'perceptible'
        which comes to be perceived as such-and-such.

182b9   THEODORUS. Naturally I remember.

SOCRATES. So let's wave goodbye to questions about the rest of Heracleitean theory, as to what it says about whatever other issue. Let us keep our eyes fixed on the object of our discussion, by asking the Heracleiteans: So your doctrine is that everything is always changing and in flux? – Is that their doctrine?

182c3   THEODORUS. Yes.

SOCRATES. – And everything is constantly changing in both the respects we distinguished, movement and alteration?

THEODORUS. It must be, if we are to have complete flux.

SOCRATES. If everything was only moving in space, and was not undergoing alteration too, we would presumably be able to describe how these moving things flow.

THEODORUS. We would.

182d1   SOCRATES. But that's not how it is: the flowing thing doesn't even flow white. That very whiteness-in-flow changes too: there is a flux even of the whiteness, a change into some other colour, lest that whiteness should be caught standing still. But if this is the case, then is it even possible to speak of a colour in such a way as to speak of it accurately?

THEODORUS. How could it be? Indeed how can we ever speak about anything like this, since it is forever quietly dissolving away from you even as you speak of it?

SOCRATES. Then what are we to say about the various sorts of perceptions, like those that go with sight and hearing? Can they ever remain in their own states, and go on being cases of sight or hearing?

182e2   THEODORUS. Evidently not, if everything is always changing.

SOCRATES. Then it is no better to talk of seeing than of not-seeing, nor of any other sense rather than of its privation, since everything is changing in every way.

THEODORUS. No indeed.

SOCRATES. And yet Theaetetus and I agreed that perception was knowledge.

THEODORUS. So you did.

SOCRATES. So our answer to the question 'What is knowledge?' mentioned something which can no more be knowledge than it is not-knowledge.

183a1   THEODORUS. Apparently.

SOCRATES. So much for our attempts to refine our answer to the question 'What is knowledge?'! The reason we were so avid to demonstrate that everything is always in motion was, precisely, because we wanted to show that that answer was correct. But what we *have* shown, apparently, is just this: that *if* everything is always in motion, then every answer to any question is just as right as every other answer. So you have just as much right to describe things as being thus-and-so as to describe them as *not* being thus-and-so (or as *becoming* thus-and-so, if you still want us to avoid fixing things down by language).

THEODORUS. You're right.

183a9   SOCRATES. Except that I used the terms 'thus-and-so' and 'not thus-and-so'; but one shouldn't even use these terms. For if you do, then what is 'thus-and-so' will no longer be changing. Nor, again, should you use 'not thus-and-so': for not even this word represents a changing. The truth is that those who uphold the Heracleitean doctrine are going to need some other vocabulary here. For they have no words to express their own hypothesis – unless perhaps 'Nohow' and 'Contrariwise', taken in their most indefinite senses, would be a suitable way of putting their point.

183b7   THEODORUS. Yes – that would certainly be a dialect they were at home in!

SOCRATES. So, Theodorus, we have shaken off your friend Protagoras,[17] and we do not yet admit his claim that every man is a measure of every subject – unless of course he is an *intelligent* man. And we are not going to allow that 'Knowledge is perception' in the sense that the Way of Flux gives to that claim, either – unless

183c3  of course Theaetetus here has anything to add?

# 38. THEAETETUS 184B–186E

**‹‹‹‹**

## KNOWLEDGE IS NOT PERCEPTION

184b2 SOCRATES. Theaetetus, you say that knowledge is perception; am I right?

THEAETETUS. Yes.

SOCRATES. Well, suppose someone asked you: 'By what means does a man see whites and blacks? By what means does he hear high and low notes?' Presumably you'd reply: 'By his eyes and his ears respectively'.

THEAETETUS. Yes.

184c1 SOCRATES. As a rule, it is well-bred behaviour to sit loose to the meanings of words and phrases, and not to treat them with parade-ground precision: that opposite method seems a slavish procedure. But at times it is necessary: for example, now. We need to stop and search the answer you have just made, for there is something not right about it. Ask yourself this: is it more correct to say that the eyes or ears are that *in respect of* which we see or hear? Or that *through* which?[18]

THEAETETUS. In each case I think we perceive through these organs, Socrates, rather than in respect of them.

184d1 SOCRATES. Yes, my boy; for it would be rather strange if there were many such senses sitting inside us, like the soldiers in the Horse of Troy, and if these different faculties did not tend towards some single, unified universal – a soul or whatever one should call it. So *in respect of* that soul, we perceive whatever perceptibles come our way, *by means of* these senses, which are organs – instruments.

THEAETETUS. Yes, this view seems more plausible than the alternative.

184d7  SOCRATES. I have insisted on this fine point because of its relevance to the following question. Do we – in respect of that one and the same part of ourselves – arrive at black and white by means of the eyes, and at other perceptions by means of the other senses? If you are asked, will you be able to refer all such organs of sense to the body? Perhaps I should let you speak and answer these questions yourself, rather than doing everything myself. So tell me: don't you think that the organs whereby you perceive hot and hard and light and sweet are all parts of the body? Or are they parts of something else?

184e9  THEAETETUS. No, they are parts of the body.

SOCRATES. Now are you willing to agree that what you perceive by means of one perceptual ability, you cannot perceive by means of any other? For example, sounds cannot be seen and sights cannot be heard?

185a3  THEAETETUS. How could I be unwilling?

SOCRATES. Then if you ever have a conception of both a sight and a sound together, you cannot have it just by means of the sense of sight; nor just by means of the sense of hearing.

THEAETETUS. Clearly not.

SOCRATES. But about both sights and sounds alike you have this primary conception: that both *exist*.

THEAETETUS. I do.

SOCRATES. Don't you also have the conception that each is *different* from the other, but *the same* as itself?

185b1  THEAETETUS. Obviously.

SOCRATES. And that together they are *two* things, whereas each of them alone is *one* thing?

THEAETETUS. Yes, that too.

SOCRATES. Aren't you also capable of examining whether sights and sounds are *like or unlike* each other?

THEAETETUS. That seems plausible.

SOCRATES. By means of what do you form all these conceptions about sights and sounds? It is impossible to grasp what is common to both sight and sound either by seeing it or by hearing it. Here's another proof of our thesis. Supposing it possible to examine both sights and sounds as to whether they were brackish or not, you know that you will be able to say what sense would conduct the examination. It would be neither sight nor hearing, but something else.

185c2  THEAETETUS. Of course: it will be the sensory power exercised through the tongue – taste.

SOCRATES. Exactly. But what is the power which makes clear to you what is common to all the senses, including these three? What is the power by means of which you talk of what is and what is not, and of the other things we were asking about a minute ago? Given such conceptions as these, what bodily organs can you suppose to be the means whereby the perceiving part of us perceives them?

185c8  THEAETETUS. You are talking of the application to perceptions of ideas like existence and what is not, likeness and unlikeness, identity and difference, and oneness and all the other numbers. Also, you are clearly raising a question about oddness and evenness in numbers, and whatever these ideas entail: you want to know by means of what bodily organ we could possibly perceive such things in the soul.

185d4  SOCRATES. You're hot on my trail, Theaetetus: that's exactly what I'm asking.

THEAETETUS. By Zeus, Socrates, I don't think I can answer your question; except to say at once that I don't think there is any special organ at all in this case, as there is in the others. Rather, I believe, the soul itself is its own organ in examining what is in common between all perceptions.

185e2  SOCRATES. Indeed you are handsome, Theaetetus, and not ugly, as Theodorus said! For the person who speaks so handsomely must himself be handsome – and good as well. And besides being handsome, you

have served my turn very well, releasing me from a
long argument. For it already appears to you that in
some respects the soul itself is its own organ, whereas
in others it conducts its examinations by means of the
body's powers. That was also what I thought myself;
and I wanted you to think the same.

186a1  THEAETETUS. Well, I do think that.

SOCRATES. Then in which of these two classes do you
put being? For being is what is most commonly shared
of all.

THEAETETUS. I would put it in the class of the things
which the soul reaches after in its own right.

SOCRATES. Would you do the same with likeness and
unlikeness, identity and difference?

THEAETETUS. Yes.

SOCRATES. What about beauty and ugliness, and good
and bad?

THEAETETUS. Yes: these too seem to me to be among
those things whose essences the soul considers most
directly in their relations to each other. The soul
calculates in itself about the relation of past and
present to future –

186b2  SOCRATES. Hold on a minute. The soul perceives the
hardness of what is hard, and likewise the softness of
what is soft, by means of touch?

THEAETETUS. Yes.

SOCRATES. But the being of hard and soft, the definition
of each, their opposition to one another, the being in
turn of that opposition – it is the soul itself that tries to
make judgements about all these, turning back to these
conceptions and comparing them with each other?

THEAETETUS. Yes, certainly.

186c1  SOCRATES. So isn't it possible, even for men and other
creatures which have only just come into being, that
they should naturally perceive whatever affections
come through the body to the soul? Whereas calcula-
tions about these perceptions, concerning their reality

and their usefulness, come about – if they come about at all – only through exertion and the passage of time, through many troubles and through education?

THEAETETUS. Absolutely.

SOCRATES. Is it possible for someone to hit on the truth when they cannot even manage to hit on being?[19]

THEAETETUS. No, it isn't.

SOCRATES. But will anyone ever have knowledge of something, if he always misses the truth about it?

186d1  THEAETETUS. How could he, Socrates?

SOCRATES. Then knowledge is not to be found in our bodily affections, but in our reasonings about them. For in the latter it is, it seems, possible to lay hold of being and of truth; but in the former, it is not.

THEAETETUS. So it appears.

SOCRATES. When they differ so widely from each other, will you call bodily affections and reasonings by the same name?

THEAETETUS. No – that would hardly be appropriate.

SOCRATES. What name *would* you give to the whole of the former class: to sight, hearing, smelling, feeling cold and heat?

186e1  THEAETETUS. I'd call it 'perceiving' – what other name is there?

SOCRATES. Taken together, you call these things 'perception'?

THEAETETUS. I have to.

SOCRATES. By means of which (we have agreed) it is impossible to lay hold of truth, since you cannot even lay hold of the idea of being by this means.

THEAETETUS. No indeed.

SOCRATES. In which case, you can't lay hold of knowledge this way, either.

THEAETETUS. No, you can't.

SOCRATES. So, then, Theaetetus, perception and knowledge could never be the same thing.

186e8  THEAETETUS. Apparently not, Socrates.

# 39. THEAETETUS 200D–201C

## ✦

## KNOWLEDGE IS NOT TRUE BELIEF

200d4   SOCRATES. We are back at the beginning again! Who will tell us: *what is knowledge?* Surely we're not stuck already!

THEAETETUS. Far from it – at least, so long as *you*'re not stuck, Socrates.

SOCRATES. Well, then, you tell me what we can say about it that will put us in least danger of contradicting ourselves.

200e1   THEAETETUS. I can't see what else I could offer except the definition we tried before.

SOCRATES. Which was?

THEAETETUS. That knowledge is true belief. After all, presumably true believing is infallible, and everything that it causes is fine and good.[20]

SOCRATES. Well, Theaetetus, 'try it and see' – as the river-guide said when they asked him if the ford was deep. Likewise if we go on and explore this suggestion. Perhaps we'll stumble upon the very thing we're after straight away; but certainly nothing will become clear if we don't go on.

201a2   THEAETETUS. Quite right; so let's go on, and consider the suggestion.

SOCRATES. Not that it will take long to consider it. For there's an entire profession which shows that knowledge is not what you say it is.

THEAETETUS. How do you make that out? – What profession?

SOCRATES. Why, the profession of the greatest men of wisdom – the ones they call orators and advocates. For evidently their profession involves advocates in persuading jurors: yet they don't *teach* them anything. Rather they *cause them to believe* – whatever they want them to believe. Or do you really think that there are any teachers clever enough to be able to teach others satisfactorily the truth about what happened to those who (with no eye-witnesses present) were robbed of money, or assailed in some other way – to teach all this while a little water drips through the clock?[21]

201b4   THEAETETUS. It's clear that they can't; all they do is persuade, not teach.

SOCRATES. By 'persuade', you mean 'cause to believe'?

THEAETETUS. What else?

SOCRATES. But jurymen can justifiably arrive at a view about things which one can only *know* by seeing them, and not in any other way – basing their verdicts on what they hear in court. If the lawyers persuade them of the truth, and if they reach the right verdict, then don't the jurors judge without knowledge, but by forming a true belief?

201c2   THEAETETUS. Yes, that seems altogether correct.

SOCRATES. But, my friend, if true belief and knowledge were the same thing in courts, even the sharpest juror could not form a correct belief without knowledge. So now it has become clear that true belief and knowledge

201c7   are not the same thing.

# 40. THEAETETUS 206c–210b

## ⇥⇤

## KNOWLEDGE IS NOT TRUE BELIEF WITH AN ACCOUNT

206c2 SOCRATES. Let's not forget the main question we are looking at: namely, the meaning of the view that properly formed knowledge comes about when an account is added to true belief.

THEAETETUS. No: that's what we must consider.

SOCRATES. So what do we think this 'account' is supposed to mean? It seems to me that it must mean one of three things.

THEAETETUS. Which?

206d1 SOCRATES. The first alternative would be that 'account' refers to the way in which you make your own thought clear by speech, with phrases and names. You reflect what you believe in the stream of speech, as if it were in water, or in a mirror. Don't you think that this sort of thing is an 'account'?

THEAETETUS. Certainly. For we say that anyone who does this is 'giving an account' in the sense that they are speaking.

SOCRATES. But anyone can learn to speak, can't they? Though some learn faster than others, anyone can give an explanation of how each thing appears to him – unless he has been deaf or dumb from the beginning. But then, it seems, everyone who has a correct belief will also have it 'with an account'! In which case correct belief will be sufficient for knowledge.[22]

206e3 THEAETETUS. True.

SOCRATES. Still, let us not glibly accuse the person who gave this present definition of knowledge of talking nonsense. For perhaps the speaker did not mean this. Perhaps he rather meant that, if someone is asked to say what anything is, he must be able to give the questioner an answer which mentions the *natural parts* of the thing in question.

207a2 THEAETETUS. What would be an example, Socrates?

SOCRATES. An example would be Hesiod, speaking of a wagon as 'a wagon of a hundred timbers'.[23] Now I couldn't enumerate all those hundred parts, and I don't suppose you could either. But if someone asked us what a wagon is, we might be content if we were able to reply that a wagon is: 'Wheels, axle, frame, rails, yoke'.

THEAETETUS. Indeed we might.

207a8 SOCRATES. Really? But our questioner might think this was just as ridiculous of us, as if we should reply to a question, asked about you, 'What is his name?', by listing the syllables in your name! Saying this would be giving a correct belief; and it would, in our present sense, be 'giving an account'. But it would be as if we took ourselves to be grammarians – as if we thought we had the account of the name of Theaetetus, and could express that account, just by grammar. The questioner might just reiterate what was said before: that no one can give an account of the sort relevant to *knowledge* until he has been right through each one of the natural parts of whatever is in question, with true opinion.

207b8 THEAETETUS. Yes – that is what was said before.

SOCRATES. So in this case, about Hesiod's wagon: this critic will say that we have correct belief about it, but that the person who can *express its being* by going through its hundred parts – the person who adds that is the one who has added an account (in the proper sense) to his true belief. He is the one who has replaced mere belief about that wagon with knowledge and a craftsman's understanding of the very being of the wagon. This he has achieved by getting to the wagon as a whole by way of its natural parts.

207c6   THEAETETUS. Do you think this view is right, Socrates?

SOCRATES. Well, my friend, if *you* think it is right, and accept the notion that an 'account' of anything means an enumeration in their order of each of the natural parts of that thing – whereas it would be an unaccountable account which went by way of the syllables of the words, or some still grosser units[24] – if that is *your* view, then tell me, so that we can discuss it.

207d2   THEAETETUS. I am happy to accept it.

SOCRATES. But you don't think – do you? – that any person has knowledge of some whole thing if they think that the same natural part is present in that whole at one time, but not at another time? Or if they think that the same whole contains one natural part at one time, but does not contain it at another?

THEAETETUS. Zeus, of course not.[25]

SOCRATES. But haven't you forgotten that this is exactly what you thought when you were first learning your letters – as did everyone else too?

THEAETETUS. Are you talking about how we sometimes thought, when we were learning to write, that a given syllable contained a given letter, and sometimes thought it didn't contain that letter? And how we sometimes put a given letter into the right syllable, and sometimes into the wrong one?

207e3   SOCRATES. Yes, I am.

THEAETETUS. By Zeus, of course I haven't forgotten. And I don't think that anyone who is still in that sort of process of learning can yet be said to know what they are learning.

SOCRATES. What then? Suppose someone who is at this stage of learning is writing 'Theaetetus'. He thinks (correctly) that he ought to write theta, epsilon; so he writes that. Then he tries to write 'Theodorus'. He thinks (incorrectly) that he ought to write tau, epsilon;

so he writes that. Then should we say that this learner knows the first syllable of your name?

208a4   THEAETETUS. No: for we've only just agreed that someone in this state does not yet know.

SOCRATES. But what's to stop someone from making the same mistake about the second syllable, or the third, or the fourth?

THEAETETUS. Nothing at all.

SOCRATES. Well, in that case, supppose a person grasps the enumeration in their order of each of the natural parts of your name. When he writes 'Theaetetus' correctly, he will do so only on the basis of correct belief, won't he?

THEAETETUS. Clearly, yes.

208b1   SOCRATES. So isn't he still, like we said, in a state of correct belief rather than of knowledge?

THEAETETUS. Yes.

SOCRATES. And this is so even though he has an account to go with that correct belief. For he wrote your name with a grasp of the way through its natural parts – which is what we decided constituted an account.

THEAETETUS. True.

SOCRATES. So, my friend, there is a kind of 'correct belief with an account' which none the less is not to be called knowledge.

THEAETETUS. It rather looks like it.

SOCRATES. So apparently our philosophical jackpot was just an illusion: we were wrong to think that we had found the most trustworthy account of the nature of knowledge imaginable. – But perhaps we should suspend judgement. For possibly this is not the definition we ought to adopt; rather we should take up the one remaining idea of the original three from which we said the definer of knowledge as correct belief with an account had to choose.

208c4   THEAETETUS. You're right to mention that, for there is still one possibility left. The first was (so to speak) the image of thought in speech. The second (which we've just discussed) was the way to the whole through its natural parts. But what do you mean by the third?

SOCRATES. Just what the majority would say: that knowledge of whatever is in question means being able to specify some sign whereby that thing can be differentiated from everything else.

THEAETETUS. Can you explain the account by giving an example of something that differs from something else in this way?

208d1   SOCRATES. If you like, there is the example of the sun. I suppose you will accept it as sufficient if I say that it is the brightest of the bodies that go round the earth across the heavens.

THEAETETUS. Certainly.

SOCRATES. Here's why I say this. As we were saying just now, it's because some people believe that if you get hold of the differentia of anything, meaning the respect in which it differs from everything else, then you will also get hold of the account of that thing. So long as you hold on to anything it has in common with other things, your account will not be about *it*: it will be about everything that shares that common feature.

208e1   THEAETETUS. I understand. It seems a very plausible proposal to call something like this 'an account'.

SOCRATES. The proposal is this: someone who previously only had beliefs about something will have acquired knowledge about that thing once he adds, to his correct belief about that thing, a grasp of its difference from other existents.

THEAETETUS. That's what we say, anyway.

SOCRATES. But really, Theaetetus, for my part I'm afraid I don't understand this proposal one bit – now that I have come up close to it, like a man with his nose against the canvas of a painting. And it seemed so promising, too: until I began to examine it closely.

THEAETETUS. How has this happened?

209a1 SOCRATES. I'll tell you – if indeed I'm up to it. According to the proposal, whenever I have correct belief about you, then I also have knowledge of you, if I add an account of you to that belief; otherwise not.

THEAETETUS. Yes.

SOCRATES. But the 'account of you' in question is the explanation of your differentia – what makes you different.

THEAETETUS. Just so.

SOCRATES. So as long as I only had correct belief about you, I didn't have a grasp of any of the ways[26] in which you differ from all other people.

THEAETETUS. Evidently not.

SOCRATES. So what I had in mind, in my beliefs about you, was one of those common features which is no more distinctive of you than of anyone else.

209b1 THEAETETUS. Right.

SOCRATES. Then for heaven's sake, what could it possibly be about my situation, when I merely had beliefs, which made my beliefs *beliefs about you*, rather than beliefs about anyone else? For imagine me thinking that 'Theaetetus is the one who (a) is a human, (b) has a nose, (c) has eyes, (d) a mouth' – and so for each of your bodily parts. Is this description of my thought sufficient to make it true that my thought is any more a thought about Theaetetus than about Theodorus? Or about the most distant barbarian?

THEAETETUS. No – it couldn't be.

209c1 SOCRATES. But even if I think about someone who not only has a nose and eyes, but has a *snub* nose and *goggle* eyes – in what way will my thought be more a thought about *you* than a thought about *me*, or a thought about anyone else who also looks like we do?

THEAETETUS. In no way at all.

SOCRATES. No; in fact I don't think that *Theaetetus* will be what is thought of in me, until his very own snubness of nose has laid down and established in me, as a memorial of him, some differentia which distinguishes *his* snubness from all the other snubnesses which I have seen. And likewise with all the other qualities from which you are composed. It is that memorial of a differentia which will remind me and cause me to have right beliefs about you if I encounter you tomorrow.

THEAETETUS. Very true.

209d1 SOCRATES. But then correct belief about any matter is *also* going to depend on the differentia!

THEAETETUS. So it appears.

SOCRATES. So what more is said by adding 'an account' to correct belief? For if 'an account' means that – besides one's correct belief about a thing – one also has a belief about how that thing differs from other things, then this suggestion about how to define knowledge is altogether absurd.

THEAETETUS. Why?

SOCRATES. Because it tells us that, to get knowledge of a thing, we should add an 'account' – a belief about how that thing differs from other things – to our correct belief about that thing – which is *also* a belief about how that thing differs from other things! For sheer circularity, the wrapping of a secret message round one of those special staffs, or the movement of a pestle round a mortar, would have nothing on this suggestion. In fact one might more fairly call it a case of the blind leading the blind. For the injunction to acquire what we already have, in order to learn what we already believe – this seems altogether worthy of a groper in the dark.

209e5 THEAETETUS. So what were you intending to say when you first put the question?

SOCRATES. Well, my boy, suppose the injunction to achieve knowledge of a thing, by adding an account to our true belief about that thing, means that we are to *get to know* what differentiates that thing from anything else, and not merely have beliefs about it. If that's so, a pretty story our 'finest account of knowledge' turns out to be! For presumably getting to know something means getting knowledge about it?

210a2   THEAETETUS. Yes.

SOCRATES. So if someone is asked 'What is knowledge?', apparently they will reply that 'Knowledge is correct belief plus *knowledge* of a differentia'. For on their story, this would be what the addition of an 'account' comes to.

THEAETETUS. Apparently so.

SOCRATES. Yet if we are trying to define knowledge, it is completely simple-minded to say that knowledge is 'correct belief *plus* knowledge' – whether that is knowledge of a differentia or knowledge of anything else.

So, Theaetetus, knowledge can be neither perception; nor true belief; nor the combination of true belief
210b1   with an 'account'.

# 41. SOPHIST 245E–249C

><

# THE BATTLE OF THE GODS AND
# THE GIANTS

245e5 STRANGER.[27] Well, now we have surveyed the arguments of some of those[28] who have formulated precise
doctrines about being and not-being, let that suffice
about them. It's time to look at those who argue less
precisely:[29] that will at least enable us to see that
whichever way you discuss it, it is no easier to define
being than not-being.

246a2 THEAETETUS. Then we should definitely go on to these
others.

STRANGER. But even these philosophers' disagreements about What Is seem to have caused a sort of
battle of the gods and the giants among them.

THEAETETUS. How's that?

STRANGER. One side in this battle drags everything
down to earth from the heavens and the invisible
realm, holding on with extraordinary insistence to
the reality of rocks and trees in their hands. They
hold on fast to everything of that sort, and aver with
the greatest force that nothing exists unless it is
possible to touch it or press it in some way. And
they say that What Is is the same as what is physical: if anyone claims that anything that has no body
exists, they have absolute contempt for him, and will
hear no more from him.

246b4 THEAETETUS. Yes, they are fearful men you speak of;
I have met quite a few of them myself.

STRANGER. Accordingly their opponents defend themselves with the greatest caution from their position
somewhere on high: the claim on which *they* forcefully

insist is that What truly Is, is some kind of intelligible, bodiless Forms. As for the giants' bodies, and 'the truth'[30] that the giants speak of – the gods chop these up by logic, referring to them not as Being, but only as what becomes and changes. A terrible battle it is, Theaetetus, continually raging about such questions between these gods and giants!

246c5 THEAETETUS. Indeed!

STRANGER. So let us get from each side in turn a proper statement in defence of their account of Being.

THEAETETUS. How shall we get that?

STRANGER. Well, it is easy to get such a statement from those who claim that Being consists of Forms, for they are courteous people. It is harder to get a statement from those who insistently reduce everything to the physical – I might say, virtually impossible. Still, I think I know how we should deal with them.

246d3 THEAETETUS. How?

STRANGER. Best of all would be an actual reformation of their characters – if only we could manage it. Failing that, we must settle for an imaginary reformation, and proceed as if they were more inclined to abide by the rules of debate than they actually are. For if they were better men in that sense, the doctrines they have agreed on would carry more weight than they actually do. However, their ill manners are no real concern of ours: what we are after is the truth.

246e1 THEAETETUS. Absolutely.

STRANGER. So, given this imaginary improvement in their debating manners, ask them to respond to your questions; and you report back their answers for them.

THEAETETUS. Very well.

STRANGER. First let them say whether they assert that any mortal animals exist.

THEAETETUS. Of course they assert that.

STRANGER. And they agree that a mortal animal is an ensouled body?

THEAETETUS. Yes, certainly.

STRANGER. So they admit that soul is one of the things that are?

247a1  THEAETETUS. Yes.

STRANGER. Then do they agree that one soul is just but another unjust, and one soul wise but another foolish?

THEAETETUS. Why, yes.

STRANGER. And that it is by the possession and presence of justice or injustice that each of these souls becomes just or unjust?

THEAETETUS. Yes, they assent to that too.

STRANGER. But won't they agree that whatever is capable of becoming present or absent must, itself, *wholly* exist?

THEAETETUS. Yes, they do agree.

247b1  STRANGER. Then justice and wisdom and all the other virtues exist, as do their opposites; and so also does the soul in which these virtues and vices come to be. Now do the giants claim that any of these existents is *visible*? Or *tangible*? Or are they all invisible?

THEAETETUS. They are more or less bound to admit it: none of these things is visible.

STRANGER. Then what about this – do they say that these sorts of existents have bodies?

THEAETETUS. They begin to make distinctions in their answers here. They say that the soul *does* possess some sort of body. But they are in some embarrassment about wisdom and the other qualities which you asked about. For they dare not concede that these qualities are no real things at all; nor yet dare they insist that all such qualities are bodies.

247c2  STRANGER. Well, Theaetetus, clearly our giants at least have reformed their characters by now. After all, there are *some* earth-born sons of Cadmus' sowing[31] who would not be embarrassed by a single one of these claims, but would maintain to the bitter end that if you can't squeeze it, then it doesn't exist in any sense whatever.

THEAETETUS. Yes – some of them do hold pretty much the doctrine you describe.

STRANGER. So let us ask our giants some more questions. If they are willing to concede that even the smallest portion of the things that exist is not bodily, that will be enough. For if they say that any non-physical things at all exist alongside physical things, then they have to explain to us what inherent characteristic there is that physical and non-physical existents share, and which is what they have in mind when they say that both exist.

247d4    It is difficult to see what *they*, being physicalists, could say about this. If they do find that difficulty oppressing them, let's see if we can offer them a way out. Perhaps they would agree to accept something like the following sort of definition of being.

THEAETETUS. What sort? Go on, and we'll soon see.

STRANGER. I have this in mind. What really exists is anything whatever that possesses any sort of causal power – either a power of the sort to affect something else in whatever way, or else a power to be affected; even if it is in the smallest way, by the meanest cause, and only on one occasion.

247e5    THEAETETUS. Since the giants themselves have nothing better than this to offer at the moment, they say they accept it.

STRANGER. Good. Perhaps some other definition will occur to us and them at a later stage: but for present purposes, let's take this definition as agreed between us and the giants.

248a2    THEAETETUS. Yes, let's.

STRANGER. Now let us turn our attention to the other party – the friends of the Forms. Please report back to me their answers, too.

THEAETETUS. Very well.

STRANGER. You friends of the Forms distinguish in your discourses between Being and what comes to be, don't you?

THEAETETUS. Yes.

STRANGER. And you assert that it is by way of the body, through perception, that we share in coming to be; whereas it is by way of the soul, through reasoning, that we share in genuine Being. That, according to you, is always in the same state and the same relations; whereas coming to be is in different states at different times.

248b1 THEAETETUS. Yes, this is what we[32] assert.

STRANGER. But, you most excellent of men, how are we to understand your assertion that humans *share* in both Being and coming to be? For isn't sharing an example of what we have just been talking about?

THEAETETUS. Of what?

STRANGER. Of a kind of being affected or of affecting, which arises from some causal power that is at work when different things come together?

Well, Theaetetus, perhaps you can't hear what their answer to this will be. But, from old experience of the friends of the Forms, I can.

THEAETETUS. So what answer do they make?

248c1 STRANGER. They reject the statement we made just now, in our conversation with the giants, about Being.

THEAETETUS. What statement?

STRANGER. Didn't we propose that this would be an adequate demarcation of the things that exist: that they are those things in which there lies a causal power of affecting or being affected, however slight its effects?

THEAETETUS. Yes.

STRANGER. The friends of the Forms retort that, although coming to be participates in both the causal powers of affecting and being affected, neither of these powers has any application to Being.

THEAETETUS. Haven't they got a point there?

248d1  STRANGER. Yes. A point to which we should respond that we still need to learn from them more clearly whether they admit that the soul comes to know, or that Being is known.

THEAETETUS. Why yes, they certainly assert those claims.

STRANGER. But look what follows, friends of the Forms; consider knowing and being known. Either both are ways of affecting, or both are ways of being affected; or both are both; or one is a way of being affected, and the other is a way of affecting; or else neither knowing nor being known has any share in either affecting or of being affected. Which alternative will you take?

THEAETETUS. Clearly they would take this last alternative, on pain of contradicting themselves.

248d9  STRANGER. I see: their point is that, if (say) knowing *was* a way of affecting, then being known would turn out to be a way of being affected. Now suppose that Being is known by someone's knowledge. Then if being known means being affected, it follows that, just to the extent that it is known, *Being* is changed. But, as we noted, this could not happen to anything that was naturally unchanging.

248e7  THEAETETUS. That's right.

STRANGER. And yet, by Zeus! – Are we so easily to be persuaded that change and life and soul and wisdom are not present to What truly Is? That it is not alive, does not think, but remains unchangingly fixed in one place – holy and reverend, and yet mindless?

249a2  THEAETETUS. That, Stranger, would be a dreadful admission.

STRANGER. Or are we to say that it has mind, but no life?

THEAETETUS. How could we?

STRANGER. Or are we rather to say that both mind and

life are present in it – and yet also claim that it is not within a soul that it possesses its mind and life?

THEAETETUS. But how else could it possess them?

STRANGER. Or again, should we say that perfect Being possesses mind and life and a soul, but that it is altogether unchangeable, staying frozen in one place even though it is ensouled?

249b1   THEAETETUS. For my part I find all these claims equally unreasonable.

STRANGER. So we must concede the existence both of what is changed, and of change itself.

THEAETETUS. Yes – we can't avoid that.

STRANGER. But then, Theaetetus, the result is this: if *nothing* is changing, then no thought about anything is present to anyone anywhere.

THEAETETUS. Indeed it is.

STRANGER. Yet if we affirm that *everything* is in motion and undergoes change, by that affirmation too we end up prising mind out of its place among existents.

THEAETETUS. Do we?

STRANGER. Yes: do you think that there can ever be anything which keeps the same relations, the same state, and the same subject, unless there is such a thing as unchangingness?

249c2   THEAETETUS. No, there couldn't possibly be.

STRANGER. But mind couldn't exist or come into being anywhere unless there were these sorts of permanence, could it?

249c3   THEAETETUS. Absolutely not.

# 42. SOPHIST 254B–258E

## ✦

## THE GREATEST KINDS

254b8  STRANGER. So we agree that some of the classes are not disposed to share in each other, whereas others are so disposed, to a greater or lesser extent; and that there are even some classes which nothing prevents from sharing universally in all the other classes. Next, then, let us pursue the argument by looking together, not at *all* the Forms – there are so many that that would be overwhelming – but at a selection of some of them, which we may call the greatest ones. First let us consider the qualities of each of these greatest Forms; then at the question of how they are disposed as to their causal powers of interrelation. That way we may not, perhaps, be able to grasp What Is and What Is Not with total clarity: but at least we shall have done as much as we can, on our present method of inquiry, to make reasonable sense of them. Perhaps we shall even find a way to say that What Is Not really is, even though it is not, and get away with it unscathed!

254d2  THEAETETUS. Yes, this is what we should do.

STRANGER. So surely the greatest classes are those we have just discussed: What Is, Unchangingness, and Change.

THEAETETUS. Yes, these are by far the greatest.

STRANGER. And as we have said,[33] two of these, Unchangingness and Change, cannot possibly mix with each other.

THEAETETUS. Emphatically not.

STRANGER. What Is, on the other hand, can mix with both of them – since, one supposes, both Unchangingness and Change *Are* – they *exist*.

THEAETETUS. Of course they do.

STRANGER. So that makes three different classes.

THEAETETUS. Obviously.

STRANGER. This means that each of What Is, Unchangingness, and Change is *other than* the other two, but *the same as* itself.

254e1   THEAETETUS. Just so.

STRANGER. But what have we just said? What is this 'other than' and 'the same as'? Aren't these two further classes different from the first three – even though these two are always and necessarily mixed with the first three? So shouldn't we consider the greatest classes to be five in number rather than three?

255a1   Or are we, in fact, still speaking about one of the first three classes when we refer to the Other and the Same, even though we do not realise it?

THEAETETUS. Yes, possibly we are.

STRANGER. Because anything which we say in common of both Unchangingness and Change – for example, Other and Same – cannot possibly be identical with either Unchangingness or Change.

THEAETETUS. Why?

STRANGER. Because in that case, to apply Other or Same to both Unchangingness and Change would be to apply either *Unchangingness or Change* to both Unchangingness and Change. But then Change would be unchanging and Unchangingness would change! For if either member of the pair, Change or Unchangingness, could properly be applied to both of the pair Change and Unchangingness, then that member would forcibly mutate the other member into the opposite of its own nature; since that other member would participate in the opposite member.

255b2   THEAETETUS. Absolutely.

STRANGER. But, in fact, Change and Unchangingness both partake of both Same and Other.

THEAETETUS. Yes.

STRANGER. Therefore we shouldn't say that Change *is* Same or Other; and likewise with Unchangingness.

THEAETETUS. No, we shouldn't.

STRANGER. Then should we conceive What Is and Same as one thing?

THEAETETUS. Possibly.

STRANGER. No. For if there was no difference in meaning between 'What Is' and 'Same', then to say (as we have) that Change and Unchangingness Are would be to say that they are the Same.

255c2 THEAETETUS. Oh yes – and that would be impossible.

STRANGER. It follows that Same and What Is cannot possibly be one thing.

THEAETETUS. Yes, that must be about right.

STRANGER. So shouldn't we take it that Same is a fourth Form, alongside the other three – What Is, Unchangingness, and Change?

THEAETETUS. Yes, certainly.

STRANGER. And are we to say that Other is a fifth class? Or are we to conceive 'Other' and 'What Is' as two names for a single class?

THEAETETUS. Yes, that might easily be true.

STRANGER. No it mightn't. Presumably you agree that some things are said to be in their own right, whereas others in relation to other things?

THEAETETUS. Of course.

255d1 STRANGER. And Other is always related to something else, isn't it?

THEAETETUS. Yes.

STRANGER. But that could not be so unless What Is and Other were entirely different from each other. If Other, like What Is, had a share of both forms, relativity and absoluteness, then there could be some particular thing that was, absolutely, *other*, and yet which was not, relatively, *other than* anything else. But, in unaccountable fact, we see that whatever is other, turns out to be so through the compulsion of something else *relative to which* it is other.

THEAETETUS. Yes, it's just as you say.

STRANGER. So we should say that the nature of the Other is the fifth among the Forms which we are selecting as the greatest.

255e2   THEAETETUS. Yes.

STRANGER. We shall say that the Other runs through all the other Forms. For each of them is other than the others, not by its own essential nature, but by participation in the universal of Otherness.

THEAETETUS. Definitely so.

STRANGER. So, let us make the following statements about these five Greatest Classes, taking them one by one.

THEAETETUS. Namely?

STRANGER. First, about Change, we say that it is entirely other than Unchangingness; what else would we say?

THEAETETUS. Nothing else.

STRANGER. So Change is not Unchangingness.

THEAETETUS. No, by no means.

256a1   STRANGER. But Change Is, because of its participation in What Is.

THEAETETUS. Yes.

STRANGER. Again, Change is other than the Same.

THEAETETUS. That is more or less so.

STRANGER. So Change is not the Same.

THEAETETUS. No.

STRANGER. Yet, as we saw, Change itself is the Same, because everything participates in the Same by being the Same as itself.

THEAETETUS. Absolutely.

256a7   STRANGER. Therefore we should agree that Change both is the same and is not the Same, and we should not feel uneasy at this statement. For in saying 'Change is the same' and 'Change is not the Same', we are speaking in two different ways. Change *is* the same in the sense that it participates in the Same with respect to itself. Change is *not* the Same in the sense that it shares in the Other, and is separated by that sharing in the Other from the Same, so that it does not coalesce with the Same, but comes to be other than the Same. That is the sense in which it is correct to say that Change is not the Same.

256b3 THEAETETUS. Yes, certainly.

STRANGER. So if there was also some sense in which Change itself had a share in Unchangingness, it would not be inappropriate to call Change 'unchanging'.

THEAETETUS. Yes: if we are going to affirm that some of the classes are such as to mingle with one another, whereas other classes are not, that would be absolutely correct.

256c1 STRANGER. We proved *that* point before we started on our present inquiries: we established that it was in the nature of things that it should be so.

THEAETETUS. Of course we did.

STRANGER. Again, let us say this: Change is other than Other, just as it is other than Same, and other than Unchangingness.

THEAETETUS. Necessarily.

STRANGER. So our present argument shows that, somehow, Change is both other and not Other.

THEAETETUS. True.

STRANGER. So what is the next point? Are we to say that Change is other than these three Forms (Other, Same, Unchangingness), and yet not other than the fourth Form (What Is)? Shall we say that, when we agreed that there were five greatest Forms which we were undertaking to inquire about in their own terms?

256d2 THEAETETUS. How could we? We can hardly admit at this point that the number of the greatest Forms is less than we saw it was just now.

STRANGER. So we may fearlessly contend that Change is other than What Is.

THEAETETUS. Absolutely fearlessly.

STRANGER. Then isn't it clear that Change really *is not* What Is? Yet also that Change *is* What Is – in so far as it partakes of What Is?

THEAETETUS. Yes – that is perfectly clear.

256d8  STRANGER. Then it logically follows that it is possible for What Is Not to Be; for What Is Not Is in the case of Change, and in the case of all the other classes too. Throughout all these classes, the nature of the Other is at work to make each of them other than What Is – and so to make each of them a thing That Is *Not*. Across the whole range of these classes, then, we will be right to say the same, that they are not What Is – and again also that they are What Is, since they participate in What Is.

256e7  THEAETETUS. That may well be right.

STRANGER. So What Is has many different relations to each of the Forms; yet What Is Not has *infinitely* many different relations to each of the Forms.[34]

THEAETETUS. Evidently so.

257a1  STRANGER. Now we must also say that What Is is itself other than the other Forms.

THEAETETUS. We must.

STRANGER. So on our account, What Is is not in just as many respects as there are things other than What Is. For What Is is not those things because it is its own single self; but all those other things are not What Is – and there are indefinitely many of them.

THEAETETUS. That must be roughly correct.

STRANGER. These claims should not cause us any dismay either, given that it is in the nature of the classes to associate with each other. If anyone won't accept them, he will not only have to turn all our previous arguments to his own purposes; he will have to do the same with what comes next as well.

THEAETETUS. You're quite right.

257b1 STRANGER. Then let us also look at this point.

THEAETETUS. Namely?

STRANGER. When we speak of what is not we aren't, apparently, referring to something *opposite to* What Is; all we mean is something *other than* What Is.

THEAETETUS. How do you mean?

STRANGER. I mean, for example, that when we say that something is not big, we evidently don't mean by that description to pick out something which is small rather than middle-sized.

THEAETETUS. No, we don't.

257b7 STRANGER. So when it is claimed that negating something means referring to *its opposite*, we shall refuse to accept that claim. All we shall accept is this: that to prefix 'not' or 'non-' to a word is to signify what is *other than* the word. (More accurately: it is to signify whatever things are other than whatever thing is signified by the utterance to which the word signifying negation is prefixed.)

257c3 THEAETETUS. Yes, absolutely right.

STRANGER. Let us also have a look at this point, to see if you agree with me here too.

THEAETETUS. Which is that?

STRANGER. It seems to me that the Other, by its nature, is a capital sum cashed out in small denominations – just like knowledge.

THEAETETUS. How do you mean?

STRANGER. Well, presumably knowledge too is one thing; but each portion of knowledge which is divided off to become knowledge *of some particular subject* has its own particular title. That is why, in common parlance, there are many skills and many types of knowledge.

257d2 THEAETETUS. Yes, quite so.

STRANGER. Doesn't exactly the same happen to the different portions of the nature of the Other, even though that nature is a unity?

THEAETETUS. Quite probably – but if so, we ought to say how.

STRANGER. Is there a part of the Other which is set over against the Beautiful?[35]

THEAETETUS. Yes, there is.

STRANGER. Shall we describe this part as nameless? Or has it a name?

THEAETETUS. It has one: 'What is not Beautiful'. For whenever we use that name, what we refer to by it will not be other than anything else but the nature of the Beautiful.

STRANGER. Come then, tell me something else.

257e1  THEAETETUS. What?

STRANGER. Doesn't it follow from our argument that What is not Beautiful is a demarcated part of some class of things that exist, which is set over against some other part of that same class?

THEAETETUS. It does, yes.

STRANGER. So What is not Beautiful comes about by an antithesis of what is to what is.

THEAETETUS. Absolutely right.

STRANGER. Then on this argument, is it our view that the Beautiful is more truly one of the things that Are, while What is not Beautiful is less truly one of the things that Are?

THEAETETUS. Not at all.

258a1  STRANGER. Then mustn't we say the same about What is not Big and What is Big?

THEAETETUS. We must.

STRANGER. And we shall apply the same view in all cases, given that the nature of the Other is evidently one of the things that Are. Since the Other itself Is, it is clearly necessary for us to say that its parts are no less real.

THEAETETUS. Yes, they must be.

258b1  STRANGER. Then evidently even that part of the nature of the Other which is set over against What Is – even *that* part is, if we dare to say it, no less really existent than Being itself. For 'other than What Is' does not mean *opposite to* What Is; all it means is *different from* What Is.

THEAETETUS. Clearly so.

STRANGER. What name shall we give to *this*?

THEAETETUS. Clearly this is the thing itself that our inquiries about the sophist set us to find: this is *What Is Not*.

258b8 STRANGER. And isn't it, just as you were saying, in no way deficient in reality compared with other things? Mustn't we now pluck up our courage and say that What Is Not most certainly Is, and has a nature of its own? For we found that big *is* big; beautiful *is* beautiful; What is not Big *is* not big; What is not Beautiful *is* not beautiful. Mustn't we now add, in the same way, that What Is Not *is* What Is Not, and is to be counted as just another one of the many Forms of things that Are? Or, Theaetetus, are we still reserving judgement in any way about this question?

258c5 THEAETETUS. In no way at all.

STRANGER. Then do you realise that our rejection of Parmenides' doctrines goes even beyond what he forbade?

THEAETETUS. What do you mean?

STRANGER. Our researches have brought us to problems far beyond the limit which he set to inquiry – and we have solved them for him.

THEAETETUS. How's that?

258d1 STRANGER. Because Parmenides, as we know, says this:[36]

> Never submit to this claim, that What Is Not Is;
> Rather, drive your mind away from that road
>    of search.

THEAETETUS. Yes, that's what he says.

STRANGER. But we have not merely shown that What

Is Not Is; we have actually revealed the very Form and nature of What Is Not. For we have demonstrated that the nature of the Other Is, and is cashed out in the small coin of every existing thing's relation to every other existing thing. Finally, regarding each part of What Is Not which is set over against What Is, we have even dared to say that *that* is what What Is Not itself 258e3 really is.

# 43. TIMAEUS 51D–E

### ❥❥

## UNDERSTANDING AND TRUE BELIEF

51d3    TIMAEUS. . . . This then is my verdict: *if* there is a real distinction between understanding[37] and true belief, then by all means these Forms do exist: they exist as things in their own right, not accessible to our senses, but only to our understanding. Whereas *if* they are right who think that there is no respect in which true belief differs from understanding, then whatever we perceive through the body should be taken to be what is most certainly dependable.

51e1    But, in fact, we should say that understanding and true belief *are* distinct. For they have come into existence separately, and their natures are not alike. Understanding arises in us through teaching,[38] true belief through persuasion; understanding is always accompanied by a true account, whereas true belief lacks an account; understanding does not change under the force of persuasion, but a belief can be changed into an opposite belief by persuasion. Moreover everyone, we should say, has a share in true belief; but only the gods and some small part of humanity has

51e8    a share in understanding.

# 44. PHILEBUS 58D–62D

## ✦✦

## LETTING IN OPINION

58d1  SOCRATES. Now let's consider the matter with great care, and argue it through properly. Let's not look at the usefulness or good reputation of any supposed form of knowledge; let us simply ask if there is by nature any ability in the soul which consists in loving the truth and doing everything else for the sake of the truth. Then when we have examined this ability, let us say whether we think it most likely that this ability will have possession of the pure form of mind and intelligence: or whether we should rather look for some other ability which the soul has which is superior to this love of the truth.

58e2  PROTARCHUS. I am considering; and I believe it would be difficult to allow that any other form of knowledge or skill could be more closely connected to the truth than this.

SOCRATES. In saying what you have just said, are you bearing in mind that (in the first place) the majority of skills, and likewise those who pursue them, make use of mere opinions, and are for ever looking into matters related to opinion? And (second) that, as you know, even the person who takes himself to be investigating natural philosophy is spending his whole life looking into questions about this world – whence it came, how it is affected in any manner, and how it behaves? Isn't this what we should say?

59a6  PROTARCHUS. Yes.

SOCRATES. Then such a person does not direct his efforts to What Is, but to what has and will and did come into being?

PROTARCHUS. Exactly so.

SOCRATES. Well, shall we say that, in the strictest sense of truth, anything like this achieves clarity and distinctness? Anything which never was, nor ever will be, nor at any present time ever is, in a stable condition in its own right?

59b3 PROTARCHUS. How could we?

SOCRATES. For how can we attain any sort of properly stable grasp of things which possess no sort of stability?

PROTARCHUS. I don't think we can.

SOCRATES. Then no mind or knowledge which has to do with them will have hold of what is most true.

PROTARCHUS. No – not likely.

SOCRATES. Then you, me, Gorgias, Philebus – we must all of us bid a lingering farewell to that sort of mind or knowledge, and make this testimony on behalf of the argument.

59c1 PROTARCHUS. Namely?

SOCRATES. That stable and pure and true and (as we call it) unalloyed knowledge is either about those things which are eternally in the same relations in the same way, and are in their condition as unmixed as they can be; or else it is about whatever is most closely akin to such things. Every other sort of knowledge is to be regarded as secondary and posterior to these.

PROTARCHUS. Quite right.

SOCRATES. Now wouldn't it be most just for us to give the most honourable names that have to do with these matters to the most honourable things?

PROTARCHUS. Probably, yes.

59d1 SOCRATES. Aren't 'mind' and 'intelligence' the names to which one attaches the most honour?

PROTARCHUS. Yes.

SOCRATES. Then these names are most fittingly and precisely applied to those states of awareness which have to do with what truly Is.

59d7    PROTARCHUS. Absolutely.

[59d8–61d9]

SOCRATES. So there was a division between two sorts of knowledge: one which looks towards what is generated and corrupted, the other towards what never comes to be nor passes away, but is eternally in the same relations in the same way. We considered these as to their truth; and we decided that the latter was more truthful than the former.

61e3    PROTARCHUS. And we were quite right.

SOCRATES. Why not see what happens if we combine together the truest parts of both? If we mix these together, will they be sufficient, working together, to provide us with the most desirable life? Or do we still need something else, of some other sort?

62a1    PROTARCHUS. Well, at any rate I think we should try this.

SOCRATES. Then let us imagine a man who has wisdom about The Just Itself, and knows its essence, and has reason in accordance with his wisdom; and has a similar understanding about every other kind of reality.

PROTARCHUS. Very well.

SOCRATES. Will such a man have enough knowledge, if he has an account of the divine Circle and Sphere [the Forms], but has no knowledge of this man-made sphere and of circles like these protractors here, even though he uses circles like these – and other similar geometrical instruments – in building a house?

62b2    PROTARCHUS. Well, Socrates, we consider it a laughable state to be in, when someone only possesses divine forms of knowledge.

SOCRATES. Are you serious? Is this unstable and impure skill in handling the inexact ruler or protractor really to be thrown into our mixture of sorts of knowledge – along with everything else?

PROTARCHUS. Well, I think it will have to be, if any of us is ever going to find his way back home.

SOCRATES. And music too – which we've just said[39] is riddled with guesswork and imitation, and quite without purity?

62c2 PROTARCHUS. Yes, I think we have to, if our life is ever to be any sort of life at all.

SOCRATES. So you want me to succumb, like a doorkeeper under the pushing and shoving of the rabble? You want me to throw back the gates, and allow every sort of knowledge to surge in and mix with one another – the great unwashed together with the pure?

62d1 PROTARCHUS. Well, really, Socrates, provided one only has hold of the *primary* sorts of knowledge, I don't see what harm it does to be open to all the other sorts as well.

SOCRATES. So *shall* I let them all stream in together, 'to be harboured at the meeting of the glens' as Homer so poetically puts it?[40]

PROTARCHUS. Go ahead.

62d7 SOCRATES. Very well then: in they come!

## NOTES

1. 127d ff.

2. Socrates first suggests that, for any kind X, there is a Form for X only if a distinction between appearance and reality applies to X (this is often called the Argument from Opposites for the Forms: cf. reading 31). No such distinction applies to hair, clay, wax, etc.; therefore there are no Forms of such things.

   But then he recalls the One over Many argument for the Forms: 'given any number of particulars to which we apply the same name, there is a single Form in each case' (see reading 32). Surely this argument *does* entail that there are Forms of hair, clay and mud?

3. I.e., Socrates will come to see that even the lowliest sorts have Forms, and so are worth studying (cf., differently, Aristotle, *de Partibus Animalium* 1.5). For Parmenides, the fact that all sorts have Forms entails that even the things that seem least 'ideal' – like hair and clay – are, essentially, just objects of thought: hence, it entails *idealism*.

4. And possibly not. As is shown by what follows, Socrates would be

well advised *not* tamely to let Parmenides substitute his sailcloth metaphor for Socrates' night metaphor.

5. The first full statement of the Third Man Argument (but cf. reading 32):
   1. There is a Form Bigness set over {all big things}
   2. Bigness is (a) itself a big thing – yet (b) not one of the big things it is set over
   3. So there is a Form Bigness* set over {{all big things} plus the Form Bigness}
   4. Bigness* is (a) itself a big thing – yet (b) not one of the big things it is set over
   5. So there is a Form Bigness** set over {{{all big things} plus the Form Bigness} plus the Form Bigness*}
   6. Bigness** is (a) itself a big thing – yet (b) not one of the big things it is set over . . .

   Usually the regress is avoided by denying either or both of 2(a) – the doctrine of the self-predication of the Forms – and 2(b) – the doctrine of the separation of the Forms. Plato consistently refuses to deny 2(a) (cf. reading 13). But to deny 2(b), as Aristotle did and as Parmenides here tries to push Socrates into doing, apparently entails giving up the distinctively strong claims about the Forms which Plato is so determined to insist on.

6. Question: How could psychologising the Forms help avert the Third Man?

7. Cf. *Rep.* 477a ff. in reading 31.

8. Parmenides argues: 1. Forms are really concepts (Socrates' suggestion); 2. all concepts are concepts of contents; 3. all contents must be real and general; 4. only universals are real and general; 5. so all contents are universals (3, 4); 6. all universals are Forms; 7. so all contents are Forms (2, 5, 6); 8. so all concepts are concepts of Forms (2, 7); 9. so all concepts are concepts of concepts (1, 8). If Parmenides proves (9), he proves that Socrates cannot psychologise the Forms without accepting Parmenides' own view (as understood by Plato): that thought thinks nothing but itself, and indeed that there *is* nothing, and so nothing to think, except thought.

9. A second application of the Third Man Argument.

10. Plato signals clearly that he does not think even this 'greatest objection' to the theory of Forms insurmountable, even if it proves difficult to answer. The *Parmenides'* critique of the theory of Forms does not prove that Plato has rejected it.

11. Socrates now casually rejects the idea of psychologising the Forms which, at 132b–c, he claimed was *the* way to avoid the Third Man.

12. Cf. *Sophist* 247e in reading 41.

13. The classic Greek theologians held that prayer influences the gods.

14. Cf. *Theaetetus* 182d in reading 37.

15. *Does* Protagoras concede that his opponents (i) have an unquali-fiedly true belief that 'Protagoras' view is false without qualifica-tion'? Two other possibilities are: that Protagoras concedes that his opponents (ii) have a *true-to-them* belief that 'Protagoras' view is false without qualification'; or (iii) have a *true-to-them* belief that 'Protagoras' view is false-to-them'.

   (iii) seems to misrepresent the subjective content of Protagoras' opponents' belief. But if Protagoras allows that his opponents hold the belief mentioned in (ii), will the objectivity of this belief 'infect' its context and so refute his theory?

16. The Heracleitean must deny that there are even any genuine percep-tions or qualities, if these are things which exist in their own right; for the Heracleitean denies that *anything* exists in its own right.

17. Socrates refers back to reading 36.

18. Plato means: 'Is seeing (a) an affection essential to some separable part of the human organism? Or is it (b) something that an indivisible mind just happens to do *by means of* such a part?'. (b), which suggests dualism, is Plato's answer. (a), which has physicalist overtones, seems to be Aristotle's: *de Anima* 425a15 ff.

19. You cannot lay hold of truth without *first* laying hold of being, because before you can assess a proposition for truth or falsity, you first have to assess its meaning – which means finding out what it says *is* (the case). 'Any judgement . . . calls upon the capacity to think that something is thus or that it is not thus . . . the inability of perception to get at being is its inability to frame any proposition at all' (Burnyeat, *The Theaetetus of Plato*, 59–60). Cf. *Sophist* 241a1, and Aristotle, *Metaphysics* 1011b27.

20. True belief, as such, is a perfectly reliable guide to action: so *other things being equal*, 'everything that it causes is fine and good'. Cf. reading 27.

21. The Athenian official clock (the *clepsydrion*) worked like an egg-timer, only with water in it not sand.

22. Which, as we already know, it isn't: reading 39.

23. Hesiod, *Works and Days*, 456.

24. For example, 'phrases and names' (206d2).

25. Theaetetus thinks we cannot be anywhere near a permanently valid 'account' – the only sort of account that could accompany knowledge – if the key terms of that account are mutable in the way Socrates describes. For if X is a *natural* part of Y, then X is *always* a part of Y; Y cannot cease to include X without ceasing to exist altogether.

26. Plato suggests a second objection to the idea of 'account' as differentia: why should there be one and only one important way in which any individual differs from any other?

27. In the *Parmenides*, Socrates – significantly – becomes the victim of Parmenides' questioning; in the *Sophist*, Socrates – significantly – is not even the respondent. Here the questioner is a Stranger from Parmenides' city, Elea; and Theaetetus is the respondent.

28. In particular the Stranger has been considering Parmenides' and Heracleitus' views.

29. Plato refers ironically to his contemporaries. As *Sophist* 242c proves, he does not really believe that the Presocratics were more precise thinkers than his own generation.

30. Possibly a reference to Protagoras' book with this title. Cf. *Theaetetus* 170e in reading 36.

31. The mythical Cadmus – founder of Thebes – sowed dragon's teeth in the soil of the Boeotian plain, and an army of fierce warriors sprang up. The metaphor refers both to the extreme physicalists' earthy fixations, and to their ferocity.

32. Is Theaetetus still just reporting? Or is he himself a friend of the Forms?

33. *Sophist* 252d.

34. 'What Is has many different relations to each of the Forms' because many particular things may exist which partake of any given Form. 'What Is Not has *infinitely* many different relations to each of the Forms' because there are infinitely many things, both particulars and other Forms, which any Form is *not*, and which do not partake of it.

35. Here the Stranger has to deal with an obvious objection to his claim that 'not X' does not mean 'opposite to X', merely 'different from X'.

36. Parmenides, DK B7.

37. Apparently 'understanding' here is a synonym for 'knowledge'.

38. Is this remark consistent with the doctrine of the *Meno* that nothing can be taught (reading 5)?

39. *Philebus* 56c.

40. Homer, *Iliad* 4.453.

# EPILOGUE: PLATO ON WRITING PHILOSOPHY

## 45. PHAEDRUS 275c–e

275c5   SOCRATES. So anyone who imagines that he has left posterity any craftwork in the form of his writings – and anyone who takes them up in the belief that there can be anything accurate or certain in any written form – such people will be full of their own naïveté, and ignorant of the oracle of Ammon.[1] Their mistake is to think that the writing-down of words could have any use except to remind someone who understands them already of what those words are about.

275d2   PHAEDRUS. Quite so.

275d3   SOCRATES. In truth, Phaedrus, writing seems to have a remarkable property which it shares with painting. For the painter's productions stand upright as if they were alive; but if you ask them something, they are as silent as a sanctuary. Likewise words. You would think that they would speak out with some wisdom. But when someone, who wants to understand one of the points which they discuss, questions them, they have only one thing to say, and that is the same thing always. Every written word, though it has been written only once, is all at sea – rolled around[2] everywhere by the learned and the utterly unfitted alike. The written word has no idea whom it should address itself to, and whom it should not; and when it is traduced or unjustly abused, it needs its progenitor's protection;

275e8   for it is quite unable to defend or protect itself.

# 46. SEVENTH LETTER 344c

344c1  Everyone who is serious about the subjects which are
most truly serious should avoid as far as he can the
possibility that, by writing about these things, he
might expose them to be the objects of envy and
perplexity among men . . . whenever one sees the
things that a person has *written*, whether these are
works on laws or whatever else, one knows that – if
he is serious – then these works are not what he takes
most seriously among his productions. His most
serious productions are elsewhere, in the most honour-
344c8  able realm available to him: his own mind.

## NOTES

1. Which says that writing things down merely atrophies our ability to
remember them: *Phaedrus* 275a.
2. Cf. *Rep*. 479d in reading 31.

# SUGGESTIONS FOR FURTHER READING

Longer bibliographies can be found, e.g., in Bostock's and Kraut's works, as listed below.

**Historical background:**

For the sources on Socrates' life (*c*.470–399 BC), which I do not discuss here, consult J. Ferguson, *Socrates: A Source Book* (Macmillan: for the Open University, 1970).

On Plato's life (427–347 BC), which I do not discuss here either, W. K. C. Guthrie, *A History of Greek Philosophy* (Cambridge: CUP, 1975) vol. 4, ch. 10.

On the chronology of Plato's works, also not discussed here, begin with the Introduction to D. J. Bostock, *Plato's Phaedo* (Oxford: OUP, 1986).

Plato frequently cites the Presocratic philosophers in the selections in this book. Footnote references of the form 'DK B' + number are to the standard edition of the Presocratics: H. Diels and W. Kranz, *Die Fragmente der Vorsokratiker*, 11th edn (Zurich: 1952).

But more accessible to the Greekless reader is G. Kirk, J. Raven and M. Schofield, *The Presocratic Philosophers*, 2nd edn (Cambridge: CUP, 1983).

**General**

A good general introduction to Plato's thought and its context is R. Kraut, (ed.), *The Cambridge Companion to Plato* (Cambridge: CUP, 1992).

A very useful collection of essays is G. Vlastos (ed.), *Plato: A Collection of Critical Essays* (Garden City: Doubleday, 1971).

The following items might be read alongside the individual Parts of this *Reader*:

Part I: For a magisterial study of the question of 'Socrates' philosophy', see G. X. Santas, *Socrates: Philosophy in Plato's Early Dialogues* (London: RKP, 1979).

Specifically on Socratic definition, there is the debate begun by P. T.
Geach, 'Plato's *Euthyphro*: An Analysis and Commentary', *Monist*
1966, pp. 369–82.

Part II: Some good editions of *Meno* and *Protagoras*, with commentary:
R. S. Bluck, *Plato's Meno* (Cambridge: CUP, 1961);
R. W. Sharples, *Plato: Meno* (Warminster: Aris & Phillips, 1985);
C. C. W.Taylor, *Plato's Protagoras* (Oxford: Clarendon Press, 1976);
G. Vlastos, *Plato: Protagoras* (Indianapolis: Bobbs-Merrill, 1956).

Part III: Two excellent editions of the *Gorgias* are E. R. Dodds, *Plato:
Gorgias* (Oxford: Clarendon Press, 1959) and T. Irwin, *Plato: Gorgias*
(Oxford: Clarendon Press, 1979).
On the moral issues raised in Parts II–III, see especially T. Irwin, *Plato's
Moral Theory: The Early and Middle Dialogues* (Oxford: Clarendon
Press, 1977).
There is also an interesting study of pleasure: C. C. W. Taylor and
J. C. B. Gosling, *The Greeks on Pleasure* (Oxford: Clarendon Press,
1979).

Part IV: the argument of reading 22 is discussed in D. J. Bostock, *Plato's
Phaedo* (Oxford: OUP, 1986) ch. 3. On the argument of reading 23, see
B. Williams, 'The Analogy of City and Soul in Plato's *Republic*', in
H. D. P. Lee, A. P. D. Mourelatos and A. O. Rorty (eds), *Exegesis and
Argument: Studies Presented to Gregory Vlastos* (Assen: van Gorcum,
1973).
A very useful guide to the *Republic* is N. P. White, *A Companion to
Plato's Republic* (Indianapolis: Hackett, 1979).
An excellent edition of the *Phaedrus* is C. J. Rowe, *Plato: Phaedrus*
(Warminster: Aris & Phillips, 1986).
On Plato's attitude to the gods, see R. Kraut (ed.), *The Cambridge
Companion to Plato* (Cambridge: CUP, 1992) ch. 7.

Parts V–VI: the bibliography on Plato's epistemology and on the theory
of Forms is vast. Begin with D. J. Bostock, *Plato's Phaedo* (Oxford:
OUP, 1986) chs. 4 and 7–10, and R. Kraut (ed.), *The Cambridge
Companion to Plato* (Cambridge: CUP, 1992) chs. 6 and 9. Then try
either N. P. White, *Plato on Knowledge and Reality* (Indianapolis:
Hackett, 1976) or, more briefly, H. Cherniss, 'The Philosophical
Economy of the Theory of Ideas', in G. Vlastos (ed.), *Plato: A
Collection of Critical Essays* (Garden City: Doubleday, 1971).
One good discussion of problems raised in reading 35 is C. Strang, 'Plato
and the Third Man', in Vlastos, *Plato*.

There are some marvellous recent discussions of the *Theaetetus*. Especially recommended are a translation (by M. J. Levett) with a 240-page introduction: M. F. Burnyeat, *The Theaetetus of Plato* (Indianapolis: Hackett, 1990). And a book-length study: D. J. Bostock, *Plato's Theaetetus* (Oxford: OUP, 1988).

The *Sophist* has also had a good run recently. One must-read is N. Denyer, *Language, Thought and Falsehood in Ancient Greek Philosophy* (London: RKP, 1991) – not exclusively about the *Sophist*, but see chs. 8–9.

On the *Timaeus*, it is probably still best to try F. M. Cornford, *Plato's Cosmology: The Timaeus of Plato* (London: Kegan Paul, 1937).

For the *Philebus*, see R. Hackforth, *Plato's Examination of Pleasure* (Cambridge: CUP, 1945).

Finally, to Plato himself. The best, indeed about the only, widely available single-handed translation of the whole of Plato is B. Jowett, *The Dialogues of Plato*, 5 vols., 4th edn. (Oxford, Clarendon Press, 1953), which will, DV, eventually be joined by Allen's excellent work in progress: R. E. Allen, *The Dialogues of Plato* (New Haven: Yale University Press, 1984) vol. 1.

For those who read Greek, two good options are: the Loeb parallel-text translations, published by Harvard University Press, and J. Burnet, *Platonis Opera* (the Oxford Classical Text), 5 vols. (Oxford: Clarendon Press, 1900–7).

1095